Thinking Through the Problem of Hell

# Thinking Through the Problem of Hell

## The Divine Presence Model

R. Zachary Manis

CASCADE Books • Eugene, Oregon

THINKING THROUGH THE PROBLEM OF HELL
The Divine Presence Model

Copyright © 2024 R. Zachary Manis. All rights reserved. Except for brief quotations in critical publications or reviews, no part of this book may be reproduced in any manner without prior written permission from the publisher. Write: Permissions, Wipf and Stock Publishers, 199 W. 8th Ave., Suite 3, Eugene, OR 97401.

Cascade Books
An Imprint of Wipf and Stock Publishers
199 W. 8th Ave., Suite 3
Eugene, OR 97401

www.wipfandstock.com

PAPERBACK ISBN: 978-1-6667-7143-5
HARDCOVER ISBN: 978-1-6667-7144-2
EBOOK ISBN: 978-1-6667-7145-9

*Cataloguing-in-Publication data:*

Names: Manis, R. Zachary [author].

Title: Thinking through the problem of hell : the divine presence model / by R. Zachary Manis.

Description: Eugene, OR: Cascade Books, 2024| Includes bibliographical references and index.

Identifiers: ISBN 978-1-6667-7143-5 (paperback) | ISBN 978-1-6667-7144-2 (hardcover) | ISBN 978-1-6667-7145-9 (ebook)

Subjects: LCSH: Hell—Christianity. | Sin—Christianity. | God—Love. | Theodicy. | Hidden God. | Self-deception—Religious aspects—Christianity. | Eschatology.

Classification: BT836.3 M36 2024 (paperback) | BT836.3 (ebook)

VERSION NUMBER 08/22/24

All Scripture quotations, unless otherwise indicated, are taken from the Holy Bible, New International Version®, NIV®. Copyright ©1973, 1978, 1984, 2011 by Biblica, Inc.™ Used by permission of Zondervan. All rights reserved worldwide. www.zondervan.com The "NIV" and "New International Version" are trademarks registered in the United States Patent and Trademark Office by Biblica, Inc.™

Scripture quotations marked (ESV) are from The ESV® Bible (The Holy Bible, English Standard Version®), copyright © 2001 by Crossway, a publishing ministry of Good News Publishers. Used by permission. All rights reserved.

Scripture quotations marked (NASB) are taken from the (NASB®) New American Standard Bible®, Copyright © 1960, 1971, 1977, 1995, 2020 by The Lockman Foundation. Used by permission. All rights reserved. lockman.org

*To Dad, who always encouraged my questions.*

# Contents

*Preface* | ix
*Acknowledgments* | xiii

**What Is the Problem of Hell?**

Chapter 1: Introduction to the problem | 3
Chapter 2: The problem of justice | 8
Chapter 3: The problem of love | 15
Chapter 4: The problem of coercion | 23

**How (Not) to Solve the Problem of Hell**

Chapter 5: The Calvinist appeal to divine sovereignty | 31
Chapter 6: The problem of faith for Calvinists | 38
Chapter 7: More misguided solutions to the problem of hell | 43
Chapter 8: A final misguided approach—and the way forward | 54

**The Divine Presence Model of Hell**

Chapter 9: Heaven and hell on the divine presence model | 67
Chapter 10: The presence of God as truth and life | 80

## Soul-Making and Self-Deception

Chapter 11: The problem of evil and the soul-making theodicy | 95

Chapter 12: Developing a natural consequence model of hell | 103

Chapter 13: Answering the universalist's objection, part I | 113

Chapter 14: Answering the universalist's objection, part II | 123

## Divine Hiddenness and Divine Disclosure

Chapter 15: The interconnected problems of divine hiddenness and hell | 135

Chapter 16: The usual explanations of divine hiddenness— and their inadequacy | 141

Chapter 17: Hiddenness on the divine presence model | 151

## The Biblical Case for the Divine Presence Model

Chapter 18: The first and second unveilings | 167

Chapter 19: The third unveiling (the judgment of transparency) | 181

Chapter 20: Apocalyptic visions | 194

*Recommended further reading* | 205
*Glossary of terms* | 209
*Bibliography* | 217
*Subject Index* | 219
*Author Index* | 223

# Preface

IN THE SUMMER OF 2015, I began writing a philosophical work on the problem of hell. As the arguments were formulated and the topics developed, the book eventually became quite long and in places somewhat technical. It was eventually published by Oxford University Press in 2019 under the title *Sinners in the Presence of a Loving God: An Essay on the Problem of Hell*. Due to its size and limited printing, the book was rather expensive and—for those not connected to a university or seminary whose library held a copy—difficult for the average reader to obtain. Among those who read it, however, the response was encouraging. I'm convinced that the problems addressed in the book are ones with which many reflective Christians struggle and are earnestly seeking answers. The present book is my attempt to make the main ideas of *Sinners in the Presence of a Loving God* accessible to a wider audience.

By "wider audience," I mean anyone who has an interest in theological issues in general or the doctrine of hell in particular. The book takes an ecumenical approach; my hope is that it will appeal equally to Catholic, Orthodox, and Protestant Christians of all stripes, and that my respect for all three Christian faith traditions will be evident in the pages that follow. My intended audience is not limited to Christians, however. I understand that many people have reservations about Christianity precisely because they find its doctrine of hell to be morally offensive. One of the primary objectives of this book is to demonstrate that the Christian doctrine of hell, rightly understood, is fully compatible with the doctrine that God is perfectly good and maximally loving—moreover, that it's compatible with the view that God does everything in His power to save everyone.

However, for reasons I will explain, especially in chapter 8, the version of the doctrine of hell that I will develop and defend is one in which some people are finally lost.

In saying that the book takes an ecumenical approach, I do not mean that I will limit my discussion to what C. S. Lewis calls "mere Christianity": that is, the core Christian doctrines about which all orthodox believers agree. Rather, I will discuss—and defend—certain views that, while perfectly at home in some Christian traditions, will likely be challenging to Christians of other traditions. One example is the doctrine of theosis, the view that salvation is a process of coming to participate in the life of God. On the other hand, there are certain theological views that I will argue against, on the grounds that they are—I will contend—incompatible with a solution to the problem of hell. Foremost among these is theological determinism, the view that God determines everything that happens in the world: a view that is central to the theological system known as Calvinism. The extended critiques of Calvinism in chapters 3, 5, and 6 are not meant to be antagonistic toward those in the Reformed tradition, but rather to clarify the stakes of the issue. By drawing out the logical implications of Reformed theology, I will explain why this set of ideas intensifies the problem of hell to the point that it becomes unsolvable. My hope is that Calvinists in particular will read and consider these arguments carefully.

The group of readers who may find the contents of this book most amenable to their existing views are Eastern Orthodox Christians. The view that I call "the divine presence model" is one that begins with a core idea about hell that is already widely accepted among Orthodox Christians. The purpose of the model is to fully develop this idea and to defend it with philosophical rigor—a project that, to my knowledge, had not been attempted before *Sinners in the Presence of a Loving God*. Insofar as my own spiritual journey has taken place largely within the Protestant tradition, I expect that my approach to certain parts of Orthodox theology may differ somewhat from the perspective of Orthodox Christians. Nevertheless, it's my desire that this book might help to encourage deeper appreciation of Orthodox theology among Christians of other traditions, and to foster dialogue among the members of the three major branches of the Christian faith.

Although this book is intended for a broad audience, potential readers should be aware that I have made no attempt to "dumb down" the discussion. The book is essentially a series of interlocking arguments that methodically builds a case, first for the claim that the doctrine of hell poses a serious theological problem, then for a certain solution to the problem over and against all the current, standard alternatives. Each major section (e.g., "What Is the Problem of Hell?") is comprised of a set of short chapters that fit together tightly to form a single discussion. Chapter breaks are intended primarily to make the individual parts of the discussion more manageable to digest. Readers who do not have much prior experience with philosophy should anticipate that certain chapters may be slow going. Nevertheless, I believe that those who are willing to work through the material carefully, taking time to digest each argument, will find their efforts rewarded and worth the investment.

Above all, it is my sincere hope that this book will find its way to some who have long struggled with the doctrine of hell, and that such readers will judge the contents of the book to be not merely interesting, or even merely successful as a theological model, but to be spiritually edifying. As I'll explain in the pages that follow, I consider this to be a requirement of any adequate account of hell. If the book achieves this end with any who might read it, the project will be well worth the effort.

# Acknowledgments

I AM GRATEFUL TO all those who read the manuscript and gave me feedback, and in particular to Landon Loftin, Jason Dulworth, Robert Meyer, and an anonymous reviewer for Oxford University Press. Special thanks are due to Jim Jones, whose support of this project—in both its academic form and its present version—has been a great source of encouragement to me. Finally and most of all, I am grateful to my dad, Bob Manis, who not only read the manuscript numerous times, but also long ago helped to lay the foundation of my lifelong love of philosophical theology. The present work is lovingly dedicated to him.

# What Is the Problem of Hell?

# Chapter 1

# Introduction to the problem

WHY WOULD A PERFECTLY good and loving God permit some people to suffer eternally in hell? God is supposed to be all powerful. Doesn't He have the ability to prevent this horrible fate from befalling anyone? And God is supposed to be perfectly good and loving. Doesn't He *want* to prevent this? Why, then, will anyone suffer eternally in hell?

These are troubling questions. But matters are even more disturbing than this, because in the usual understanding of the doctrine, it is God Himself who consigns some to hell, meaning that God deliberately acts so as to bring it about that some people suffer for all eternity. In other words, God doesn't simply *permit* some to suffer in hell; He *causes* it. And it's very difficult to see how this conclusion can be avoided, since God is supposed to be in control of everything that happens in the world. But why would a loving God do such a terrible thing?

This set of questions conveys, in brief, the **problem of hell**.

One of the most common initial reactions to the phrase "the problem of hell" that I've encountered is this callous remark: "It's only a problem for those who are in it." But in fact, it isn't. It's a problem for every reflective Christian, because it poses a serious challenge to the internal coherence of the Christian worldview, and an even more serious challenge to the practical task of trusting—that is, *believing in*—the God whom Christians profess. The problem of hell is no mere philosophical puzzle. It's a hindrance to many who are contemplating coming to the faith, and a source of doubt for many who profess it. This book is an attempt to solve the problem, or at least to make some significant headway on it.

Before we begin trying to develop a solution, we need to make sure we really understand the full extent of the problem. The problem of hell is even more difficult, and much more complex, than what has been conveyed in these opening reflections. Let's begin by situating the problem.

## General and Specific Problems of Evil

The problem of hell is a specific form—arguably, the most difficult form—of a more general problem known as the **problem of evil**.[1] The problem of evil is the most famous objection to belief in God and the most celebrated argument for atheism. It's a problem for all monotheists (often abbreviated as "**theists**"): all those who believe there's an all-powerful, all-knowing, and perfectly good Creator of everything that exists.[2] To understand the problem of evil, we need only generalize the opening questions with which we began: Why does God allow *any* evil or suffering to exist in the world? Since God is all-powerful (**omnipotent**), He could eliminate all evil and suffering. Since God is all-knowing (**omniscient**), He's aware of all the evil and suffering in the world. And since He's perfectly good (**omnibenevolent**), He surely desires that there be no evil and suffering in the world. Why, then, doesn't God eliminate all of it? More to the point, why did God allow evil and suffering in the first place? His limitless power and knowledge surely were adequate to prevent anything He didn't want from coming into existence. Why, then, did God allow evil and suffering to mar His good creation?

Like the problem of hell, the problem of evil is certainly an academic problem—one that has preoccupied philosophers and theologians for thousands of years—but it isn't *merely* an academic problem. Nearly every theist considers the problem at some point, and some struggle with it considerably. Evil and suffering are all around us, and in appalling types and quantities. Anyone who has watched a loved one suffer daily with a terrible

---

1. Although I have tried to keep jargon to a minimum in this book, there are some philosophical and theological concepts that are essential to the discussion. Wherever such terms are first introduced, I have placed them in boldface and included them in the glossary at the end of the book for ease of reference.

2. Strictly speaking, God is the Creator of everything that exists *other than Himself*. And even this claim is controversial. Some philosophers hold the view that there are "abstract objects" that exist necessarily—numbers are a good example—and that such things are neither created nor dependent upon anything, even God, for their existence. This is the sort of technical issue that I will ignore in this book. To any readers who are interested in a discussion of the problem of hell that takes such issues into account, and that strives for the level of philosophical precision and rigor which such a discussion requires, I recommend my previous work, *Sinners in the Presence of a Loving God: An Essay on the Problem of Hell*.

and chronic illness, anyone who has been the victim of a grave injustice, anyone who has lost someone close to them, has been personally affected by evil and suffering. For those who believe in God, these experiences raise disturbing questions about the extent of God's goodness and love, which in turn raise the question of whether God can truly be trusted. And since trust is essential to faith, the problem of evil has led many a believer into a personal crisis of faith. This is the problem faced by all theists even before the doctrine of hell is introduced.

There are many books that attempt to address the problem of evil in its general form, but this book isn't one of them. Having identified the more general problem of which the problem of hell is a specific form, we'll now focus entirely on this specific form. Our guiding question will not be *Why does God permit evil and suffering of any kind?* but rather *Why does God permit the suffering of hell?*

## Traditionalism

Let's begin with the most common answer. The usual explanation for the doctrine of hell is presented in terms of divine justice: God consigns some people to an eternity in hell as a retributive punishment for their earthly wrongdoing. This explanation of hell is based on a theory known as **retributive justice**, according to which justice is achieved through the retributive punishment of wrongdoers. A retributive punishment is one that inflicts some penalty, loss, pain, or harm upon those individuals or groups who have done something wrong. The idea is that the initial wrongdoing caused some loss, pain, or harm, so the appropriate response—the response that achieves justice—is one that causes the wrongdoer(s) to themselves experience something like what they caused. This is what's fair, and justice is a matter of fairness and giving each person what they are due. Those who cause harm *deserve* to suffer a reciprocal harm; those who cause suffering should themselves be made to suffer, etc. Bringing this about is the proper way to "balance the scales of justice." Justice is among the most important and worthwhile moral goods, so in consigning some to hell, God is doing something good: He's restoring the moral order of creation. In this way of viewing things, the doctrine of hell in no way exacerbates the problem of evil. In fact, just the opposite: it's a *solution* to the problem of evil.

This is a very common way of thinking about the logic of hell. It's also a traditional way of understanding these matters—so traditional, in fact, that it rightly deserves the name **traditionalism**. In order to facilitate our discussion of this view, we'll list and label each of its essential components:

- **The consignment thesis:** some people are (or will be) consigned to hell.

- **The no escape thesis:** once consigned to hell, there's no possibility of escape; consignment to hell is a final, irreversible, and everlasting condition.

- **The conscious torment thesis:** existence in hell involves intense suffering of some kind.

- **The retribution thesis:** the purpose of hell is retribution—consignment to hell is a punishment that God freely selects and imposes upon some people as a just recompense for the evil deeds they committed during their earthly lives.

In its developed forms, traditionalism usually includes further claims about the nature and purpose of hell. Some claim that hell includes literal fire and physical tortures. Others claim that the scriptural language of hell is metaphorical: that the language of fire and brimstone and gnawing worms is not to be taken literally but is simply meant to convey a state of psychological, emotional, and spiritual torment. Many traditionalists assume that these various ways of understanding hell are significantly different from one another. But as far as the *problem* of hell is concerned, they are not.[3] All forms of traditionalism present the basic logic of hell in terms of God's inflicting eternal retribution as a way of bringing about justice and restoring the moral order of the universe, regardless of whatever further embellishments they add to this foundation.

We've seen that traditionalism tries to turn the table on the critics of the doctrine of hell: not only is hell not a problem, it actually *solves* the problem of the rampant evil and injustice that we currently observe in the world. Is this analysis enough to lay to rest the supposed problem of hell? Unfortunately, it is not. But the traditionalist analysis does make it clear that a vague appeal to our expectations of what a good God would do—that is, our expectations of what's consistent with perfect goodness

---

3. Insofar as there's a problem of hell, nothing is improved by insisting that the descriptions of hell are metaphorical. If anything, it makes the problem worse. Insofar as the scriptural metaphors are apt, they're obviously meant to convey a state of extreme suffering, and if metaphors must be employed to describe hell, this is presumably because the suffering of hell is *even worse* than anything that can be experienced on earth. In other words, it's a type or magnitude of suffering that's beyond the ability of humans to fully comprehend. The metaphorical view of hell, no less than the literal view, suggests that hell is the worst suffering possible for human beings. Whatever problems are introduced with the doctrine that God consigns some people to this final state, these problems aren't solved merely by insisting that the scriptural language of hell is not to be taken literally.

and love—isn't enough to demonstrate that hell is morally or theologically problematic. To demonstrate this, we'll need to develop in detail some of the more specific problems generated by the doctrine of hell in its traditionalist interpretation.

# Chapter 2
# The problem of justice

THE TRADITIONALIST'S RESPONSE TO the problem of hell is that hell is not itself a moral or theological problem, but rather a *solution* to a theological problem: the problem of evil. Consigning the wicked to hell is the way that God restores justice in the world. In this chapter, we'll begin to explore the reasons that this answer is not satisfactory, at least not as the traditionalist develops it. When we think more carefully about the traditionalist's understanding of hell and their response to the general problem, we find that other, more specific problems quickly emerge.

## A disproportionate punishment

As it turns out, there are *many* such problems. For present purposes, we'll focus on three of the most important. Each problem can be framed as an objection to the traditionalist's understanding of the doctrine of hell, and the most common and widely recognized of these is *the problem of justice*.

According to this objection, God's consigning some individuals to hell does not bring about a moral balance in the world, contrary to the claims of traditionalists. The reason it fails to do so is that justice requires that "the punishment must fit the crime." It's not enough that a punishment is meted out *in response to* a person's wrongdoing; the punishment must also be *proportionate to* the wrongdoing.

This a simple moral principle, and one with a good deal of intuitive support. To make this clear, we'll consider a simple **thought experiment**, the term philosophers use for a description of a possible scenario—whether real or imaginary—whose features highlight or help to clarify something of philosophical significance. Throughout this book, thought experiments will be used to support key philosophical claims. The following thought experiment illustrates the plausibility of the moral principle just cited.

Suppose that a young child is caught stealing candy by a grocery store manager. The child is old enough to know that stealing is wrong and that taking candy without paying for it constitutes stealing. The manager confronts the child and the child's parent about what he has witnessed, and insists that the child's hand be cut off as a just punishment for the crime the child has committed. Obviously, were such a punishment carried out, this would not be an example of justice served. Justice requires that the severity of the punishment not exceed (or at least not egregiously exceed) the severity of the wrongdoing. The punishment must be proportionate to the crime. Call this the **proportionality principle**.

Once this principle is grasped, the problem of justice for traditionalism becomes obvious. Hell is an unjust punishment, because those in hell suffer without end; in terms of the quantity of suffering inflicted, the punishment is literally infinite. But the "crimes" for which the damned are sentenced to hell involve only a finite amount of wrongdoing. Even in the cases of history's worst perpetrators of evil, the amount of harm, while enormous and likely beyond human calculation or understanding, is nonetheless finite. Consequently, the punishment of eternal suffering is always far out of proportion to the severity of the earthly wrongdoing that it's a response to. In short, the punishment of hell is never one that fits the crime, no matter how egregious or numerous those crimes might be.

## The traditionalist response

This is a simple and powerful objection to the traditionalist understanding of hell. But traditionalists are not without reply. Among those who have thought about the problem carefully, the most popular traditionalist response contends that hell *is* in fact a fitting punishment for those consigned to it, because it's a punishment not simply for wrongdoing, but for *sin*, a distinctly theological category whose very possibility requires the existence of a God to whom we are morally accountable. (There would be, according to this view, no sin in a world without God, however much evil or suffering there might be.) This traditionalist response is developed in three steps.

The first step is to argue that when a person sins, they are not simply doing something wrong; they are *wronging God*. This is the case because sin involves a violation of God's commands or requirements. Sin is a kind of rebellion: a matter of willfully disobeying the very author of the moral law, who is also the sinner's Creator. For this reason, acts of disobedience are dishonoring to God. In disobeying and dishonoring God, humans wrong God every time they sin, regardless of whether or to what degree these acts cause harm to other people.

The second step is to argue that all acts wronging God are infinitely blameworthy: that is, a single sin is enough to make a person incur a literally infinite quantity of guilt. In popular presentations of the traditionalist view, this idea is often stated vaguely: "All sin is infinitely bad because it's committed against an infinite God." Clearly, this will not suffice. An adequate defense of traditionalism requires an explanation of *why* the infinitude of God is supposed to render any action of wronging God to be infinitely bad. To explain this, the most adept defenders of traditionalism typically present some version of the following thought experiment.

Imagine the same wicked action carried out against different kinds of creatures; suppose the action-type is *killing for the fun of it*. Such an action might or might not be wicked in all cases, but it's clear that the degree of wickedness varies widely depending on what kind of being it's directed toward. Killing a houseplant for fun might, in some circumstances, not be wicked at all; likewise for killing a horsefly. Killing a goldfish for fun seems worse, though many people would say that it doesn't attain to the level of being truly wicked. But suppose the creature in question is a dog, or a dolphin, or a chimpanzee. It's obvious that killing one of these animals for fun is much worse than killing a plant or a horsefly or a goldfish for fun. And it would be even worse than this—much worse—to kill a human being for fun. What the thought experiment is meant to show is that the same action can vary widely in its degree of wickedness depending on the type of being that it's directed toward, and the greater the level of wickedness, the greater the **culpability**—the moral guilt or blameworthiness—of the perpetrator.

It's important to reflect on *why* the degree of culpability changes with changes in the type of creature harmed. The reason it's so much worse to kill dolphins than dandelions for fun is that dolphins are *significantly greater beings* in all of the ways that are morally relevant: dolphins (but not dandelions) are conscious, intelligent, capable of experiencing pain, capable of forming relationships, capable of complex emotions, etc. As we go up the "great chain of being," as some philosophers have called it, the moral significance of the action increases. At the very top of the chain of being is God, who is infinitely greater than any and all created beings in every morally relevant way. For this reason, any action that wrongs God is infinitely worse than the same action would be if directed against another creature. Perhaps killing for fun is not an action that anyone could carry out against

God.¹ But other kinds of actions—especially those involving disobedience and dishonor—are certainly ways that a creature can wrong God. And whenever God is wronged in these or any other ways, the act in question is always infinitely bad, and thereby incurs for the sinner infinite culpability. In short, because of the kind of being God is, all sin renders the sinner infinitely guilty, and since the punishment of hell is an infinite punishment, it's a punishment that "fits the crime"—regardless of what the specific crime might happen to be, for any given person.

The third and final step of the traditionalist response to the problem of justice is to argue that no one is altogether without sin.² Most people commit a great many sins in the course of their earthly lives—perhaps even in the course of an average day—but even a single sin is enough to justly warrant the punishment of hell.

This completes the three-step traditionalist response to the problem of justice: all sin is against God, every action that wrongs God causes the wrongdoer to incur infinite culpability, and every person commits at least one sin. It follows that all are infinitely guilty and justly deserving of the infinite punishment of hell. It's purely by the grace of God that some will avoid the fate of being eternally consigned to hell; those who are consigned to it are simply receiving their just deserts.

## Why the traditionalist response fails

This is an impressive and influential response to the problem of justice, and many who have considered it find it compelling. But does it really solve the problem?

It doesn't, for two related reasons.³

---

1. It's important in Christian theology that Jesus is God, and he was killed by crucifixion. However, what the present argument requires is that there are ways of wronging God that *anyone* can perform, not just those who lived in Judea in the first century. So we can put aside questions about whether anyone's actions against God have ever qualified as "killing for fun."

2. All orthodox Christians consider Jesus to be an exception to this rule, of course, and many Christians consider Mary the mother of Jesus to be a second exception. These exceptions—and any in-house disputes that Christians of different faith traditions might have about them—can safely be ignored for present purposes.

3. There's a third possible reason that I won't discuss in the main text: namely, that the traditionalist response seems to have the absurd consequence that all sins are equally bad (since all are infinitely bad). The claim that all sins are equally bad—or "equal in God's eyes"—is fairly common among Evangelicals, many of whom, I suspect, feel compelled to say this in order to maintain consistency with other, traditionalist views about hell and divine justice. But it's as obvious as anything could be that the claim is

The first is that a person's level of culpability is not a simple function of the amount or type of harm caused by that person's actions. Intentions matter a great deal, and a person's intentions in performing a certain action are directly connected to their own understanding of *what it is that they're doing*. In general, lack of knowledge or understanding—at least in cases where this lack of knowledge is not willfully chosen or the result of self-deception[4]—tends to mitigate (lessen) a person's level of guilt. This is why we take into account whether a person is intellectually disabled or mentally ill in deciding whether they're blameworthy for some harmful action and whether punishment is a morally appropriate response. It's also why, to take a different sort of example, we wouldn't consider a person guilty of murder who flips a switch that they reasonably believe to control the lights but which, due to some terrorist meddling, instead detonates a bomb. To be responsible for your actions, you have to know what it is that you're doing. And to be *completely* responsible for your actions—responsible in a way that is wholly unmitigated by any extenuating consideration—you would have to *completely* or *perfectly* understand what it is that you're doing. Since (non-willful) ignorance diminishes a person's level of culpability, a maximum or infinite level of culpability would require that the individual has a perfect understanding of what they're doing in performing some wrongful act.

The problem for traditionalists is that, with actions wronging God, this condition could never be met. Because of the limited capacities of human understanding, no one could possibly understand *fully* what they're doing in wronging God, because no mere human can fully comprehend God.

It might not be immediately obvious why it would be necessary to fully comprehend God in order to possess perfect understanding of what one is doing in wronging God. An example will help to illustrate the reason for this requirement. Imagine a person who is pulling the legs off a live insect. In order for this person to fully know what they're doing, in the morally relevant sense, they must have sufficient knowledge about the creature that their actions are affecting; that is, they must know something about the *nature* of insects. Among other things, they must know whether insects (or insects of this particular type) are capable of pain, since this

---

false. Pirating movies and murdering children are not equally bad, and any theological argument that implies otherwise should be rejected. Fortunately, the traditionalist is not actually committed to this absurd claim. Even if the traditionalist were right that all sin is infinitely bad, it would not follow that all sins are equally bad; surprising as it might at first seem, it is mathematically provable that not all infinities are equal.

4. Readers who are unfamiliar with the idea of self-deception can ignore this qualifier ("at least in cases . . .") for now. We'll return to the concept of self-deception to explore it in detail in a later chapter.

bears directly on the question of what harm (if any) the action causes, which partially determines the action's moral status.

The point can be generalized: moral understanding requires knowledge of the natures of the beings whom one's actions affect. At the upper limit, *complete* or *perfect* understanding would require complete or perfect knowledge of these natures. And this is the conclusion that's relevant to the discussion at hand: since everyone's understanding of the divine nature is far less than complete, no one can *fully* know what they're doing in wronging God. Consequently, the quantity of guilt that a person accrues in wronging God could never be literally infinite. It might be some very large finite amount—perhaps an amount far greater than what we ordinarily assume—but insofar as this amount is less than infinite, it cannot warrant an infinite punishment, given the proportionality principle. This is the first reason that the traditionalist response to the problem of justice fails.

The second reason it fails is that culpability is *decreased* whenever the perpetrator of a wrong or harmful action is a lesser type of being than the victim. Once again, a thought experiment is helpful for illustrating the point. Compare several cases of killing: in the first, a human is killed by another human; in the second, a human is killed by a dog. Would we judge the dog to bear equal guilt to the human killer? Now consider a third case, in which a human is killed by a scorpion. Is it reasonable to blame (in the moral sense) the scorpion as much as the human killer? What the thought experiment is meant to highlight is that culpability decreases whenever the perpetrator of some harm is a lesser kind (type, category) of being than the victim, and decreases *in proportion to* the size of the "gap" between the two types.

This insight casts doubt on the fundamental logic of the traditionalist response to the problem of justice. From the fact that God is infinitely greater than humans, it does not automatically follow that humans incur infinite guilt in wronging God. The infinite difference in levels of greatness between humanity and divinity seems to be a mitigating factor.

Note that this second reason for doubting the traditionalist response is connected to the first: part of the reason for judging that the dog is less blameworthy than the human killer is that a dog cannot really understand what it's doing in killing a human being (and all the more so for a scorpion). More generally: in cases where a lesser being wrongs a greater being, part of the reason that culpability decreases is that the widening gap between the types of beings correlates to less and less understanding on the part of the wrongdoer. The dog doesn't really know what it's doing in killing a human, because it has little or no understanding of the *nature* of human beings. Of course, the gap between dog and human is infinitely less than the gap between human and God. All the more, then, it follows that the guilt of human beings in wronging God is diminished (certainly not increased) by our infinitely lesser status.

Our discussion has revealed that the problem of justice is not adequately answered by the usual traditionalist response, and this is the case for two related reasons. First, levels of culpability are diminished by lack of understanding on the part of the wrongdoer, and since humans are incapable of fully comprehending God, it's impossible for humans to be fully or infinitely culpable for acts wronging God, regardless of the level of objective badness these acts might otherwise have. Second, the level of culpability of a wrongdoer decreases as the difference in the respective levels of greatness between the wrongdoer and his/her/its victim increases. For these two, related reasons, the problem of justice is not adequately answered by the traditionalist response that we've considered, and since this response is the best one that traditionalists have so far produced, the problem of justice remains unsolved for traditionalists.

## Chapter 3

# The problem of love

ALONGSIDE THE CONCERNS ABOUT justice that we explored in the previous chapter, philosophers and theologians have long been concerned about whether the doctrine of hell is compatible with the doctrines of God's perfect goodness and love. Different types of objections are possible here, and one common type focuses on the duration of a person's consignment to hell and the magnitude of the suffering experienced in hell. The concern here is that it would be bad, or at the very least unloving, for God to consign a person to *so much* suffering. This objection is closely tied to the problem of justice, insofar as it focuses on the quantitative facet of the punishment of hell. A different—and perhaps less appreciated—form of the problem, which will be developed in this chapter, focuses on a *qualitative* feature of the punishment of hell. What drives this objection is a concern about what the punishment of hell is, and especially what it is *not*, intended to accomplish, on a traditionalist account.

## An unloving punishment

To begin, recall that traditionalism is a retributive model: the *purpose* for the suffering of hell, the reason that God wills it, is to balance the scales of justice by returning harm upon those who have caused harm—whether to others, to God, or even to themselves—by the wicked actions they committed during their earthly lives. What hell is *not* intended to accomplish, according to this account, is the reform or moral improvement of those consigned to it. More generally, the punishment of hell is in no way intended to promote the good of the damned.

In this way of understanding matters, the punishment of hell is *unloving*, even if—contrary to the arguments of the previous chapter—it turned out to be perfectly just. In order for a punishment to be loving, it must be intended to promote the good of the one who is punished. Good and loving parents understand and appreciate this principle, which guides their approach to disciplining their children. The purpose of punishing a child's bad behavior is not to balance the scales of justice, but rather to shape the child's character, to promote their moral and spiritual growth and maturing, toward the end of helping them eventually to become a good person. All of this is for the child's good. This is the motive for punishment that love requires, because, in general, *to love someone is to will their good*, insofar as one is able. At the very least, this is the case if we restrict the meaning of "love" to **agape**, the selfless and sacrificial kind of love that, according to the Bible, God has for us and commands us to have for one another.[1]

Insofar as God is perfectly loving, we can expect that any punishment that He inflicts will be both *directed at* and *intended to promote* the good of those whom He punishes. But on a retributive model of hell, such as traditionalism, the punishment of hell doesn't meet this condition. There's no possibility that it will promote the good of the damned, and it's not intended to do so. For this reason, it is an unloving punishment. Insofar as God is the one who imposes the punishment, traditionalism implies that God does not love the damned, or, at the very least, that He does not love the damned perfectly. Traditionalism is thus incompatible with the doctrines of God's perfect goodness and love.

### Response #1: God doesn't love the damned

Like the problem of justice, the problem of love in this version is simple, but it poses a very difficult challenge to a retributive view of hell. There are various ways of trying to respond to the problem, and some are clearly better than others. We'll consider three possible lines of response, beginning with the one that's surely the worst strategy, despite its likely being the most popular.

The first response is simply to "bite the bullet" and insist that God does not love the damned. There are many Christians who hold this view—albeit for reasons slightly different than the ones suggested by the previous argument. Almost always, these Christians are **Calvinists**, whose main theological emphasis is the **sovereignty** of God, and who understand

---

1. See, for example, Jesus' famous parable of the good Samaritan in Luke 10:25–37, noting especially the command that Jesus gives at the end: "Go and do likewise."

divine sovereignty to be a matter of both authority and *control*. On the Calvinist understanding of matters, for God to be absolutely sovereign is for God to be in complete control of everything that happens in the world.[2] The way in which God exerts this control over creation, on the Calvinist account, is by God's directly determining all of the events that occur within it, a view known as **theological determinism**.

In this way of understanding God's relation to the world, creaturely free will is no obstacle to divine sovereignty, because God can *make* a person choose something *freely*. This is so, says the theological determinist, because freedom and determinism are compatible: an action can be *both* free *and* determined. This view of free will—which philosophers call *compatibilism*—is highly controversial, but this is not the place to pursue the debate. For present purposes, what matters is that on Calvinist theology nothing in creation functions as an impediment to God's will; the world is *exactly* as God desires and wills it to be.

Since Calvinists believe that many people (perhaps most people) are finally lost, it follows from their theology that it is God's will for many (most) to be finally lost.[3] But if it's God's will that many people meet a final, ruinous end—an eternal state of unrelenting and unsurpassable misery—when it's perfectly within God's power to save everyone, without so much as violating anyone's free will, then it's obvious that God does not will the highest good for everyone. In the Calvinist scheme of things, God is perfectly able to save everyone; He simply chooses not to. (The usual Calvinist explanation for this is that God desires instead to maximize His own glory, which requires that many people be chosen to suffer the fate of eternal damnation. The details of this account will be saved for a later chapter.)

We noted previously that loving a person requires willing that person's highest good, insofar as one is able. If God doesn't will the highest good of every person, but instead wills that some suffer the worst fate imaginable,

---

2. In the memorable words of R. C. Sproul, "If there is one single molecule in this universe running around loose, totally free of God's sovereignty, then we have no guarantee that a single promise of God will ever be fulfilled" (Sproul, *Classic Teachings on the Nature of God*, 172).

3. I should clarify that I am discussing Calvinism in its mainstream version, both here and in later chapters. There is a minority version of Calvinism, inspired by the great twentieth-century theologian Karl Barth, which rejects the view that it is God's will that some people will be finally lost. In this minority view, divine election—God's selection of a person for salvation—extends to everyone, and since God is capable of saving whomsoever He chooses, it follows that all will be saved. The great advantage of this form of Calvinism is that it's capable of retaining the doctrines of God's perfect goodness and love (unlike the mainstream version of Calvinism, as I'll presently argue). Nevertheless, the view has been widely rejected by Calvinists outside of academia, and for this reason I'll ignore it in the remaining discussion of Calvinism in this book.

it follows that God doesn't love everyone. Endorsing a *consistent* form of Calvinism requires one to simply embrace this conclusion—and many prominent Calvinists do exactly this.[4] Of course, if one is willing to embrace the conclusion that God doesn't love the damned, then the problem of love is easily answered. In formulating the problem of love, we were assuming that it's objectionable for a view of hell to imply that God doesn't love the damned. The consistent Calvinist rejects this assumption, thereby removing the barrier to embracing traditionalism.

This "solution," however, comes at a theological cost that no Christian should find acceptable. To claim that God doesn't love everyone is to deny central teachings of Scripture: that "God so loved the world," that God "wants all people to be saved and to come to a knowledge of the truth," that God is "not wanting anyone to perish, but everyone to come to repentance," that God loved us "while we were still sinners," that "God *is* love," and so on.[5] The claim that God doesn't love everyone is also, significantly, a rejection of the mainstream of Christian tradition. The way of understanding God's nature that dominates the history of Christian thought is called **perfect being theology**. In this view, God is the greatest possible being; His perfection is *unsurpassable*. To say that it's unsurpassable is not simply to say that there is no being greater than God (in other words, that God's greatness is *unsurpassed*); it's to say that no being could *possibly* be any greater than God, and that God could not *possibly* be any greater than He is. In the philosophical parlance, what perfect being theology requires is that the divine nature is comprised of all "great-making properties" in their "maximal forms." Knowledge, power, and goodness are three prominent examples of great-making properties—properties the possession of which makes a being greater—and God possesses the greatest possible amount of each. He possesses these properties in their maximal forms, which are omniscience, omnipotence, and omnibenevolence, respectively. Likewise for whatever other great-making properties there might be: if a property contributes to perfection, then God possesses that property in its maximal form.

In some cases, there is theological controversy as to whether a certain property counts as great-making: the properties of timelessness and

---

4. Jonathan Edwards is perhaps the most famous historical example of a Calvinist who clearly and explicitly embraces the conclusion that God loves only the elect; Herman Hoeksema and Arthur Pink are prominent twentieth-century examples. Among contemporary Calvinists, John Piper and Mark Driscoll are especially outspoken proponents of this view, but examples could easily be multiplied.

5. John 3:16; 1 Timothy 2:4; 2 Peter 3:9; Romans 5:8; 1 John 4:8–16, respectively. Throughout this book, all quotations from Scripture are taken from the New International Version (NIV) unless otherwise noted. All italics in quotations from Scripture are added, unless otherwise noted.

impassibility are two important examples. However, Christians are clearly committed to the claim that the property of *being loving*—where "loving" is understood in its agapeistic sense—is a great-making property. This is the property perfectly exemplified by Jesus and for which he is the archetype of all Christian ethics.

It might come as a surprise to some Calvinists, but the simple admission that being loving is a great-making property is devastating to Calvinist theology. To see why, compare two divine beings,[6] perfectly similar in every way—knowledge, power, etc.—except for one crucial difference: the first being has the property of loving every person it creates, and the second has the property of loving some, but not all, of those whom it creates. The divine being who loves only some of its creatures displays the property of being loving to a limited degree, a degree that is surpassable, and in fact is surpassed, by the first being, whose love is unbounded toward those whom it creates. Given the requirements of perfect being theology, this fact alone is enough to establish that the second being is not God. To be God, a being must possess the property of being loving in its maximal form, and any being whose love could be greater or more perfect in any way does not meet this condition. Accordingly, Calvinists and any other Christians who claim that God loves some (the "**elect**," the saints) but not others (the non-elect, the damned) are forced either to reject the traditional understanding of God's nature or to admit that the god of their theology is not the God of Christianity.

## Response #2: Loving someone doesn't require willing their good

So much for the first proposed solution to the problem of love. But other responses are possible and perhaps more plausible. A second strategy of response that a traditionalist might adopt is to argue that the punishment of hell is loving even though it's not directed at the good of the damned. Let's now consider this view.

The first thing to say about this view is that one of the ways of trying to argue for it is clearly misguided. Suppose someone claimed that the

---

6. A thought experiment doesn't have to be a description of the world as it actually is; it can be a description of something merely possible. This thought experiment invites a comparison of two divine beings. For theists, who believe there's only one *actual* divine being, at least one of the beings described in this thought experiment is purely imaginary (a merely possible being). This in no way undermines the thought experiment.

punishment of hell is loving toward those who have been wronged by the damned—in other words, that punishing the damned is a way of honoring their victims, a way of showing respect for the dignity and worth of those who have suffered injustice. The problem with this response is that it simply misses the point. The challenge for traditionalists is not to explain how there could be *something* loving about the doctrine of hell; the challenge is to explain how God is behaving lovingly *toward the damned* in consigning them to hell. Otherwise, we're back to the problem discussed above: if God fails to love the damned, then His love could be greater than it is, in which case He's not the greatest possible being, in which case He's not God—which is clearly absurd.

In order to argue that the punishment of hell is loving even though it's not directed at the good of the damned, a traditionalist will have to go further, rejecting altogether the fundamental principle on which the problem of love rests: namely, that to love someone is to will their good, insofar as one is able. But this strategy also appears to lead to self-contradiction. In formulating this principle, we specified that "love" is to be understood in the biblical sense of *agape*. But it's part of the very concept of agape that it is a self-sacrificing love that wills the good of the beloved, even at great personal cost. Claiming that agape love doesn't require willing the good of the beloved is like claiming that being square doesn't require having right angles. So much for the second strategy of response to the problem of love.

### Response #3: Hell is good for the damned

The remaining option for traditionalists is to try to argue that the punishment of hell is good for the damned (and thus loving) even though it is not, and is not intended to be, reformative. In short, it's good for the damned that they suffer an eternal retributive punishment.

But how could this be? The most common explanation given by traditionalists is that punishing those in hell is actually a way of *respecting their dignity*. To be a **moral agent** is to be capable of making morally significant choices and to be held accountable for those choices. If God were to ignore or excuse without consequence the wrongdoing of the damned, He would not be treating them as competent moral agents. (Note the way that we sometimes excuse the harms caused by very young children, those with intellectual disabilities, the mentally ill, etc.) By consigning to eternal punishment those whose actions deserve it, God is recognizing and respecting the dignity that humans possess in virtue of being moral agents.

This is perhaps the most plausible strategy of response to the problem of love, but it too turns out to be seriously defective. One problem will be mentioned only in passing. There's at least a worry that consignment to a state of eternal suffering would be destructive of human personality, and thus dehumanizing. To put it starkly: How much suffering could a person realistically endure without descending into madness? But if the punishment of hell has, or tends to have, any such effect, it's hard to see how it could be a way of promoting the dignity of the damned.

There's an even bigger problem for this strategy of response, however. Even if it could be established that an eternal retributive punishment somehow promotes the dignity of those in hell or is an expression of God's respect for the moral agency of the damned, this wouldn't be enough to solve the problem of love. Love requires more than willing *some* good of the beloved; it requires willing the beloved's *highest* good. But hell, understood as an eternal retributive punishment, in no way promotes the highest good of those consigned to it.

Another thought experiment will help to illustrate the first part of this counterargument: that love requires willing the *highest* good of the beloved. Imagine a recovering drug addict who is going through withdrawal. The addict must go cold turkey to have any chance of overcoming his addiction, let's suppose, but his withdrawal symptoms are severe. In order to relieve the pain of his withdrawal symptoms, his wife gives him more of the drug. She knows that her husband's continued use of this drug will eventually lead to his death, but her intention is simply to promote her husband's good by relieving his immediate pain. Clearly, this woman is failing to love her husband properly. The goodness of relieving the man's immediate pain is vastly outweighed by the badness of feeding his addiction, with all its dire consequences.

There's an important lesson here for traditionalists. To be successful, the proposed strategy of response to the problem of love would have to contend that God is willing the *highest* good of the damned in consigning them to eternal retributive punishment in hell in order to promote their dignity. But this strategy is doomed to failure, because it conflicts with basic assumptions of Christian theology. On any orthodox version of Christianity, the highest good of every human being, and the condition of true and permanent happiness, is a state of eternal **communion** (fellowship, union, friendship) with God. Attaining this state of communion with God requires that the individual first be made holy, or righteous, or sanctified, or perfected in love; in biblical terms, they must be "conformed to the image" of Jesus Christ (Romans 8:29).[7] There are various accounts of how this is possible, and the details of these various accounts have at times divided different versions of Christianity from one another. But there's no need to enter into this dispute for present purposes, since on *any* such account, it involves the individual's undergoing some sort of moral and spiritual transformation and improvement. And this is precisely what a traditionalist account denies to be a feature of hell. No one in hell is in any way morally or spiritually improved thereby, on the traditionalist account. It follows from this that hell does not promote the highest good of those consigned to it, even if it manages to promote some lesser good, such as human dignity. Since it fails to promote the highest good of the damned, not only in its effect, but in its intent, the punishment of consignment to hell is one that does not properly express love for the damned.

Note, finally, that it will not improve matters to try to come up with some *other* good—something other than respect for human dignity—that hell supposedly promotes. Regardless of what good might be proposed, and regardless of how successfully it might be argued that hell promotes this good, the resulting view will always face the same problem. Insofar as consignment to hell neither achieves nor even aims to promote the highest human good, it is an unloving punishment, regardless of whatever other goods it might achieve.

In the end, all of the available traditionalist responses to the problem of love come up short. Even more than the problem of justice, it seems, the problem of love poses a very difficult challenge to traditionalism.

---

7. This idea is prevalent throughout the New Testament. See, for example, 1 Corinthians 15:49; 2 Corinthians 3:18; Galatians 3:27; Ephesians 4:13; Philippians 3:21; Hebrews 12:14; 1 Peter 1:13–16; 1 John 3:2.

# Chapter 4

# The problem of coercion

THE THIRD SPECIFIC PROBLEM of hell that we will consider is importantly different from the first two. The problem of justice and the problem of love are logical problems, in the sense that they reveal a deep tension, and perhaps even a logical contradiction, between the traditionalist version of the doctrine of hell and other doctrines of orthodox Christianity. The problem that we will now consider is one that reveals a deep tension between *belief in* the traditionalist doctrine of hell and other beliefs, attitudes, and actions that are essential to Christian faith.

### The edification principle

In order to develop this problem, let's first consider what we would expect to be true of any doctrine that God has revealed to human beings. Many Christian beliefs are known (or knowable) on the basis of common experience and reason. An example is the belief that there is much evil in the world. This is obviously implied by various passages in Scripture, but it's also known to be true independent of Scripture. There are, however, important theological teachings in the Bible that are not known to be true on independent grounds; these are known as **revealed doctrines**. The doctrines of the Trinity, incarnation, and atonement are important examples of this in Christian theology. Crucially for the present discussion, the doctrine of hell also falls into the category of revealed doctrine. The primary reason many Christians believe that some people will suffer eternal punishment in hell is that they take this to be revealed in Scripture (for example, in Matthew 25:46).

Those committed to the inspiration and authority of Scripture are obliged to accept any teaching they take to be a genuine revealed doctrine, even if it's something they cannot know on independent grounds such as reason or personal experience. Nevertheless, there are certain things that we would, and would not, expect to be true of any revealed doctrine. We wouldn't expect a revealed doctrine to be scientifically verifiable, for the reason just discussed, so the fact that the doctrine of hell doesn't meet this standard isn't surprising or problematic. But we would expect that anything God reveals to be true would be *edifying* for believers to accept. For something to be edifying is for it to "build up" a person or community: to strengthen a person's faith, to promote moral and spiritual growth, to encourage believers in the pursuit of godly things, etc. We would reasonably expect that all revealed doctrines would have this effect in the lives of those who believe them sincerely, *especially* those who reflect on these doctrines very carefully and internalize them deeply. Furthermore, we would expect this to be true at both the individual level and at the corporate level: that is, at the level of the church, the collective body of all true believers. Let's give a name to this set of expectations about revealed doctrines: let's call it the **edification principle**.

One of the most disturbing and problematic features of the doctrine of hell, in its traditionalist version, is how flagrantly it seems to violate the edification principle. It turns out there's a whole set of problems of this form—a multitude of ways that sincere and deeply internalized belief in the traditionalist doctrine of hell seems to be the very opposite of edifying. Indeed, such belief in hell seems actually to undermine other beliefs, attitudes, and actions that Christian faith requires.[1] For present purposes, we will develop only one of these problems, the most severe problem of this type for traditionalism.

## The threat of hell

Let's begin with another thought experiment. Imagine a man who's in love with a woman who doesn't love him in return. Frustrated and eventually driven mad with desperation by his failure to court her affections, the man finally resorts to threats of violence. He takes his beloved hostage, points a gun to her head, and demands that she either love him or be killed. Notice the position the woman now finds herself in. It's *impossible* for her to

---

1. I have elsewhere developed numerous problems of this type under the heading "The Doxastic Problem"; see especially chapter 2 of *Sinners in the Presence of a Loving God*.

comply with this man's demand. Even if she might have come to love him under other circumstances, she cannot possibly begin to do so now, under threat of being killed. She may *say* that she now loves him, or try to *act as if* she loves him, in order to increase her chances of surviving this ordeal, but she certainly cannot begin to *genuinely* love him under these circumstances. And the reason she cannot do so is obvious: she's being coerced.

The problem for traditionalism is that the revelation of hell, as the traditionalist interprets the doctrine, seems to function much like the gun at this woman's head. What the doctrine specifies is that those who fail to act in a certain way will be punished by God for all eternity. This is a kind of threat: assuming that Scripture is inspired, the revelation of the doctrine of hell (on the traditionalist interpretation) is a matter of God's telling human beings that He will inflict a certain harm on anyone who fails to comply with a certain requirement. Traditionalists of different stripes disagree with one another about which actions, exactly, are required for compliance—that is, which actions one must take to avoid the punishment of hell.[2] Regardless, these actions include, at a minimum, repenting of one's sins and believing in God, where "believing in" does not mean merely believing true propositions about God, but rather trusting, obeying, loving, and worshiping God. What the doctrine of hell specifies, then, is that God will inflict an eternal punishment upon all those who fail to repent of their sins and believe in Him. By revealing this doctrine to us, it appears that God is making a threat of the greatest possible magnitude.

The problem is not that God is doing something wrong, or violating our rights, or otherwise mistreating humans by threatening us in this way. For present purposes, we can assume that God has no moral obligations at all, that we have no rights in relation to God, and that nothing God could do to us would count as mistreatment. The real problem for traditionalism is that, by issuing a threat of such magnitude, God appears to be bringing about a situation in which anything humans do in response to the revelation will count as coerced. More precisely, anyone who *truly believes* the revelation and whose response is motivated by this belief will be acting under coercion. But acts performed under coercion are not free. So by issuing the threat implicit in the revelation of the doctrine of hell, God is thereby eliminating the possibility of a free response for anyone who truly believes it.

This is an alarming and disturbing conclusion, because at least some of the actions that are demanded by God to avoid hell—namely, repenting

---

2. Here I'm referring to disputes about the nature of the sacraments (baptism, the Eucharist, etc.) and the role of individual works in achieving salvation—the kinds of disputes that historically have tended to separate Protestants from Catholic and Orthodox Christians.

of one's sins and believing in God—are actions that *cannot* be coerced; they must be performed freely to be performed at all. It's logically impossible to *make* a person repent, because repentance is, of its very nature, an act of *freely* turning from one's own sins. The same is true of love, worship, and trust: these cannot be coerced, because any response that's coerced will not qualify as *genuine* love, *genuine* worship, or *genuine* trust.[3]

The conclusion we have reached, then, is that the very revelation of hell, as traditionalists understand it, makes it impossible for those who truly believe the doctrine to do what's demanded of them in order to avoid hell. The only people who can do what's necessary to avoid hell, it seems, are those who don't really believe the revelation. Consequently, sincerely believing the revelation of hell and deeply internalizing the doctrine is the exact opposite of edifying: it apparently makes it impossible to be saved!

## Possible lines of response

This is a disastrous result for traditionalism. Is there any way to avoid it? Once again, it's worth considering some possible lines of response. There appear to be four: traditionalists can (1) reject the edification principle, (2) contend that the doctrine of hell is somehow edifying even though it's coercive, (3) deny that freedom is required for repentance or belief in God, or (4) argue that the doctrine of hell is not actually coercive (or not coercive to a degree that undermines a free response). This list of possible responses can be immediately winnowed, since the first and second are so implausible as hardly to warrant serious consideration. How could any Christian seriously claim that some core Christian doctrines are unedifying to believe? Likewise, the claim that it's edifying to be coerced in a way that makes repentance or belief in God impossible is self-evidently absurd.

The third option might appear to be better. Calvinists, in particular, might be tempted to deny that freedom is required for repentance or belief in God, on the grounds that humans have no free will, since God determines everything that occurs in the world. But any Calvinist who adopted such a line would be confused. The clear-headed Calvinist is not someone who denies the reality of free will, but rather someone who claims that free will is compatible with determinism (as discussed in chapter 3). All Christians are committed to the reality of free will in *some* form, because free will is

---

3. The novel *1984*, and in particular its closing scene, is an instructive example of what kind of "love" could be elicited through coercion. It's safe to conclude that a theology is deeply flawed if it implies that the believer's love for God is like Winston's "love" for Big Brother.

a necessary condition of moral responsibility, and all Christians agree that God holds us morally accountable for our actions, and that He acts justly in doing so. Once this is recognized, there's no good reason to deny that freedom is required for the specific actions of repentance and belief in God.

This leaves the fourth and final option, which comes in two forms. The traditionalist could deny altogether that the revelation of hell is coercive. Or, while admitting that the doctrine is coercive to *some* degree, the traditionalist could argue that it's not so coercive as to undermine a free response. The first strategy is a nonstarter. It's true by definition that threatening to inflict severe harm for failure to comply with one's demands constitutes coercion. Insofar as the doctrine of hell is understood to be a threat of this kind—which, on the traditionalist account, it clearly is—there's no avoiding the conclusion that the revelation of hell is coercive to *some* degree.

There is, however, an argument to be made that coercion doesn't always undermine the possibility of a free response. Even in the face of threats that are clearly coercive, some people refuse to comply, which seems to demonstrate that free will remains intact under such circumstances. Perhaps, then, the coercive feature of God's revealing the doctrine of hell is unproblematic.

Unfortunately for traditionalists, this line of response also fails. Even granting that there are levels of coercion that might leave open the possibility of a free response, it seems clear that there is *some* level of coercion at which freedom is destroyed. At the least, freedom is destroyed at (if not before) the point when the magnitude of the threat is so high that noncompliance is **psychologically impossible** for the one who's being threatened. Something is psychologically impossible for a certain person if it's something that they simply *could not bring themselves to do*, even if the action is physically within their power. The idea is best conveyed by an example: it's physically within your means to stab a loved one through the eye with an ice pick, but—assuming you're not deranged—you simply couldn't bring yourself to do such a horrible thing.

The example demonstrates that psychological impossibility is relative to individuals: what's psychologically impossible for one person might be entirely doable for another. It's clear that some people are capable of resisting even extreme threats—threats on their life, for example—so it might seem doubtful that any threat could count as freedom-destroying *in general*. What this overlooks, however, is the *kind* of threat implicit in the revelation of the doctrine of hell. Even for those who are highly resistant to threats, there is some level of coercion that renders noncompliance psychologically impossible. For the one who's prepared to resist threats on their own life, perhaps threats on the lives of their entire family would be the breaking point. Perhaps some could resist even this threat; but even worse threats are possible. What drives the problem of coercion is simply the assumption that there's *some* level beyond which a threat is so great that no sane person could *both* believe that the threat is real—that is, that the threatened harm will in fact be inflicted in the event of noncompliance—and still, nonetheless, refuse to comply. This assumption seems all but undeniable.

But if *any* threat attains this level, the threat of hell does so, since the level of harm that is threatened by consignment to hell is the greatest imaginable. Hell is the worst thing that could possibly happen to anyone. Accordingly, we could say that the threat of hell is—adopting a term previously introduced—a *maximal* threat.[4] If any threat is coercive to a degree that undermines a free response—and it's clear this is the case—a maximal threat certainly does so. In the face of a maximal threat that is *genuinely believed*, noncompliance is psychologically impossible. Under such conditions, freedom is destroyed, because freedom requires the ability to make (or to have made) a different choice in the circumstances. When the range of available options—options that are actually within one's ability to choose—is reduced to only one, there is no longer any freedom of choice. Accordingly, the only ones whose response to the revelation of hell isn't coerced are those who don't believe it (in its traditionalist form).

It appears, then, that there is no good way for traditionalists to circumvent the problem of coercion.

Each of the three problems that we've discussed—justice, love, and coercion—poses a very serious objection to traditionalism. The combination of the three appears to be fatal. How, then, should we solve the problem of hell?

---

4. Some might object that the doctrine of hell need not be conceived as issuing a threat this great. Perhaps hell isn't *that* bad. But this line of response isn't one the traditionalist can adopt. Even if the intensity of suffering in hell is, at any given moment, less than maximal, the suffering of hell goes on forever, on the traditionalist account, and is thus infinite. This alone would make any earthly suffering pale in comparison to the suffering of hell, which is enough to establish the truth of the statement that consignment to hell is the worst thing that could possibly happen to anyone. Any movement away from the claim that the revelation of hell is a maximal threat is a movement away from traditionalism.

# How (Not) to Solve the Problem of Hell

## Chapter 5

# The Calvinist appeal to divine sovereignty

WHEN TRYING TO SOLVE a difficult problem, it's sometimes helpful to first consider what *won't* work. Bad answers to hard questions can be instructive. Appreciating why these answers are problematic can help point us toward a right answer. In the upcoming chapters, we'll consider a number of misguided ways of trying to solve the problem of hell. In the course of developing these misguided approaches, we'll also consider in more detail some of the theological assumptions that generate the problem in the first place. The purpose of these considerations is to begin sketching the *general form* of a solution to the problem of hell. In chapters 9 and 10, we'll develop the model of hell that best incorporates these insights.

### Misguided approach #1: Appealing to divine sovereignty

Many Christians imagine that the problem of hell—and a great many other theological problems, as well—can be easily solved. All that's needed is a firm reminder that God is absolutely sovereign. He can do anything He wants. We don't have any right to question God. His ways are higher than ours. God is God and we are not. Once we really take this to heart, we will realize that there's no genuine problem of hell. The "problem" is really just a way of trying to judge God according to human standards.

The group of Christians most prone to this kind of response are Calvinists. Recall, from chapter 3, that on the usual way of working out Calvinist theology, sovereignty is the most emphasized and celebrated attribute of God. To say that God is absolutely sovereign is to say, on the Calvinist account, first, that God is the rightful ruler of all—He has absolute authority over all creation—and, second, that God exercises His authority by completely controlling everything that happens in the world. These two facets of sovereignty go together in the Calvinist understanding of hell: as the Creator of all that exists, God has the right to do anything He wants with any part of His creation, including human beings, and what God sovereignly decrees is that some are chosen to be saved ("the elect"), while others are determined to persist in their sins and be damned. To quote a favorite Calvinist passage from Scripture: "Has the potter no right over the clay, to make out of the same lump one vessel for honorable use and another for dishonorable use?" (Romans 9:21 ESV).

To say that God has the right to act as He does is not yet to explain *why* God acts as He does. According to Calvinists, the purpose of God's sovereign decrees—the ultimate purpose of *all* God's actions, in fact—is *to bring glory to Himself*. These two claims—that God is absolutely sovereign and that God's actions are all aimed at maximizing His own glory—form the basis of the theology that's distinctive to Calvinism, including the Calvinist understanding of hell.

If God is completely in control of everything that happens in the world, including everyone's "free" choices about whether to accept or reject Him, it follows that it's within God's power to save everyone. But Calvinists interpret the Bible, and in particular Romans chapter 9, as teaching that God has in fact created some people for the express purpose of bringing glory to Himself through their eternal suffering in hell. This is a shocking and disturbing thought to most people, at least initially. It's also confusing. Why would it bring glory to God for some people to suffer horrendously for all eternity?

The usual explanation offered by Calvinists is that this is the means by which God displays His justice. Justice is displayed by the retributive punishment of sinners. In order to display His justice, God needs some sinners to punish. So God includes these in His creation. He creates some "vessels of wrath prepared for destruction" (Romans 9:22 ESV) in order to fill this role.[1] And these vessels are chosen to fill this role *before they're even born*. From all eternity past, before any humans even existed, it was already decreed by God who would be saved and who would be damned.

---

1. A minor point that we won't linger on here is that this popular Calvinist argument is clearly invalid. Even granting the Calvinist assumption that displays of justice require the punishment of sinners, *eternal* punishment isn't needed to display divine justice. If God were to create sinners, punish them, *and then restore them*, God would thereby display His justice.

According to Calvinist theology, some people are literally created for damnation: suffering for eternity in hell is—from the perspective of God's sovereign will—their reason for existing. This idea, that God has chosen some people for eternal damnation from before the foundations of the world, is called the doctrine of **reprobation**, and it's arguably the most distinguishing feature of Calvinism.

When it's pointed out to Calvinists that their doctrine of reprobation clearly entails that God doesn't love everyone and that He even hates some people (He not only fails to will the highest good for some, He instead wills for them the most horrific fate imaginable), the typical Calvinist rejoinder is that *God doesn't owe anyone His love.* He doesn't owe it to anyone to save them. He doesn't owe anyone anything. God is absolutely sovereign, and He chooses in His sovereignty to reprobate some in order to bring greater glory to Himself. No one has any right to complain.[2] And the few He saves have great cause for giving thanks to Him. On the traditional Calvinist account, the fact that most are lost is part of what makes the elect so happy in heaven: they witness the horrendous sufferings of the great mass of the damned and delight that they, the elect, were chosen, through no merit of their own, to enjoy the eternal bliss of heaven instead.[3] The appeal to God's absolute sovereignty is the final explanation of everything, on the Calvinist account.

To those not yet in the grip of this theological system, the logic is chilling. But the problems with this approach are not limited to the visceral reactions it elicits from the uninitiated. There are deep philosophical and theological problems as well. If fact, there are *many* reasons this solution to the problem of hell is misguided. In this book, there's space to develop only a few of these.[4]

One of the problems has already been discussed, in chapter 3. Calvinism entails that God doesn't love everyone, which requires its proponents to reject the traditional way of understanding the divine nature: namely, that God is the greatest possible being. This is a very high theological price to pay. And the Calvinist response—pointing out that God doesn't owe us anything, including His love—does nothing to ameliorate this problem. In fact, it misses the point entirely. The issue is not what God owes us; the issue is *who God is.* Suppose we grant, for the sake of argument, that God

---

2. Another Calvinist favorite from Romans 9: "But who are you, O man, to answer back to God? Will what is molded say to its molder, 'Why have you made me like this?'" (Romans 9:20 ESV).

3. For a philosophical defense of the Calvinist view of hell, and the doctrine of reprobation in particular, see Hart, "Calvinism and the Problem of Hell."

4. For a more thorough critique, see Manis, *Sinners in the Presence of a Loving God*, 67–92 ("Additional Problems for Calvinists and Other Theological Determinists").

doesn't owe us anything, from which it follows that God doesn't owe us His love. It remains the case nonetheless that God *of His very nature* is perfectly loving. In response to the objection that Calvinism is incompatible with God's nature as a perfect being, it's simply a *non sequitur* to claim that God doesn't owe us His love. And yet, this is the response that Calvinists give repeatedly to their critics.

A second problem with the Calvinist solution is its reliance on the "display of justice" thesis. The problem is that reprobation isn't an effective means of displaying divine justice. To see why, imagine a judge who is sentencing two people—identical twins, let's suppose, with life histories as similar to one another as humanly possible—convicted of exactly the same crime in exactly the same circumstances on exactly the same evidence. The judge sentences one of the twins to death, and the other to ten hours of community service. Obviously, this isn't a just judge. The concept of justice includes the concept of fairness, and fairness requires *treating like cases alike*. The sentencing of the judge is egregiously unfair because of its failure to respect this principle. But this is a *principle of justice*. So the judge's sentencing is not only unfair, it's unjust.

In the Calvinist scheme, God appears to behave very much like this imaginary judge. Everyone is alike in being "totally depraved" and utterly unworthy of being redeemed, in Calvinist theology, and everyone is equally, desperately in need of divine redemption. But God chooses to save only some, and the rest He "passes over," leaving them eternally in their sins. He thereby fails to treat like cases alike. In this sense, God fails to treat His creatures fairly, and thus His actions are not displays of justice.[5]

---

5. Some readers might be concerned that the principle that justice requires fairness runs contrary to what is taught in Scripture. In particular, the parable of the workers in the vineyard (Matthew 20:1–16) might seem to refute it. But in fact, it doesn't. The landowner in the parable doesn't fail to treat like cases alike; he fails (or rather refuses) to treat *unlike* cases *differently*. He pays all the workers the same despite the differing lengths of their workdays, thereby treating unlike cases alike. This isn't contrary to the principle that fairness requires treating like cases alike, and it doesn't refute the principle that justice requires fairness. So there's no support for Calvinism to be found in this parable. And in fact, a more careful consideration of the parable reveals that it actually *refutes* Calvinism. In the parable, all of the workers are poor day laborers who need a full day's wages to provide food for themselves and their families. The landowner pays every worker what they need, regardless of whether it was earned. Insofar as the landowner in the parable represents God, the lesson is that God provides us—the poor day laborers—everything we truly need, and that He does so because He is gracious, not because we are deserving. But every human being is desperately in need of being saved from their sins. So the conclusion to be drawn from the teaching of this parable is that God in His grace provides *everyone* with what is needed for their salvation. In the Calvinist scheme of things, God doesn't do this: He provides some people what they need and "passes over" others. The parable of the

In reply, Calvinists insist that God doesn't owe us fair treatment; He's not obliged to treat everyone the same. He treats humans justly in that no one gets anything worse than what they deserve. But this reply is problematic in at least two different ways.

First, justice requires more than simply not treating anyone worse than they deserve. It also requires fairness, as demonstrated by the unjust judge thought experiment. Calvinism entails that God doesn't treat everyone justly: He fails to treat some people the same way He treats others in relevantly similar circumstances. So the Calvinist response really comes down to the claim that God doesn't owe His creatures anything, even fair treatment. And this response runs into the same problem discussed above, pertaining to divine love. Even granting that God doesn't owe us fair or just treatment, it remains the case that God *of His very nature* is perfectly just. The doctrine of reprobation is inconsistent with this fundamental tenet of Christian orthodoxy.

Furthermore, the Calvinist response is inconsistent with Calvinism's own "display of justice" thesis. Even granting that God owes us absolutely nothing, the question remains whether His actions manage to *display* justice, nonetheless. They do so only if they are displays of fairness. And in the Calvinist scheme, God's actions do not display fairness.

Some Calvinists take a different approach to this issue, however. Instead of denying that God treats everyone justly,[6] some Calvinists instead claim that God's justice is simply *beyond human comprehension*. God's ways are higher than ours. He isn't limited by human conceptions of justice, and His justice doesn't accord with human expectations. Likewise, divine love and divine goodness aren't like their human counterparts. This is why we struggle to recognize benevolence in the doctrine of reprobation or love in God's punishment of the damned. In general, divine attributes are *inscrutable* (beyond understanding) to finite, limited creatures like ourselves.

In order to assess whether this is a better line for Calvinists to take, we should first note a clearly misguided way that it's sometimes developed, especially in regard to the attribute of justice. Many Calvinists speak as if divine justice *simply is* God's displaying His awesome power and unlimited sovereignty. God is perfectly just *because* He's absolutely sovereign. This is clearly confused; it amounts to the claim that "might makes right." Justice

---

workers in the vineyard thus refutes a core tenet of Calvinism.

6. Calvinists are reticent to admit outright that, according to their theology, God fails to treat everyone justly. But they admit that God doesn't treat everyone in similar circumstances alike, so their view entails that God doesn't treat everyone fairly. And as we've seen, fairness is an aspect of justice. So Calvinists are committed to the claim that God fails to treat everyone justly, whether they're willing to admit it or not.

isn't simply the power to impose one's will unimpeded. Being able to get away with anything one chooses, like a tyrant, doesn't automatically make one's actions just. The "God's ways are higher than ours" strategy will never work if it's held that justice is reducible to something else we comprehend, such as power or control. Instead, Calvinists must make a bolder claim: that divine justice is *altogether* inscrutable—that is, *completely* beyond human capacities of understanding—and likewise for divine goodness and love.

But as it turns out, this approach fares no better. For one thing, to adopt it is to abandon the idea that God reprobates for the sake of displaying His justice. If divine justice is beyond human ability to grasp, then it's simply not true that God's actions manage to be displays of justice. In order for an action to be an effective *display* of something, those to whom it's displayed must be able to recognize it as such. So in order for God's actions to display justice to human beings, it must be that they accord with a *human* conception of justice; they must be recognizable as just actions as we humans understand the concept.

But suppose the Calvinist were to go further with this strategy, abandoning the "display of justice" thesis altogether in order to retain the claim that justice and other divine attributes are beyond human comprehension. Even this wouldn't improve matters. The claim that the divine attributes are beyond human comprehension undercuts the basis of human love, obedience, and worship as proper responses to God. If we cannot recognize God's actions as good, just, and loving *by our own lights*, then we have no legitimate basis for responding to God with praise and worship. In fact, we'd have no basis for reasonably believing that the being claiming to be God is actually God, rather than, say, the devil. In order to be justified in believing that a certain being is actually good (or just, or loving), it must be that the being's actions are good as *we* understand goodness (and likewise for justice and love).

It's also worth pointing out that the Calvinist approach we're now considering is thoroughly unbiblical. Throughout Scripture, divine justice, goodness, and love are presented as qualities that humans can easily recognize and for which we should rightly give God praise.[7] All of this would have to be abandoned if one adopted the view that divine attributes are completely mysterious and utterly unlike their human counterparts.

---

7. There are far too many such passages to list here, but the following are some representative samples: 1 Chronicles 16:34; Psalms 23; 27:13; 33:5; 34:8; 69:16; 86:15; 92:15; 107:8–9; 119:103–5, 68; 145:5–9; Proverbs 21:15; 28:5; 29:7; Isaiah 30:18; 51:4–5; 54:10; 61:8; Micah 6:8; Nahum 1:7; Zechariah 7:9; Matthew 7:11; John 3:16; 15:13; Romans 5:8; Ephesians 2:4–5; 1 John 3:1; 4:7–21; James 1:17.

Finally, we should also ask of the Calvinist who adopts this view: If the nature of divine justice, goodness, and love are so mysterious as to be inscrutable, why isn't the same true of divine sovereignty? It's a striking feature of Calvinism that its proponents are so confident in their understanding of this particular divine attribute. It is of course inconsistent to claim that all divine attributes are mysterious and then to regard one attribute as perfectly comprehensible. But the problem is deeper than this. Calvinists seem to get the categories exactly reversed. Justice, love, and goodness are qualities familiar to ordinary human experience. For Christians, in particular, there's nothing mysterious about the very concepts of perfect goodness and love. Christians *recognize* these qualities, displayed in their perfect forms, in the words, actions, and character of Jesus Christ; Christians *experience* these qualities firsthand in their relationship with their Savior. But nothing comparable can be said of divine sovereignty, as Calvinists understand this attribute. We have nothing but the faintest glimmer of an idea of what it's like for God to create the world from nothing and then guide its unfolding history—including the history of all human lives—across endless eons. If there is any divine attribute that is truly mysterious, and even inscrutable, in virtue of being so far removed from anything in human experience, it is sovereignty.[8] The Calvinist insistence that divine love, goodness, and justice are inscrutable, in combination with their implacable commitment to a *very particular* understanding of divine sovereignty, is evidence that Calvinists are in the grip of a theory.

---

8. More precisely: if there's any attribute that is mysterious and inscrutable, it is sovereignty *as Calvinists construe this attribute*. Sovereignty in its ordinary sense—its sense apart from the framework of Calvinism—is just rightful rule or absolute authority, which carries with it the implication of being subject to no one. This is something familiar to human experience; consider the ordinary concepts of a sovereign (ruler) or a sovereign nation. But in its Calvinist construal, sovereignty also includes the property of *absolute control of everything that happens in the world*.

## Chapter 6

# The problem of faith for Calvinists

ALL OF THE PROBLEMS discussed in chapter 5 involve internal tensions or incoherencies in Calvinist theology; these are problems of logical consistency. There's a further reason the Calvinist understanding of hell is seriously flawed, and it resembles the problem of coercion (discussed in chapter 4) in being a problem pertaining to *belief*. But in this case, the problem is with belief in Calvinism. This problem is especially worth developing because, unlike some of the previous problems, it's one that has rarely been appreciated or even discussed.

The problem begins with the observation that trust is an essential component—likely the *most* central component—of faith. Judging from the way that many people talk about faith, both believers and unbelievers alike, it's clear that the concept is widely misunderstood. Faith is not a matter of *believing without evidence*, as many apparently assume. The theological term for this view is *fideism*, and it's both irrational and self-defeating.[1] To arrive at a better understanding of faith, we need only pay attention to the way that we use the term, and related ones like "believing in," in nonreligious contexts. When a parent tells her child, "I believe in you," is she telling her child that she believes things about him that she has

---

1. Fideism is a claim about the nature of faith and the proper way of holding religious beliefs. If it were true, it would be a *religious* truth, and thus a belief that fideism is true is a religious belief. But what fideism claims is that religious beliefs should not be held on the basis of reason. To defend a view (including fideism) is to present *reasons* on its behalf. Thus fideism is, quite literally, indefensible: to defend fideism is implicitly to reject fideism. In order to be consistent, the fideist would have to adopt their religious beliefs *arbitrarily*, that is, without any reasons at all. Obviously, to adopt beliefs in this way is irrational.

no evidence to support? Of course not. If you say to your friends, "Have a little faith in me," are you asking your friends to believe things about you for which they have no evidence? Of course not. To have faith in someone, to believe in someone, is first and foremost to *trust* them and to have *confidence* in their character. Whatever else faith involves, it clearly includes trust as an essential component.

There's something interesting that follows from this. Reasonable faith isn't possible for a Calvinist who sincerely believes and deeply internalizes Calvinist theology.

To see why, consider what's required for reasonable trust as an absolute minimal condition. In order for you to reasonably trust someone, it must *not* be the case that, for all you know, that person is presently orchestrating your death or your complete and utter ruin. Try it out as a thought experiment. Suppose you have a neighbor whom you've overheard talking about "the list." From what you've been able to put together, you know the list contains the names of people your neighbor is planning to kidnap, torture, and murder, and you know there are a lot of names on the list. But you don't know *who*, specifically, is on the list, and you have no idea what the neighbor's reasons are for putting any particular person on it. For all you know, *you're* on the list—and for all you know, you're not on it. Under these conditions, could you reasonably trust your neighbor? Obviously not.

And yet, this is the situation of the Calvinist in relation to God. Given Calvinist theology, it's true, for all one knows, that God is presently orchestrating things so that one will finally meet the most horrific end imaginable.[2] For anyone who truly and sincerely believes this, God cannot be reasonably trusted. But trust is essential to faith. So for Calvinists, reasonable faith in God is impossible.

Most Calvinists assume they have good reasons for thinking that they're among the elect, and thus that God is *not* orchestrating a ruinous

2. As a reminder: on Calvinist theology, God is in complete control of everything that occurs in the world, such that *everything* that happens is an expression of His own, sovereign will, for His own, sovereign reasons—reasons that are, in most if not all cases, inscrutable to human beings. To be among the reprobate is for God to have decreed that one will be "passed over" for the grace that leads to salvation, and that one is instead determined to persist in one's sins and eventually be consigned to hell. So if someone rejects Christ, persists in their sin and rebellion, and is eventually consigned to hell as an eternal punishment, the *entire series of events* is orchestrated by God for His own reasons. Being chosen for reprobation is thus analogous to being put on "the list": in both cases, the selection has nothing to do with one's own merits or demerits (in the case of reprobation, the issue is settled *before one is even born*). Whether or not one is selected for reprobation is entirely due to the inscrutable reasons of God, much like whether or not one is put on "the list" is entirely due to the inscrutable reasons of the neighbor.

end for them. They imagine they have good reasons to believe they're not on "the list," so to speak. These reasons have to do with the "signs of election" they're confident they observe in themselves: a past experience of conviction and conversion, a present hatred of sin and love for God, a desire for holiness and communion with God, etc.

Ironically, however, the great reformer John Calvin himself provides a powerful reason for anyone who adopts his theology to reject the assumption that the aforementioned inner states are, in fact, good evidence of election. According to Calvin, there's a "special" call—an experience of conviction and illumination by the Holy Spirit—that God for the most part gives only to the elect, but that He sometimes gives to the reprobate, whom He later causes to reject Him and ultimately to be damned.[3] What this means is that there's no state you could observe in yourself that would count as good evidence of election. The experience of a false conversion that will eventually lead to apostasy (an explicit rejection of the faith) and, ultimately, to eternal damnation is *introspectively indistinguishable* from an experience of genuine, saving conversion and the life of faith. So you can't possibly know whether or not you're a true believer. Regardless of your past or present experiences, for all you know God is setting you up for future apostasy and judgment.

This might seem to be a very puzzling feature of Calvin's theology. But there's actually a good reason for it. Given the other theological commitments of Calvinism, something like this is required to explain the fact that some people commit apostasy. There's no denying that some people confess the faith at some point in their lives, in all apparent sincerity, but later come to explicitly reject the faith. Given the Calvinist assumption that God is in control of everything, some explanation is needed for why God would cause anyone to do such a thing. Calvin's explanation, it seems, is that it brings greater glory to God if there are some people who commit the worst of all possible sins, so that God might have the opportunity to

---

3. Calvin writes the following in his magisterial *Institutes of the Christian Religion*: "There is the general call, by which God invites all equally to himself through the outward preaching of the word—even those to whom he holds it out as a savor of death [cf. II Cor 2:16], and as the occasion for severer condemnation. The other kind of call is special, which he deigns for the most part to give to the believers alone, while by the inward illumination of his Spirit he causes the preached Word to dwell in their hearts. Yet sometimes he also causes those whom he illumines only for a time to partake of it; then he justly forsakes them on account of their ungratefulness and strikes them with even greater blindness" (Calvin, *Institutes*, Book 3, chapter 24, section 8). For further discussion of this passage, see Walls and Dongell, *Why I Am Not a Calvinist*, 168–69.

inflict the worst of all possible punishments, which constitutes the most perfect display of justice.[4]

Many Calvinists apparently wish to part ways with Calvin himself at this point, insisting that there *are* in fact reliable signs of election that can be observed in oneself and others. But even if this were true, it wouldn't help much. The reason it wouldn't help is that, for each of us, there's someone we love who doesn't even appear to display these signs of election. These loved ones appear to be lost. And in the Calvinist scheme of things, this is so because God is orchestrating it. This is enough to generate the problem under discussion. We previously stated that, as a bare minimum, reasonable trust requires that it *not* be the case that, for all you know, the trusted one is orchestrating your ruin. But this is clearly too minimal. Reasonable trust also requires that it not be the case that, for all you know, the trusted one is orchestrating the ruin *of any of your loved ones*. (Go back and reconsider the thought experiment about the neighbor with "the list," this time imagining that you know you're not on the list, but you suspect that some of your loved ones are on it.) Given that some people you love appear to be lost, you can't rule out the possibility that God is orchestrating their eternal damnation. Even if there are reliable signs of election, these loved ones don't display them. Of course, it's possible they'll repent and be reconciled to God at some point in the future. But it's also possible they won't. And given Calvinist theology, that's equivalent to the claim that *for all you know*, God is presently orchestrating the ruin of some of your loved ones. And of course you cannot reasonably trust anyone who, for all you know, is presently orchestrating the ruin of some of your loved ones.[5] For anyone who sincerely believes and deeply internalizes Calvinist theology, reasonable trust in God is impossible, regardless of whether the supposed signs of election are recognized in themselves. And since trust is essential to faith, the conclusion we've finally reached is that Calvinism is incompatible with reasonable faith in God.

---

4. See also *Institutes*, Book 3, chapter 2, section 11, where Calvin explains why God gives some people an experience of faith which He later causes them to reject: the reason is "to render them more convicted and inexcusable."

5. Perhaps a few people are in the fortunate situation that all of their loved ones appear to be saved; they all display the supposed signs of election. Even in such a remarkable and rare situation, however, the problem would remain. Christians are called to love their neighbors, and it's widely recognized that the meaning of "neighbor" in the biblical commandment extends to *everyone*, without exception—even to one's enemies. So for any Calvinist who actually obeys this command, it's guaranteed (given Calvinist theology) that some loved ones are *actually* lost, that God is *actually* orchestrating the final ruin of some people they love. It's not just that *for all one knows* God is doing so; given the Calvinist doctrines that some are lost and that God is completely in control of everything, it's *certain* that God is doing so.

It has become clear that appealing to the sheer magnitude of divine sovereignty is the wrong way to try to solve the problem of hell. The Calvinist understanding of hell and related doctrines is fatally flawed in numerous ways. Looking back on the discussion so far, we can see that all of these problems are fundamentally rooted in the idea that God is orchestrating (sovereignly controlling) everything that happens in the world. This idea—which we previously termed *theological determinism*—is philosophically and theologically disastrous when combined with the doctrine that some are finally lost. In order to solve the problem of hell, it will be necessary to reject theological determinism.

## Chapter 7

# More misguided solutions to the problem of hell

WE'VE SEEN THAT IT'S a mistake to think that the problem of hell can be solved simply by appealing to God's sovereignty. Our discussion of Calvinism over the past two chapters revealed just how problematic this type of approach is. The second mistake that an adequate model of hell will need to avoid is simpler to develop than the first, but it's equally common.

### Misguided approach #2: Mitigating (rather than solving) the problem

Because of the number and the severity of the problems associated with the doctrine of hell, it can be tempting to move the goalposts in trying to formulate an adequate solution. Certain models of hell are regarded by their proponents as adequate when in fact they only mitigate the problem of hell in various ways without actually solving it. This can happen in two ways. First, a model of hell might solve some of the problems but make no progress at all on others. Second, a model might lessen the severity of certain problems without actually solving them.

Both of these types of problems are on display with **annihilationism**, the view according to which those consigned to hell are completely annihilated, either immediately or following a finite period of punishment.

In its most popular form, annihilationism retains the retribution thesis—the claim that God consigns people to hell as a retributive punishment for their earthly sins—but regards consignment to hell to be like a prison sentence that ends in capital punishment. In claiming that the final destiny of the damned is utter destruction rather than eternal torment, annihilationism rejects the no escape thesis (introduced in chapter 1). There is no escaping hell for someplace better, on the annihilationist view, but there is an end to suffering, so consignment to hell is not an everlasting condition. The punishment of hell is eternal in its *effect*, not its duration: that is to say, the consequence of being annihilated is permanent.

Because the suffering of hell is not everlasting (and thus not infinite) in this model, annihilationism seems to have a straightforward solution to the problem of justice, and this is typically touted by its proponents as a compelling reason to prefer it over traditionalism. What is commonly overlooked, however, is the fact that these annihilationist models at most lessen the severity of the problem of coercion, and they make no progress at all on the problem of love.

Let's consider each of these in turn. The threat of annihilation does indeed seem to be less than the threat of eternal torment. But it's far from obvious that the corresponding reduction in the level of coercion is enough to restore freedom of choice for the one who understands and believes the threat implied in the revelation of the doctrine of hell, construed in annihilationist terms. The "desperate lover" thought experiment, discussed in chapter 4, actually models annihilationism closer than traditionalism: the deranged man is threatening his beloved with death for noncompliance, which is more analogous to a threat of annihilation than eternal torment. Insofar as the thought experiment describes a level of coercion that destroys the free will of the woman who is threatened, and thereby destroys her ability to comply with her captor's demand (the demand that she *genuinely* love him), this suggests that annihilationism makes no significant headway on the problem of coercion. In short, threatening someone with annihilation is enough to undermine the possibility of a free response, so a divine revelation of an annihilationist doctrine of hell would still be coercive.

In regard to the problem of love, annihilationism makes no headway at all. The fundamental problem, recall, is that a purely retributive punishment is unloving, and thus any model that regards hell as a purely retributive punishment has the implication that God fails to love the damned. Swapping out annihilation for eternal suffering as the retributive punishment that God inflicts does nothing to solve this problem.

These considerations suggest that annihilationism—in its standard forms, at least—is a misguided approach to the problem of hell.

As it turns out, annihilationism faces another serious problem: in all its forms, not just its retributive ones, it is a rejection of the mainstream of Christian tradition. We'll return to this issue shortly, in chapter 8. The lesson of the present section is that a successful model of hell must actually solve, rather than merely mitigate, the various problems discussed in chapters 2–4.

## Misguided approach #3: Conceiving of hell as an artificial and arbitrary punishment

We have now catalogued two misguided approaches to solving the problem of hell: one that adds something to traditionalism (Calvinism's acceptance of theological determinism) and one that subtracts from it (annihilationism's rejection of the no escape thesis). In this section, we're going to further explore traditionalism itself. Specifically, we'll diagnose the fundamental source of traditionalism's most intractable problems. Once we identify the source, we'll be much better positioned to construct an alternative model of hell that avoids these problems.

The single, common source of all the major problems for traditionalism—the problem of justice, the problem of love, and the problem of coercion—is not hard to identify: it's the retribution thesis. The retribution thesis is a claim about the *purpose* of hell, the *reason* that God consigns some people to eternal suffering. It generates the problem of justice, because retributive justice requires that a punishment "fit" the crime in order to be just, and this "fitness" involves a proportionality between the degree of wrongdoing and the severity of the punishment. The punishment of hell vastly outweighs any amount of culpability a person could accrue in their earthly lives, which implies that consignment to hell is unjust, on the assumption that this consignment is to be understood as a retributive punishment for earthly wrongdoing. The retribution thesis is likewise the source of the problem of love. Here the problem is that a purely retributive punishment is not intended to promote the good of the one punished, which makes it unloving *even if* it were just. Construed as a retributive punishment, consignment to hell is an unloving punishment for God to impose on someone. But if God does not love the damned, it follows that He is not maximally loving—a conclusion that conflicts with long-standing Christian tradition. Finally, the retribution thesis is the source of the problem of coercion. Insofar as consignment to hell is a retributive punishment, the revelation that this punishment will be imposed by God for noncompliance (however "noncompliance" might be construed) is coercive, at least for anyone who genuinely believes the revelation.

Having identified the common source of the problems for traditionalism, the next step is to figure out what it is about the retribution thesis, exactly, that makes it so problematic. The answer, in short, is that it construes the punishment of hell to be both *artificial* and *arbitrary*.

First, retribution is a way of understanding punishment in terms of **artificial consequences** rather than **natural consequences**. To see the difference, compare two possible consequences of reckless driving: one might get a ticket and have to pay a fine (an artificial consequence), or one might lose control of the vehicle and wreck it (a natural consequence). A natural consequence is one that follows an action in virtue of the laws of nature: the laws of physics, chemistry, and biology. An artificial consequence is one that's imposed by a person or group. On a retributive model, punishment is a matter of some individual or group imposing a certain consequence artificially; the punishment is not a consequence that follows naturally from the action to which it's a response. In general, the infliction of artificial punishments requires an exercise of free will on the part of at least one person (for example, a law enforcement officer or a judge).

In addition to being artificial, retributive punishments are also arbitrary. This is not to say that these punishments are random or senseless or without justification for their infliction. Rather, to say that a certain punishment is arbitrary is to say that, to some extent, it's up to the discretion of some person or group to decide the punishment's type and severity. The punishments of the legal system in the United States are arbitrary in this sense. Not only does a judge exercise a degree of discretion in sentencing (say, a prison term of three years rather than the maximum five allowed by law for the crime committed), but also those who crafted the law selected the punishments arbitrarily, in the sense that they could have chosen a different punishment for breaking the law in question (say, fifty lashes with a cane pole) rather than the one they actually chose (say, a maximum fine of $10,000). There might be good reasons for restricting the range of possible penalties: most people would agree that it's a positive feature of United States law that it forbids the use of such punishments as public flogging, amputation of limbs, crucifixion, or other forms of torture. Nevertheless, the punishments imposed by penal law are arbitrary in the specific sense we've just defined.

These two features of retributive punishments—their artificiality and their arbitrariness—are the reasons that a doctrine of hell becomes problematic when it's construed as a retributive punishment. But it's important that we not miss the point here. The problem isn't necessarily the concept of retribution itself. There may be cases in which justice requires retribution. And the problem isn't necessarily with the idea that God sanctions or even carries out retribution. There are many passages in Scripture where—on a "straightforward" reading, at least—God is depicted as inflicting artificial punishments on some person or group in response to their sins. (Whether these punishments are *purely* retributive depends in part on whether they are aimed at the correction of the ones punished, in addition to serving a retributive function.) The retribution thesis of traditionalism claims something far more specific, and far more problematic, than that retribution is sometimes morally justified or that God sometimes imposes retributive punishments. The retribution thesis is the claim that *consignment to hell* is a purely retributive punishment.

As noted above, the infliction of artificial punishments requires someone (or a group of people) to exercise free will. If damnation is an artificial punishment, then consignment to hell is something that God freely chooses to inflict on certain people, and it's fully within His power to refrain from doing so. If the punishment of hell is arbitrary, then God could have chosen a different punishment to inflict upon those who are unrepentant of their sins. And this is the problem with traditionalism: we're left to wonder why God chooses to inflict a punishment so severe that it seems far out of proportion to the wrongdoing committed, and the advance revelation of this policy for dealing with sin seems coercive, when it was perfectly within God's power to have chosen some other punishment instead. We're left to wonder, moreover, why God chooses to inflict a purely retaliatory punishment rather than a punishment that's at least *intended* to promote the moral and spiritual betterment of those subjected to it. And as we've seen, these are the foundations of the problems of justice, coercion, and love. In order to construct a model of hell that avoids these problems, it will be necessary either to abandon or to revise the retribution thesis.

## Misguided approach #4: Failing to accommodate the full scriptural revelation

The conclusion we've just reached might seem as problematic as the difficulties it's meant to avoid. After all, the idea of hell as a retributive punishment appears to enjoy strong scriptural support. We've already noted that hell is described in the Bible as "eternal punishment," and this description is attributed to Jesus himself (Matthew 25:46). There's also the foundational Christian doctrine of the final judgment, according to which the righteous and the wicked will be separated from one another at Christ's return, and the latter consigned to hell. Given these teachings, how else could hell be conceived if not as a retributive punishment?

To answer this question, we'll first need to consider whether there could be such a thing as a non-retributive punishment. If we can make sense of this idea, we'll then need to assess whether the idea of hell as a non-retributive punishment can be squared with the full revelation of Scripture. These issues will be crucial to the remainder of our project in this book.

Some people understand punishment to be necessarily retributive: the very concept of retribution is built into their analysis of what it is for something to qualify as a punishment. In this view, a non-retributive punishment is a contradiction in terms. But this analysis seems mistaken. We've already noted that loving parents typically punish their children not with the primary intention of balancing the scales of justice, or any such purely retributive motivation, but rather for the purpose of correcting their children and helping them to grow morally and spiritually. This type of punishment is *corrective* or *reformative*.

There's an important type of model that understands the punishment of hell to be of this type: it's called **universalism**. According to universalists, the punishment of hell is reformative not only in its intent but in its actual function. Everyone who's consigned to hell will *eventually* be led to repentance, sanctified, and ultimately delivered from hell—though this process could, for some people, take a very long time. In this view, hell functions in a way similar to **purgatory** in Catholic theology: it's a necessary waystation for many people, but everyone who's consigned to it eventually winds up in heaven. The universalist view, in short, is that everyone will *finally* be saved.

This understanding of the doctrine of hell rejects not only the retribution thesis, but also the no escape thesis. Because of this, it represents a significant deviation from the majority view of historic Christianity. We'll return to this issue in the next chapter, where we'll consider whether such deviation from the mainstream of Christian tradition is problematic. For now, let's instead ask a different question: Is there any way to understand the punishment of hell to be non-retributive *without* embracing universalism?

In fact, there is. To understand how, we need to consider further the idea of natural consequences.

We previously characterized natural consequences as those that follow a certain action in virtue of the laws of nature. This needs to be expanded a bit. Natural consequences concern not only the laws of nature (the laws of physics, chemistry, and biology) but also the laws of *human* nature. Humans are developmental beings: each of us is constantly in the process of becoming a certain kind of person. Among the most important natural consequences for a non-retributive model of hell are the ways that a person's actions shape their character. In terms of moral and spiritual development, some people become more virtuous over the course of their lives, while others become more vicious. Making repeated choices of the same type results in the formation of habits, and these habits—especially those having moral and spiritual significance—help to shape a person's character over time. To be a virtuous person is in part to be a person who's disposed to behave in certain characteristic ways: ways that are just, courageous, honest, benevolent, loving, etc. To say that a person is disposed to behave in a certain way is to say (roughly) that a certain kind of response is the one that is most likely for them. In most cases, the reason this behavior is most likely is that it's the most "natural" behavior for that person, given the particular habits and character they've formed up to that point. There's also an *affective* component to character. Part of what it is to be a virtuous person is to have the right kinds of attitudes and emotions and to desire the right things: for example, to love justice, to hate evil, to desire the happiness of others, to want to do what's right, and so on.

It's a basic and widespread theological assumption of orthodox Christianity that sin *naturally* leads to unhappiness, at least in the long run. This is the case because sin is contrary to the fulfillment of human nature; in philosophical terms, it's contrary to **human flourishing**. According to Christianity, we are creatures *made for* communion with God and communion with other people. This is the end for which humans are created, and the only state in which humans can be truly and lastingly happy is a state in which our natures are fulfilled. Because of this, anything that orients people in the opposite direction—anything that promotes disunion with God or other people—*naturally* leads to unhappiness, at least in the long run.

Putting these ideas together, we arrive at the following view. When someone persists in sin and rebellion against God, they form a character over time that is marked by the vices: pride, selfishness, dishonesty, greed, envy, intemperance, etc. The longer they persist in sin, the more ingrained these traits become in their character. Eventually, whether in this life or the next, these vices are so thoroughly entrenched in their character that it's psychologically impossible for them to behave morally—to do what's right for the right reasons—or even to repent of their sins. (Recall the notion of *psychological impossibility* from our discussion of the problem of coercion in chapter 4.) In biblical terms, their heart is hardened—and to such an extent that no further change is possible given the constraints of human nature. In theological terms, this is the state of damnation.

It's important to notice that, in this model, damnation is not something God artificially or arbitrarily imposes on someone as a punishment. It's the *natural* consequence of persistence in sin and rebellion. Those who are in hell are reaping what they have sown; God has given them over to their sins.[1] In a very real sense, they are experiencing what they have chosen for themselves, albeit indirectly. Through their own exercises of free will, the damned are those who have gradually formed themselves into the kinds of people who are incapable of communion with God and other people. Because their characters are solidified to the point that no further change is possible—at least, not in a positive direction—their state is final; and because their final state is an entrenchment in sin, a state contrary to human flourishing, it's a state of misery. The natural trajectory of persistence in sin is to arrive, eventually, at a state of eternal suffering, forever alienated from God and other people, which is the state of damnation.

The general type of view we've just sketched is called a **natural consequence model of hell**, and the most popular specific form of it is the **choice model**. Perhaps most famously, we find this view (though not the label) in the writings of C. S. Lewis.[2] It's called "the choice model" by some contemporary philosophers because of its key idea that damnation is not a state that God imposes on the damned against their wills, but rather a state that the damned freely choose for themselves. In consigning some to hell, God is merely respecting human free will, allowing people to experience the natural consequences of their own wicked choices.

The most impressive feature of the choice model is its plausible working out of the logic of damnation without any reliance on the retribution thesis. Because it understands the eternal suffering of hell to be a natural consequence of sin rather than an artificial and arbitrary punishment imposed by God, it's able to avoid all of the major problems for traditionalism discussed in chapters 2–4. If damnation isn't a retributive punishment, the problem of justice doesn't even get off the ground. The disproportion between the actions (earthly sin and rebellion against God) and the consequence (eternal damnation) does not constitute an injustice, because the consequence is a state that the damned *bring upon themselves*, not something that God inflicts upon them.

The problem of love is likewise avoided on the choice model, for two reasons. First, the crucial premise that motivates it—namely, that a purely retributive punishment does not aim at the good of the one punished—has no application to the choice model since it does not construe the punishment of hell in retributive terms. Second, God's motive in allowing the

---

1. The teaching that a person reaps what they sow is found in Galatians 6:6–8. A discussion of God's giving over certain people to their sins is found in Romans 1:18–32. Neither passage mentions hell; the idea developed in the main text is a way of *applying* this set of biblical ideas to the doctrine of hell.

2. See especially Lewis, *The Great Divorce*, and the chapter on hell in Lewis, *The Problem of Pain*.

damned to consign themselves to a state of eternal damnation—namely, in order to respect their free will—is a loving motive.

Finally, insofar as the doctrine of hell is a revelation about the natural consequences of persistence in sin, rather than an artificial and arbitrary punishment freely selected and imposed by God, the problem of coercion is avoided as well. On the choice model, the revelation of hell is a warning, not a threat: it reveals in advance the horrific natural consequences of willful persistence in sin, thereby allowing the recipients of the revelation to take proper measures to avoid it. This is a good thing for God to do, regardless of how disturbing the revelation might be. A simple thought experiment makes this clear. Imagine a doctor who kept from her patient the news that he had cancer, in order to spare him the distress of the bad news. The doctor's behavior would be negligent, not praiseworthy. The patient needs to know his condition, in its full severity, in order to be motivated and guided in seeking a cure. Likewise, we need to know the severity of our present spiritual disease and the inevitable trajectory of its progression if left untreated. The divine revelation of the doctrine of hell thus promotes the highest good of human beings, on the choice model.

In these ways, the choice model demonstrates an effective way of circumventing each of the major problems of hell. Clearly, the choice model has a number of important benefits, and the significance of these should not be underestimated. The central insights of the choice model are ones that a successful model of hell must somehow incorporate.

Despite these benefits, however, the choice model also has a significant deficiency: it fails to accommodate some key scriptural teachings about hell.

First, it's not entirely clear that the choice model can account for the scriptural teaching that hell is a state of eternal *punishment* (Matthew 25:46). It's easy to see how turning people over to the natural consequences of their sins could result in their experiencing great suffering, even profound and lasting misery. But it's not so easy to see how this would count as a punishment. Recall the prodigal son, from Jesus' famous parable (Luke 15:11–32). In the parable, the father is respecting his son's wishes in giving him his share of the inheritance; he's respecting his son's freedom in allowing him to squander it all. The parable doesn't depict a father who's *punishing* his son, especially insofar as the father stands ever ready to receive his son back again. On the choice model, the damned are like prodigal sons, with the crucial difference that they've so hardened their hearts that they're no longer capable of "returning home" to their heavenly Father. It's not God who prevents the damned from returning; it's their own character that prevents it.

(Hence Lewis's famous line that "the doors of hell are locked on the *inside*.")³ This feature of the choice model makes it clear that God is not behaving unlovingly toward the damned, which is a significant benefit. The problem, however, is that this very same feature makes the choice model unable to account for a key scriptural teaching about hell.

This is not the only scriptural teaching that the choice model struggles to accommodate. Throughout the New Testament, the biblical language describing the final judgment suggests that the damned are consigned to hell *against their wills*. The wicked are said to be "shut out" from the heavenly banquet, "cast" into outer darkness, "thrown" into the lake of fire, and so on.⁴ But insofar as the damned are consigned to hell not of their own free choice but rather against their wills, the foundation of the choice model is compromised. This problem for the choice model is connected to the previous one, because the very idea of punishment implies something that is contrary to the will of the one punished.

We could multiply examples of biblical themes that the choice model struggles to accommodate. Consider the recurring motif of "the fear of the Lord." The choice model certainly suggests that we should fear sin, given the dire consequences of persisting in it. And the model can make sense of the biblical idea that salvation is a matter of God's saving us from our sins. But the fear of sin is not the same as the fear of the Lord, and being saved from one's sins is not the same as being saved from the wrath of God—another prominent biblical motif.

Finally, in the usual way of developing it, the choice model includes the claim that hell is a state of *separation* from God, a freely chosen self-exile from heaven and all its inhabitants. But this idea, despite its popularity, appears to be inconsistent with certain key biblical passages about hell. One such verse, from the book of Revelation, suggests that the punishment of the damned will take place *in the presence of Jesus and the angels*.⁵ It's not at all clear how the choice model could accommodate such a teaching.

In light of these omissions and discrepancies, it seems a bit of a stretch to say that the choice model is a biblical view of hell. Our discussion of "misguided approaches" has revealed yet another problem that an adequate model of hell must avoid: it must not fail to accommodate the full spectrum

---

3. Lewis, *The Problem of Pain*, 130.

4. See, for example, 2 Thessalonians 1:9; Luke 12:5; Revelation 22:14–15; Matthew 3:10–12; 5:29–30; 7:19–23; 8:12; 13:30–50; 18:8–9; 22:13; 24:50–51; 25:10–12, 30.

5. Revelation 14:10. Another key verse, 2 Thessalonians 1:9, is translated in two very different ways, one that supports the idea of hell as separation from God, and another that flatly contradicts this idea. This verse will be the focus of special attention in chapter 18.

of biblical teachings. The choice model fails to do so, and consequently it's not a fully adequate model; it's at best incomplete.

The conclusion to which we are finally led, then, is that an adequate model of hell will need to incorporate the idea of natural consequences and reject the idea that hell is a retributive punishment. But it must somehow do so in a way that accommodates all the biblical teachings pertaining to final judgment, including the idea that hell is a state of eternal punishment. Whether or not such a combination is possible is a question we'll address in chapters 9–10. Before turning to this question, there is one final misguided approach that we need to discuss.

## Chapter 8
# A final misguided approach —and the way forward

WE'VE SEEN THAT THERE are many mistakes to avoid in addressing the problem of hell: dismissing the problem with an appeal to divine sovereignty (misguided approach #1); lessening the severity of the problem without actually solving it (misguided approach #2); conceiving of hell as an artificial and arbitrary punishment (misguided approach #3); and failing to account for the full scriptural revelation about hell (misguided approach #4). In this chapter, we'll discuss the final mistake to be avoided. It will turn out that this final issue is the most difficult one to navigate in constructing an adequate model of hell.

### Misguided approach #5: Disregarding Christian tradition

In chapters 2–4, we found compelling reasons to reject traditionalism. We eventually identified the retribution thesis as the source of traditionalism's most intractable problems (chapter 7). The choice model demonstrates the possibility of making sense of hell apart from the retribution thesis, but we found it to be an insufficiently biblical view. There are other models that reject the retribution thesis, however. There are non-retributive forms of annihilationism, and universalism is a view of hell in which the concept of retribution plays at most a supporting role. It might seem promising that one of these views could provide the best solution to the problem of hell.

The trouble, however, is that both annihilationism and universalism, in all their various forms, are nontraditional ways of understanding hell.

To embrace any version of either of these views is to reject an important part of the Christian tradition.

But what does it mean, exactly, to say that a certain view is part of, or is contrary to, the Christian tradition? And why does it matter? In trying to answer these questions, it's easy to end up in the weeds of some long-standing controversies that have tended to divide Christians from one another. But if we're careful to make the right distinctions, there's a way to sidestep most of these controversial issues—and to bring into focus the reason that it's problematic to embrace a nontraditional view of hell.

First, we need to be clear that "nontraditional" does not mean "unbiblical." In claiming that annihilationism and universalism are nontraditional views of hell, we are not making any claims about the degree to which they find support in Scripture. The best defenders of annihilationism and universalism are prepared to argue forcefully that their respective views are thoroughly biblical.[1, 2] But the fundamental problem with these views lies elsewhere, in their relation to Christian tradition. For this reason, we need not, for present purposes, be drawn into the debate about the biblical case for and against annihilationism and universalism.

But if "nontraditional" does not mean "unbiblical," then what does it mean, exactly? There are various possible answers to this question. One popular answer is that "nontraditional" means something like "contrary to the official teachings of the church, established in the ecumenical councils." Understood in this way, tradition is a potentially divisive concept. There are long-standing debates about which councils, exactly, are authoritative. There are also debates about whether annihilationism and universalism were actually condemned, in an official and binding way, at any such council.

---

1. An exhaustive biblical case for annihilationism is presented by Fudge in *The Fire That Consumes: A Biblical and Historical Study of the Doctrine of Final Punishment*. To varying degrees, the biblical case for universalism is presented by Robin Parry (under the pseudonym Gregory MacDonald) in *The Evangelical Universalist: The Biblical Hope that God's Love Will Save Us All*; by Talbott in *The Inescapable Love of God*; and by Hart in *That All Shall Be Saved: Heaven, Hell, and Universal Salvation*.

2. Many traditionalists assume that only traditionalism can accommodate the revelation of Scripture. Not only do they regard traditionalism to be *the* biblical view, they regard this to be so glaringly obvious as to be self-evident. They dismiss opposing views as simply failing to take the Bible seriously. Anyone who rejects traditionalism, they think, either willfully disregards the authority of Scripture or is self-deceived in imagining that any other view might find a basis in it. This position is at best confused, and at worst slanderous. Of course, we can find fringe versions of annihilationism and universalism that flagrantly disregard central teachings of Scripture. But the same is true of some embellished versions of traditionalism. To assess the various views of hell fairly, we must engage the versions defended by their best representatives.

Fortunately, these too are questions that we can put aside, for present purposes. Regardless of one's views about such matters, it remains the case that the doctrine of hell as eternal suffering is *the way that the vast majority of biblically informed Christians through the ages have interpreted the relevant passages of Scripture*. It is in *this* sense that the doctrine of hell as eternal suffering is indisputably the traditional view of hell[3] and both annihilationism and universalism are nontraditional views.[4]

But is it actually problematic for a view of hell to be nontraditional? Some Christians—especially Protestants of certain denominations—are inclined to dismiss not only the *authority* of tradition, but even its relevance or importance in deciding doctrinal matters. "Tradition is just peer pressure from dead people," as some like to put it. Those who hold this view often imagine that Scripture *alone* is the only authoritative source of doctrine, and "alone" is interpreted so strictly by such Christians as to rule out everything but the Bible and the inner witness of the Holy Spirit to the individual believer in guiding their interpretation of it.[5] Tradition doesn't matter, even if we're using "tradition" to refer to the dominant ways that Christians of past ages have interpreted Scripture.

In my judgment, such total disregard for tradition is certainly a mistake. There's a compelling theological reason not to dismiss the weight of tradition, at least where "tradition" is understood in the way we're now discussing. It's part of the doctrine of **providence**—a fundamental doctrine of the Christian faith—that God is actively involved in guiding His church, not only in its initial development in the first century, but also in its subsequent history. Another fundamental doctrine of Christianity is that believers are indwelt and led by the Holy Spirit. Putting these two doctrines together, it's altogether reasonable to judge that consensus or near consensus among

---

3. This way of interpreting "tradition" has an ecumenical advantage: it does not exclude more robust understandings of tradition—those defined in terms of ecumenical creeds and councils, the official teachings of the magisterium, etc.—but it does not require these. Consequently, any argument that relies only on this more general account of tradition should have broad appeal to Catholic, Orthodox, and Protestant Christians alike.

4 Hopefully it's clear by this point that a "nontraditional view," as I'm using this term, does not mean "a view that rejects the entirety of the Christian tradition" or even "a view that has no place within the Christian tradition." We find prominent and influential defenders of annihilationism and universalism in the early church; it follows that these views are a part of the Christian tradition in some sense. But they are (or eventually came to be) minority reports in the tradition; they stand outside of the mainstream.

5. To be clear, this is not the position of historic Protestantism. It is not my purpose here to make any claims about how widespread this attitude toward tradition might be today, but simply to make it clear why it's misguided as an approach to constructing a view of hell.

Christians through the ages about a certain reading of Scripture—that is, a certain way of interpreting the relevant passages pertaining to some core doctrine—is *very good evidence* that that reading is divinely inspired.

In fact, this should be one of our guiding principles in crafting a model of hell: *broad consensus in the church is evidence of divine inspiration.*

Whenever Christians find that a certain interpretation of Scripture on some issue has been held by the vast majority of Christians through the ages, and on this basis conclude that this interpretation is very likely correct, they aren't committing a logical fallacy such as "appeal to tradition" or "appeal to the masses." Because of the Christian doctrines of divine providence and the leading of the Holy Spirit, broad consensus among believers throughout the history of the church is rightly taken to be good evidence that a certain teaching has been revealed to the church by God.

It is not, however, *conclusive* evidence. As I'm using this term, conclusive evidence is evidence that's so strong, the conclusion it supports could not *possibly* be false. Widespread agreement in the history of the church, and even consensus, does not by itself constitute conclusive evidence of divine inspiration, even if it qualifies as good evidence. It's always at least possible that certain widespread beliefs are the result of political, cultural, literary, or philosophical influences rather than sound biblical interpretation or the leading of the Holy Spirit. And there are, in fact, a number of historical examples of widespread beliefs about hell that seem to be of rather dubious pedigree. The belief that hell is filled with cruel and unusual—not to mention gruesome—physical torments is common in the history of the church. Likewise for the belief that God gives the damned resurrection bodies *for the express purpose* of inflicting infinite suffering upon them. Even more shocking, perhaps, is the prevalence of the view that the saints in heaven *delight* in the experience of beholding the eternal sufferings of the damned. These kinds of considerations leave many Christians understandably hesitant to adopt every traditional idea about hell.

But perhaps there's no real problem here. The aforementioned beliefs about hell, despite their popularity at certain times and places, likely are not prevalent enough in the Christian tradition to qualify as "broad consensus" beliefs or even "beliefs that have been endorsed by the vast majority of Christians through the ages."

Unfortunately, however, there's another problematic belief about hell that very well *might* meet these descriptions. It's the belief that hell is a retributive punishment for the wrongdoings a person commits in their earthly life—that is, a belief in the retribution thesis—which we've already found compelling philosophical and theological reasons to reject.

So now we face an apparent dilemma. If widespread agreement in the tradition on a certain matter were always indicative of divine inspiration, we would have to conclude that the retribution thesis is a part of the revealed doctrine, in which case we would be back where we started, facing an apparently intractable problem of hell, for all the reasons we discussed in chapters 2–4. But if widespread agreement in the tradition is *not* always indicative of divine inspiration, we need to explain how this is reconcilable with the points we previously made about divine providence and the indwelling of the Holy Spirit. Moreover, we need to develop some sort of criteria for distinguishing, among the various widespread beliefs that we find in the tradition, what is divinely inspired from what is not. How should we go about this?

There's no easy answer to this question. Every proposed solution will come at a cost. Nevertheless, I propose the following as a helpful guide to our deliberations.

It is not, I submit, essential to the doctrine of providence that *every* widespread belief in the Christian tradition is inspired; what's essential is that every *core doctrine* of the faith is inspired, and that the church's understanding of every core doctrine is *fundamentally* correct. So the question that should guide our discussion is this: *Which consensus or near-consensus beliefs in the tradition are such that, if they were false, it would mean that the church had fundamentally misunderstood some doctrine that is central to the Christian faith?* For orthodox Christians, it's crucial that any such traditional belief is *not* in fact false, because it is of the utmost importance that the church has *not* fundamentally misunderstood any core doctrine. Consequently, any traditional belief that meets this condition should be regarded as *unrelinquishable*.

We shouldn't pretend that there's only one reasonable set of answers to the aforementioned question, however. For each reader, and for any doctrine of which we ask the question, the answer will require a series of personal judgments.

Regarding the doctrine of hell, I think it's reasonable to judge the unrelinquishable core of the traditional view to be this: *hell is a state of eternal suffering, and some will be finally lost.* Because of how widespread this belief is in the history of the church, *and* how firmly it has been held, *and* how central it is to any understanding of hell that includes it, it seems reasonable to conclude that if this belief were false, it would mean that the church has fundamentally misunderstood the revealed doctrine of hell.[6] For those

---

6. To say that this judgment "seems reasonable" is not to say that a different, contrary judgment would necessarily be unreasonable. Disagreement is pervasive in philosophy and theology, and often those on opposing sides of a debate are equally

(like myself) who are committed to the view that the church has *not* fundamentally misunderstood any revealed doctrine, it follows that any model in which hell is not a state of eternal suffering—which includes all forms of universalism and annihilationism—should be rejected.

In making this judgment about what is the unrelinquishable core of the doctrine of hell, I am of course making a subjective judgment. But it seems to me that many others make a similar judgment, regardless of whether they've thought about the issue in exactly the way I've just described. As evidence of this, I submit the following, anecdotal observation: a great many conservative Christians view the choice model as an acceptable alternative to traditionalism but consider annihilationism and universalism to be beyond the pale.[7] What this shows, I think, is that the retribution thesis is widely considered *not* to be an unrelinquishable part of the traditional doctrine of hell.[8] What's considered unrelinquishable is the belief that hell is a state of eternal suffering, and that some will be finally lost.

If I'm right about this, then an adequate view of hell must turn out to be something *very close to* traditionalism. In particular, it must include the propositions that were previously labeled (in chapter 1) the consignment thesis, the no escape thesis, and the conscious torment thesis. On the other hand, it must be different enough from traditionalism that it can avoid the problems that we discussed in chapters 2–4 and found to be fatal to *full-fledged* traditionalism. I've already indicated which part of traditionalism I think ought to be rejected: the retribution thesis.[9] The choice model

---

reasonable in holding their respective views. The claim I am making in the main text is a claim about what it is reasonable for one to conclude, not a claim about what it would be unreasonable (for someone else) to conclude.

7. Note, for example, that the current Catholic teaching on hell appears to be a version of the choice model: "We cannot be united with God unless we freely choose to love him. But we cannot love God if we sin gravely against him, against our neighbor or against ourselves. . . . To die in mortal sin without repenting and accepting God's merciful love means *remaining separated from him for ever by our own free choice*. This state of definitive *self-exclusion* from communion with God and the blessed is called 'hell'" (*Catechism of the Catholic Church*, 2nd ed., 1033, italics added).

8. There's also an important argument to be made that belief in the retribution thesis is more prominent in Western Christianity than in Eastern Christianity, and that this is traceable to the outsized influence of St. Augustine in the Western tradition. We won't pursue the issue here, but suffice it to say that if this view is correct, then the decision to reject the retribution thesis is much less weighty insofar as it is not a matter of rejecting a belief that enjoys broad consensus in the Christian tradition.

9. Even here, however, an adequate view of hell must include something *very close to* the retribution thesis, in order to account both for the scriptural language that's problematic for the choice model ("eternal punishment," "the fear of the Lord," "the wrath of God," etc.) and the pervasiveness in the Christian tradition of the belief that hell is a retributive punishment. This issue will be addressed in chapter 9 in the section titled "Retribution and eternal punishment."

demonstrates the way that a non-retributive model of hell can be a traditional view *in the sense discussed in this chapter*. What remains to be seen is whether any model of hell that combines these same features (traditional, non-retributive) could also manage to accommodate the full revelation of Scripture (unlike the choice model). In chapters 9–10, I'll argue that it's possible to construct just such a model.

In order to assess the case that I'll make for this model, the reader will be forced to make a judgment about what kinds of traditional beliefs are unrelinquishable in regard to the doctrine of hell. I've specified what I take to be the unrelinquishable core of the doctrine of hell. But I understand that many other Christians—equally sincere in their faith, equally committed to the authority of Scripture, and equally earnest in their pursuit of truth—judge things differently than I do. It's not the purpose of this book to try to refute all opposing views. My purpose, rather, is to try to demonstrate that there's a way forward for those who, on the one hand, find the doctrine of hell to be enormously problematic in its full-fledged traditionalist version, but who, on the other hand, understand tradition in such a way that alternatives to the doctrine of hell as eternal suffering—in particular, annihilationism and universalism—are ruled out.

Regardless of which claims about hell one takes to be unrelinquishable, what the preceding considerations reveal is that the issue of tradition is both one of the most important and one of the most difficult to navigate in constructing an adequate model. There's no simple formula for deciding which views about hell should be regarded as divinely inspired on the basis of how widespread they are in church tradition. And yet, tradition is an indispensable guide for orthodox Christians. The combination of these two points highlights both the complexity of the issue and the need for personal judgment in navigating it. One thing is clear, however: any approach to constructing a model of hell that simply disregards Christian tradition is misguided.

## What would count as a solution?

Before turning to the task of trying to develop an adequate solution to the problem of hell, there's one further issue that we need to address. We need to consider how high the standards are for a model of hell to qualify as a successful solution. Is it required that the model be *proven*, like the conclusion of a mathematical proof? Certainly not. A standard this high applies to very little outside of mathematics and logic. (Even your knowledge of your present surroundings fails to meet this standard, as the history of modern philosophy famously demonstrates.) Is it required that the model be proven true by a lesser standard of evidence—say, a level of evidence comparable to the one justifying your beliefs about your present surroundings? Almost certainly not. Few, if any, theological or philosophical models attain to this standard. Is it required that the model be composed entirely of propositions that can be known according to some ordinary standard of theological knowledge that most orthodox Christians would accept? For example, should all of its components be known on the basis of Scripture according to sound hermeneutical principles? Perhaps surprisingly, even this is not required.

What's required for a solution to the problem of hell is something more minimal. A successful solution to the problem of hell would be a demonstration that all of the required components—the proposition that God is maximally good and loving, the proposition that hell is a state of eternal suffering, the proposition that some are finally lost, etc.—are reconcilable under a certain model, and that the model itself is *possibly* true. The model doesn't need to be provable, or even known to be true. It just needs to be *consistent with* everything we know to be true.

Why are the standards for success so low? It has to do with a principle of logic. In order to demonstrate logical consistency among a set of propositions, all that's required is a description of a *possible* scenario in which the propositions are all simultaneously true. This is easiest to see with an example. (We'll pick one that has nothing to do with theology, to keep things simple.) Consider these two propositions:

P1: Ronald Reagan was the 40th president of the United States.

P2: The 40th president of the United States was a Democrat.

It might at first seem that P1 and P2 are logically contradictory. But they aren't, and we can prove this by describing a possible scenario in which both are true. Imagine that Reagan had run as the Democratic candidate in the 1980 presidential election, and that he had won. That's a scenario in which both P1 and P2 would be true. The scenario we've described isn't the actual world, of course. But it's a way that things *could have been*. It's a possible scenario. And that's enough to demonstrate that P1 and P2 aren't logically contradictory propositions, because propositions that are *genuinely* contradictory could never both be true in *any* imaginable scenario. (Try imagining a scenario in which the proposition that Reagan was a lifelong bachelor and the proposition that Reagan was married are both true. You can't, of course, because these propositions are genuinely contradictory.)

So now let's apply this principle of logic to the problem of hell. The reason the doctrine of hell is a problem is that it *appears* to conflict with other doctrines (other theological propositions) that Christians believe. If it can be shown that all these Christian beliefs are in fact logically consistent—that the appearance of contradiction is *mere appearance*—then the problem is solved. And now that we've specified what it takes to demonstrate logical consistency, the standard for success in our project is clear. The problem of hell will be solved if we can describe a merely *possible* scenario in which it's clear that God's actions and motives are all perfectly good, just, and loving, despite some people being consigned to eternal suffering.

In philosophical terminology, the kind of project we've just described is called a **defense**. What a defense of hell proves is that the doctrine of hell is not refuted by anything known to be true, and that it's logically consistent with everything else that's a part of orthodox Christianity—for example, the doctrine that God is a perfect being. A defense of hell doesn't offer a reason for thinking that the doctrine of hell is *actually* true. It just neutralizes the argument meant to show that the doctrine is false (the argument we've called "the problem of hell"). The reason for thinking the doctrine is actually true is something else that's already in place: a special revelation given in Scripture.

We've identified the minimal conditions of a solution to the problem of hell. But it's possible that a model of hell could be even more successful than this. Suppose we were able to produce a model that was not only logically possible, but also *plausible*. Suppose the model was not only true for all we know, but also *likely* true. Suppose the model was not only consistent with Scripture, but actually *supported by* Scripture. In this case, we would have something better than a defense; we'd have a **theodicy** of hell.

In discussions of the problem of evil, a theodicy is a plausible explanation of God's reasons for allowing evil and suffering in the world. A successful theodicy is more satisfying than a successful defense, wherever one can be produced, because it offers the prospect of actually *understanding* God's reasons for allowing evil and suffering. If we understand God's reasons, we can *make sense* of evil and suffering in the world, and we can order our lives accordingly. All of this applies to the problem of hell. A successful theodicy of hell would be more satisfying than a successful defense of hell, if we can manage to produce one, because it would help us to understand God's reasons for consigning some to hell.

We're now ready to state the project of this book in more precise terms. Its primary goal is to produce a model of hell that *objectively* qualifies as a successful defense: that is, a model that demonstrates that the doctrine of hell as eternal suffering is consistent with other theistic commitments, thereby solving the problem of hell. Its secondary goal is that the model be plausible enough that it could *subjectively* qualify as a theodicy of hell. This will be the case if the model is plausible enough that some who consider it judge it to be likely true. And this is a standard that can be attained even if the model contains speculative elements that prevent us from being confident that we *know* it's true.

One thing more is required for a model to qualify as a successful theodicy of hell. It should be *edifying*. When we considered the problem of coercion in chapter 4, we saw how the doctrine of hell can be extremely unedifying if developed in the wrong way. Not only can it raise serious intellectual doubts, it can tempt a person to distrust God, or even to despair. It can also have the feature that, if it's sincerely believed and deeply internalized, it works at cross purposes to other things that are essential to Christian faith, such as a free response to the gospel. A successful model of hell should have the very opposite effects as these. It should strengthen the individual believer and enrich their faith; it should build up the church. It should not only be consonant with other central Christian beliefs, attitudes, and actions, but should also encourage and support them, demonstrating these beliefs to be part of a coherent and rationally defensible worldview and helping to motivate the proper attitudes of worship and trust toward God, as well as the actions of loving God and being receptive to the work of His Spirit within us.

In the next chapter, we'll begin developing the model that has all of these characteristics. It's time to introduce the core idea.

# The Divine Presence Model of Hell

# Chapter 9

# Heaven and hell on the divine presence model

Let's begin by assembling the insights from our discussion up to this point. We've seen, *first*, that there are good reasons to judge that an adequate solution to the problem of hell must retain the traditional view that some will be finally lost, along with the understanding of hell as a state of eternal suffering. This is needed to respect the way in which Christian tradition is a vehicle of divine inspiration on core doctrines and thus sets the parameters within which an adequate model of hell can be constructed. *Second*, an adequate solution cannot dismiss the problem of hell through a pat appeal to divine sovereignty, but must instead regard human free will as playing a central role in both salvation and damnation. Consequently, the theological determinist model, according to which God wills, intends, and even orchestrates some people's eternal damnation, must be wholly rejected. *Third*, an adequate solution must explain damnation in terms of the natural consequences of persistence in sin, rather than as an artificial and arbitrary punishment selected and imposed by God. That is to say, it must be a natural consequence model of some type. This in turn requires that the model must reject the retribution thesis, according to which eternal suffering is a retributive punishment and the purpose of hell is to exact vengeance upon those who are consigned to it. *Fourth*, an adequate model must be able to account for the full scriptural record pertaining to hell and final judgment. In particular, it must be able to accommodate the recurring scriptural motifs of the day of judgment, eternal punishment, the fear of the Lord, the wrath of God, and language implying that the damned are, in many if not all cases, consigned to hell against their wills. *Fifth*, an adequate solution must account for the way that, even in consigning some to hell, God's goodness, justice, and love are perfect and unsurpassable, which requires that God not only loves the damned but that He actually wills the highest good of the damned in consigning them to hell. And *finally*, in addition to all this, an adequate solution to the problem of hell must have the feature of being spiritually edifying to those who accept and deeply internalize it.

## Introducing the core idea

Is a model of hell that has all of these characteristics even possible? I think it is. We're now ready to introduce the core idea on which we'll build a model of hell—the idea that will orient the remainder of our discussion in this book. The central premise of the model is that *heaven and hell are the various ways that the righteous and the wicked will experience the presence of God after the final judgment.*

This core idea is simple to state, but it will require a good deal of explanation to unpack. Before taking up the project, it's worth noting in passing that this idea is—perhaps surprisingly—a recurring one in Christian thought, showing up in the writings of thinkers as diverse as the twentieth-century apologist C. S. Lewis,[1] the sixteenth-century Reformer Martin Luther,[2] and the seventh-century bishop and theologian Isaac of Nineveh (St. Isaac the Syrian).[3] It is also, significantly, an idea that is currently widely accepted within Eastern Orthodoxy, one of the three major branches of Christianity. None of this proves the idea to be true, of course,

---

1. Lewis, *Mere Christianity*, Book I, chapter 5, and Book II, chapter 5. See also, among Lewis's fictional works, *The Great Divorce* and *Till We Have Faces*.

2. In his *Commentary on the Psalms*, Luther writes, "The fiery oven is ignited merely by the unbearable appearance of God and endures eternally. . . . Not as though the ungodly see God and His appearance as the godly will see Him; but they will feel the power of His presence, which they will not be able to bear, and yet will be forced to bear. . . . This chief and unbearable punishment God will inflict with His mere appearance, that is, with the revelation of His wrath." (Quoted in Fudge and Peterson, *Two Views of Hell*, 122.)

3. St. Isaac famously claims that "those who find themselves in gehenna will be chastised with the scourge of love. How cruel and bitter this torment of love will be! For those who understand that they have sinned against love, undergo greater sufferings than those produced by the most fearful tortures. The sorrow which takes hold of the heart which has sinned against love, is more piercing than any other pain. It is not right to say that the sinners in hell are deprived of the love of God. . . . But love acts in two ways, as suffering in the reproved, and as joy in the blessed." (From *Mystic Treatises*; quoted in Lossky, *The Mystical Theology of the Eastern Church*, 234.)

but it does at least show that it's not simply a notion conjured up by a philosopher to solve a philosophical problem. There's an important case to be made that this is a theological insight with deep roots in the Christian tradition, though we won't digress to try to develop this case here. It's also significant that this core idea is embraced by a large number of Christians today who regard tradition to be a source of authoritative teaching. The prospects are at least promising that the model based on this idea will turn out to qualify as a traditional view.

It's helpful to consider how the core idea is commonly elaborated in Eastern Orthodox theology. The following is taken from Fr. Thomas Hopko's four-volume work *The Orthodox Faith*, endorsed by the Orthodox Church in America:

> The final coming of Christ will be the judgment of all men. His very presence will be the judgment. . . . All men will have to behold the Face of Him . . . whom they have crucified by their sins. . . .
>
> For those who love the Lord, His Presence will be infinite joy, paradise and eternal life. For those who hate the Lord, the same Presence will be infinite torture, hell and eternal death. The reality for both the saved and the damned will be exactly the same when Christ "comes in glory, and all angels with Him," so that "God may be all in all."
>
> According to the saints, the "fire" that will consume sinners at the coming of the Kingdom of God is the same "fire" that will shine with splendor in the saints. It is the "fire" of God's love; the "fire" of God Himself who is Love. . . . For those who love God and who love all creation in Him, the "consuming fire" of God will be radiant bliss and unspeakable delight. For those who do not love God, and who do not love at all, this same "consuming fire" will be the cause of their "weeping" and their "gnashing of teeth."
>
> Thus it is the Church's spiritual teaching that God does not punish man by some material fire or physical torment. God simply reveals Himself in the risen Lord Jesus in such a glorious way that no man can fail to behold His glory. It is the presence of God's splendid glory and love that is the scourge of those who reject its radiant power and light.[4]

---

4. Hopko, *The Orthodox Faith*, 196–97. These passages can also be found on the Orthodox Church in America website, http://oca.org/orthodoxy/the-orthodox-faith/spirituality/the-kingdom-of-heaven/heaven-and-hell.

The theological assertions made in this passage are representative of a fairly standard elaboration of the core idea in Eastern Orthodoxy. It's important to note the distinct claims:

- The second coming of Christ *is* the final judgment; the final judgment *is* the revealing of Christ in glory.
- When Christ is revealed in glory, all are compelled to behold "the face of God," which is at once a source of surpassing joy to the righteous and a source of torment to the wicked.
- The presence of God "consumes" both the righteous and the wicked: the righteous experience this as the glory of heaven; the wicked experience it as the fire of hell.
- The consuming fire of God's presence is God's love, because God *is* love.

It follows from these claims that damnation is the way that the wicked experience the love of God after the final judgment.

These are provocative claims, but they also immediately raise a number of questions. Are the saints and the damned all together in the same place in this account? Why, exactly, is the presence of God a source of *suffering* to the wicked? How could love, and especially God's perfect love, be a source of torment? Why does the revealing of Christ in glory count as a *judgment*? Does God *intend* for the wicked to suffer for all eternity? Wouldn't it be more merciful for God to simply annihilate the damned in order to put them out of their misery? These questions, and many more, are ones that a developed version of the model must answer.

So now, having introduced the core idea, let's begin developing the model that builds on it. The model has no standard name, so I'll call it the **divine presence model**.

## Heaven and hell on the divine presence model

We'll start with some basics of Christian *eschatology*: the part of theology that deals with the culmination of both human and cosmic history ("the end of the world"). According to the New Testament, Jesus Christ will someday return in glory, the dead will be resurrected, and each person will be subjected to a final judgment, whereupon each will be consigned to either heaven or hell. These are the fundamental Christian teachings regarding "last things." The divine presence model is a way of fleshing out these fundamental doctrines, but its core claim is primarily about the nature of heaven and hell.

To begin unpacking this core claim, we need to first notice the important connection it has to the problem that philosophers call **divine hiddenness**. For the vast majority of people, God is neither easily nor fully perceived in this life. We don't experience God the same way we experience other people; we don't see God "face to face." This feature of human existence raises some difficult philosophical and theological questions—we'll return to this in later chapters—but according to Christian theology, it's a *temporary* feature of human existence. At the second coming of Christ—also called the *parousia*, which literally means "arrival" or "presence"—Jesus will be revealed in all his glory; the presence of God will fill the earth; God will finally be "all in all" (1 Corinthians 15:28). This event ushers in the **apocalypse**, a word sometimes translated "revelation" (the usual rendering of the title of the last book of the Bible), but whose literal meaning is "unveiling." The apocalypse is the unveiling of the glorified Christ to all the world at the final judgment, the event that marks *the definitive end of divine hiddenness*. This is the point when the presence of God becomes wholly manifest, the point when it becomes not only unmistakable but also *inescapable*.

Unlike our present experience of God, each person's experience of the divine presence after the final judgment will be *unmitigated*. The conditions that bring about a state of divine hiddenness will no longer be in place. Everyone will be unshielded, so to speak, in their permanent state of exposure to the presence of God. On the divine presence model, this will be an experience of unimaginable and unsurpassable joy for some people: the satisfaction of their deepest longings, the fulfillment of their very nature, a consummation of their union with the divine, the source of a perfect and everlasting happiness. This is eternal life—the experience of the righteous in the age to come: in a word, *heaven*. But to those who've remained stubbornly obstinate and unrepentant in their sins all the way up to the day of judgment, exposure to the presence of a holy God will be a source of torment, unmitigated as it is by any of the current conditions of divine hiddenness that permit an escape from it. The very same event of being in the presence of God—which will be experienced by the righteous as perfect bliss, what has traditionally been called *the beatific vision*—will be experienced by the wicked as horrendous suffering.

Just as important as understanding what heaven and hell *are* in this account, it's important to understand what they are *not*. First, *heaven and hell are not geographical locations*. Consignment to hell is not a matter of God's physically relocating a person to some very unpleasant place, like a prison or a torture chamber or the center of the earth or a far-off planet.

The divine presence model incorporates the teaching, found in the closing chapters of the book of Revelation, that what follows the resurrection and final judgment is a restoration of creation, "the new earth." This is the final destiny of all mankind: *this* earth, the same one we inhabit now, albeit completely healed and renewed. (Specific details about *how* creation is made new are not a part of the model.) On the divine presence model, heaven and hell are different ways—radically different ways—of experiencing resurrection life in the **new creation**.[5]

Second, *the suffering of hell is in no way artificial or arbitrary*. Consignment to hell is not a matter of God's subjecting the damned to physical tortures or any other artificial punishments. On the divine presence model, the suffering of hell is a natural consequence of the character a person forms by persisting in sin. Suffering is the way that the wicked *necessarily* experience the presence of God. There's nothing artificial about it. And there's nothing arbitrary about the punishment of hell. God doesn't freely select the punishment of hell from among a range of possible options. The way in which the damned suffer in hell is the inevitable outcome of an encounter between a sinful creature and a holy and loving God. There's no action that God takes, other than the action of being fully revealed, that causes the damned to suffer.

These two points—that heaven and hell are not geographical locations and that the suffering of hell is in no way artificial or arbitrary—are related to one another. If heaven and hell were locations, there would be an element of arbitrariness in God's consigning people to them. We would be left to wonder why there were only two options, and why God doesn't consign the damned to some other location instead. And we might also wonder why God doesn't just *leave people alone* who don't believe in Him. On the divine presence model, there's no alternative to heaven and hell, because in the new earth there's no alternative to being in the presence of God. It wouldn't help matters to be whisked away to some far-off planet. In the age to come, the divine presence will fill *all* of creation.

Third, *the purpose of hell is not retribution*. We've already noted that the punishment of hell is neither artificial nor arbitrary, from which it follows that it's not a retributive punishment. It's crucial to the divine presence model that there is no action that God takes with the *intention* of inflicting suffering upon the damned. Causing unrepentant sinners to suffer is the *foreseen but unintended consequence* of Christ's being fully revealed in glory. To say that

---

5. What I call "the new creation" or "the new earth" is also commonly referred to as "the world to come" (Nicene Creed) or "the age to come." All are ways of referring to the period that follows "the present age," which is the time from creation to the return of Christ.

this consequence is foreseen is to say that God knows in advance that it will have this effect; to say that it is unintended is to say that bringing about this consequence is not God's reason or purpose in so acting.

So what *is* the intended purpose of Christ's being revealed at the end of the age? First, its purpose is to bring glory to Jesus, which in turn brings glory to God. At the second coming of Christ, everyone will recognize the truth of who Jesus is: the Messiah, the Lord of all creation, the rightful King of the universe, the very Son of God. In returning to earth, Jesus is claiming what is rightfully his.

Second, the purpose is to restore creation. The second coming of Christ is the point when the kingdom of God is finally and fully established "on earth as it is in heaven" (Matthew 6:10). It inaugurates a state of perfect peace and justice. But it's also a restoration of all that was marred in creation by the fall of humankind. The return of Christ reestablishes the order and harmony of the original creation ("Eden") and abolishes the curse of death.

Third, its purpose is to consummate the union between humanity and divinity and thereby to bring human nature to its fulfillment. As we previously discussed (chapter 7), the purpose for which humans are created is communion with God. We are made for love, and thus union with the divine, who is perfect Love, is the fulfillment of human nature, the highest and only lasting happiness that is possible for human beings. It is thus God's intention, in fully manifesting His presence in the new creation, to bring about a state of perfect joy and fulfillment for every person. He is willing the highest good of every human being. It is unequivocally true, on the divine presence model, that God "would have all men to be saved" (1 Timothy 1:4 ASV). God *foresees* that this will not be the case, but it is fully His *intention* that it be so. God loves everyone, and He wills the highest good for everyone, even while knowing that some will use the free will He has given them to reject Him finally and thereby to thwart their own highest good forever.

It's a crucial feature of the divine presence model that *God does everything in His power to save everyone*. It doesn't follow from this that everyone will be saved, because there are some things that cannot be accomplished unilaterally, regardless of how much power a being has. As we noted in chapter 4, it's impossible for God to *make* a person repent, because repentance is, of its very nature, an action that must be performed freely to be performed at all. Any action that's coerced or determined by an outside agent or force simply does not qualify as an act of repentance. But repentance is a necessary condition of salvation; it's an essential part of the process of being saved from one's sins. So there can be no salvation without repentance.

On the divine presence model, God provides to each and every person the grace that's required to make repentance *possible*. This is crucial, because no one can repent of their sins by their own effort or power, apart from the enabling grace that only God can provide.[6] But it's likewise mistaken to think that the magnitude of divine power enables God to bring about creaturely repentance by force. Omnipotence is not the ability to do the logically impossible,[7] and the notion of God's *forcing* someone to repent is self-contradictory, and thus logically impossible.

Those who use their freedom to continually reject divine grace and the conviction of the Holy Spirit in calling them to repentance, who stubbornly persist in their sin and rebellion all the way up to the day of judgment, will finally be lost. But, on the divine presence model, no one will be lost due to a failure on God's part to call them, or to give them enough grace to enable them to repent, or, more generally, to provide whatever is needed to make their salvation possible. And not only does God do what's necessary to make everyone's salvation possible, God does everything in His power to save each and every person. Those who are finally lost are lost because of their own stubborn refusal to accept divine grace and turn from their sins. On the divine presence model, everyone who *can* be saved *will* be saved. Nevertheless, God foresees that some will finally reject Him, despite all His efforts (past, present, and future) to elicit a positive response from them. But insofar as God does everything in His power to save everyone, it is unequivocally true that God loves everyone and wills the highest good of everyone.

Some readers may have doubts that anyone would—or even could— misuse their free will so egregiously in the way just described. What could possibly be the motive for such a self-destructive choice? We'll return to this topic in chapter 13, where it will be addressed in detail. For now, what's important to appreciate is that, on the divine presence model, the extent of God's mercy, goodness, and love toward each and every person

---

6. To think otherwise is to fall into the heresy known as Pelagianism.

7. Surprising as it might be to some readers, this is the *traditional* view of omnipotence. It's within God's power to violate or suspend the laws of *nature*—this is a common understanding of what miracles are—but not the laws of logic. To think otherwise is to become immediately entangled in manifest absurdities—and even worse. The claim that God can do the logically impossible ends up entailing that *God doesn't have a nature*, which is heretical. To see why, notice that if God can do absolutely *anything*, including the logically impossible, then He could do all of the following: He could forget your name; He could do something evil; He could create a rock so heavy that He can't lift it; He could bring it about that He no longer exists. But if it's even *possible* for God to do these things, then He is not *of His very nature* omniscient, omnibenevolent, omnipotent, or self-existent (respectively). Similar considerations would lead one to reject all the other attributes that are, according to Christian orthodoxy, part of God's nature as well. Clearly, this conclusion is unacceptable. The way to avoid it is to reject the assumption that leads to it: namely, that omnipotence includes the ability to do the logically impossible.

is unsurpassable. None of the divine attributes is in any way diminished or compromised on the divine presence model; the model is fully compatible with the requirements of perfect being theology. The damned are not loved any less than the saints. The difference lies wholly on the side of the creatures, not the Creator.

## Retribution and eternal punishment

Let's turn now to the issue of how retribution and eternal punishment are understood on the divine presence model. In chapter 7, we decided that an adequate solution to the problem of hell must reject the retribution thesis, and yet it must also, somehow, manage to account for such prominent biblical themes as eternal punishment, the fear of the Lord, and the wrath of God. It must likewise account for the biblical descriptions of hell suggesting that damnation is a state that's imposed on the damned against their wills. We're now in a position to see how all of these requirements can be met.

What the divine presence model demonstrates is the way that retributive *elements* can be a part of a model of hell that nonetheless rejects the retribution thesis. Even though retribution is not the purpose of hell on the divine presence model, and the punishment of hell is neither artificial nor arbitrary, there is, nonetheless, a sense in which the punishment of hell is imposed by God upon the damned against their wills. The damned do not want to be subjected to the presence of God; it's a source of torment to them. God has compelling reasons for willing that Christ be revealed in glory—reasons that we've already discussed—but suffering is the only possible way that sinful creatures can experience the fully manifested presence of God. So even though damnation is a state that God imposes on the wicked in hell, it's not a punishment that He freely chooses for them, and inflicting suffering is not the intended purpose of God's subjecting sinful creatures to His presence.

What this means is that, on the divine presence model, exposure to the presence of God *functions* as a punishment for the wicked, even though it isn't *intended* by God to be such.

The language of eternal punishment in Scripture is perfectly apt, because this is the way that the wicked forever *experience* God's presence in the new creation. In philosophical terms, we would say that the scriptural language is *phenomenological*: it's language that describes the first-person, subjective experience of the damned.[8] Being punished is *what it feels like*

---

8. I take it that this language in Scripture is the primary reason the retribution thesis has been so widely accepted, especially in Western Christianity. Those who find

to be a sinner in the presence of a holy God. It feels like divine wrath; it feels like vengeance. The punishment of hell isn't retributive, but it feels retributive to those subjected to it. And because this condition is permanent after the day of judgment, the experience of those in hell is that of an *eternal punishment*.

There's nothing exactly like this in ordinary experience. But there's something that's close enough to be illuminating. Consider a case where parents intentionally allow their child to experience the painful consequences of disobedience in order to "teach them a lesson." There's a certain moral good that, in the parents' judgment, can be obtained in this case only (or best) by allowing the child to experience the natural consequences of their own foolishness. Typically, the good to be obtained is the promotion of the child's moral training and development. The parents have the ability to intervene and spare the child the unpleasant experience, but they instead allow—and even *intend*—the child to experience these painful, natural consequences, because doing so will help the child to learn and grow. Let's call this a **natural punishment**.

Not every natural consequence is a natural punishment. If someone forgets to tie their shoelaces and subsequently trips and falls, this is a natural consequence, but not a punishment. The concept of punishment requires the presence of some person or group who *intends* another person or group to experience the natural consequences of their actions. It further requires that the ones "inflicting" the natural punishment have the ability and authority to intervene and prevent these natural consequences from being experienced by those who are being punished, but who fail to intervene for the sake of achieving some moral good.

On the divine presence model, the suffering of hell is *not* a natural punishment, because a crucial element is missing. It is God's presence that causes the damned to experience in full the natural consequences of the character they have forged for themselves through past evil choices and persistence in sin, but it's not God's *intention* to bring about this suffering in exposing all to His presence. This is important, because the suffering of hell doesn't have a reformative function; it doesn't bring the damned to repentance or otherwise promote their moral improvement. If God

---

scriptural support for the retribution thesis are interpreting "eternal punishment" and related terms (divine "wrath," "hate," "vengeance," etc.) literally, rather than phenomenologically. This is understandable, but deeply problematic, for all the reasons discussed in chapters 2–4. It's important to highlight at this point that the divine presence model meets *both* of the requirements for an adequate model of hell with respect to the retribution thesis: namely, it rejects the retribution thesis *and* is able to explain the reason so many Christians have interpreted Scripture as supporting the retribution thesis.

intended this everlasting suffering, it would bring into question God's love for the damned, and thus compromise the doctrines of divine omnibenevolence and perfect love.

The conclusion we should finally reach on this matter is that hell functions, on the divine presence model, as something *close to* a natural punishment and *close to* a retributive punishment, without exactly being either. In terms of the way that it's *experienced* by the damned, it's more like a retributive punishment. This helps to explain the scriptural language that "the wrath of God remains" on the wicked; that they will be "thrown into the outer darkness" and "cast into hell"; that God will "repay with affliction" the enemies of His church, "inflicting vengeance upon those who do not know God," and so on.[9] Hell is also close to a retributive punishment in terms of its subjective function (the way that it functions in the lives of those consigned to hell): it does not bring about the moral improvement of the damned but only brings their evil back upon their own heads. However, hell is closer to a natural punishment when considered in terms of its existence and objective function. The suffering that the damned experience is a natural consequence of their past evil choices and the vicious characters they have formed by these choices. "The wrath of God is revealed from heaven against all ungodliness and unrighteousness of men" when God *gives the wicked over* to their sins, when He allows them to fully reap what they have sown.[10] But the suffering of the damned isn't *simply* a matter of sin running its natural course as a spiritual disease. It's the *combination* of this sickness of the soul and exposure to the presence of God that brings about the state of damnation.

We should note, finally, that this account of eternal punishment provides an answer to one of the questions we previously raised: Why is the presence of God a source of *suffering* to the wicked? The presence of God, who is Love, is a source of happiness to those who have been conformed to the image of Christ and thereby made perfect in love. It's the fulfillment of their natures and the satisfaction of their deepest desires. But to those who are incapable of true love—*agape* love—and who are instead capable only of selfish love, the presence of Love is experienced as something hostile and threatening, both to their wills and to their egos. Love is a uniting force that binds individuals to one another and to God, whereas sin and the vices that it forms in the soul have the very opposite tendency: that of disuniting and alienating people from one another and from God. The damned do not *want*

---

9. John 3:36; Matthew 8:12; Luke 12:15; and 2 Thessalonians 1:6–8, respectively. The NASB translation of 2 Thessalonians 1:8 uses the phrase "dealing out retribution."

10. Romans 1:18–32.

to be united in agape love to God or to other people. So they experience the presence of Love as an opposing force. In their earthly lives, they willed to forge their identities on their own terms, ordered around their own interests and directed toward the satisfaction of their own, selfish desires. The natural psychological and spiritual consequences of this extend into the next life. Insofar as selfishness and the vices produced by it have become so deeply ingrained in their natures as to be part of their self-identities, the presence of perfect Love is experienced as an assault upon their deepest selves. In this way, the very love of God is a source of suffering to those whose will and character have become incorrigibly bent toward evil.

## Solving the specific problems of hell

Now that we've developed the divine presence model's account of eternal punishment, we're in a position to see how the model solves each of the specific problems of hell that we discussed in chapters 2–4: the problem of justice, the problem of love, and the problem of coercion. It does so in essentially the same ways as the choice model of hell, but with the significant advantage of being able to account for the scriptural themes that the choice model struggles to accommodate.

Our discussion in chapter 7 revealed that the retribution thesis is the common source of all three of the specific problems of hell. The choice model rejects the retribution thesis, and thereby avoids all of these problems. In revealing the truth about the natural consequences of rejecting God and persisting in sin, God is giving us the information we require to avoid the worst end possible for human beings. The problem of coercion doesn't arise, because God is issuing a warning, not a threat. Likewise, rejecting the retribution thesis allows a model of hell to avoid the problem of love as it was developed in chapter 3. That problem was driven by the assumption that a purely retributive punishment doesn't aim at the good of the one punished, so hell is an unloving punishment if its purpose is retribution. And finally, the disproportion of earthly sin and suffering in hell is a problem of justice only insofar as the purpose of hell is retribution. A natural consequence model of hell—which includes both the choice model and the divine presence model—entirely avoids the problem of justice developed in chapter 2.

The divine presence model overlaps the choice model in all of these solutions because of its like-minded rejection of the retribution thesis. The principal advantage of the divine presence model over the choice model is its ability to solve these problems without compromising key scriptural teachings about eternal punishment. The divine presence model thus incorporates the most significant benefits of the choice model while avoiding its principal liability.

There is, however, a remaining problem that the divine presence model—and any natural consequence model, for that matter—still faces. The problem can be construed as a different version of the problem of justice: the concern is that it seems unjust for God to allow the damned to bring so much suffering upon themselves. But the problem can likewise be construed as a different version of the problem of love: the concern is that it seems *unloving* for God to allow anyone to bring so much suffering upon themselves. Either way the objection is formulated, the central questions that motivate it are the same. Is God being *good to* human beings in giving us so much freedom and allowing us to misuse it so egregiously? Is God *willing the highest good* of every person in treating everyone this way?

These are important questions, but we'll save them for later, because developing an adequate answer will require us to explore the issue of human free will—and a number of related matters—in detail. This we will do in chapters 11–14. Before we turn to this task, we need to finish developing the divine presence model. In the next chapter, we'll expand the model beyond the core ideas that we've introduced so far. These expansions will increase the explanatory power of the model, and also enable it to answer some important objections.

— Chapter 10 —

# The presence of God as truth and life

IN THE PREVIOUS CHAPTER, we noted that the core idea of the divine presence model in its elaborated form, such as the one we considered from Thomas Hopko, raises a number of questions. Some of these questions we have already addressed, such as:

- How could love, and especially God's perfect love, be a source of torment?
- Does God *intend* for the wicked to suffer for all eternity?

Other questions have not yet been addressed or have received, so far, only a preliminary response that needs to be further developed before the answer is complete. These include the following:

- Why does the revealing of Christ in glory count as a judgment?
- Why, exactly, is the *presence* of God a source of suffering to the wicked?
- Wouldn't it be more merciful for God to simply annihilate the damned in order to put them out of their misery?
- Do the saints and the damned exist together in the same place in the age to come?

Answering these questions will require not only clarifications but *expansions* of the divine presence model.

In this chapter, we'll consider two such expansions. These develop the divine presence model beyond the standard presentations found in the writings of Eastern Orthodox thinkers. However, these expansions are not *ad hoc*—that is, they're not simply ideas added on to solve problems that the model faces. They are, instead, ways of drawing on Scripture and tradition to further develop key parts of the model in ways that naturally fit together with the core ideas and bring about greater conceptual unity and explanatory power. For now, the two expansions will be introduced and considered primarily on the basis of their philosophical and theological merits, with only a preliminary case being offered for their support in Scripture and tradition. In the final chapters of the book, we'll return to these topics to explore in more detail the degree to which they are thoroughly biblical ideas.

## The presence of God as truth

The first expansion of the divine presence model that we'll consider is that *the presence of God reveals the inner truth about a person.*

One of the most common religious experiences reported by Christians is the experience of feeling *convicted* by the Holy Spirit. Part of what it is to be convicted is to become aware of some unflattering truth about one's own moral and spiritual condition: that one is guilty, that one has wronged God or other people, that one has sinned. A person finds an encounter with God convicting because, in it, "the secrets of his heart are disclosed" (1 Corinthians 14:25). Typically, these "secrets" are revealed to a person through their own conscience. But many Christians regard conscience to be simply the voice of God within them. If so, then feelings of conviction are a common type of religious experience.[1]

There are very different possible reactions that one can have to this experience. For some, it elicits *contrition*. In such cases, the ugly truth that's been revealed to a person is acknowledged by that person to be true. The individual accepts the reality of their guilt, turns from their sin in repentance,

---

1. It should be emphasized that not every feeling of guilt is an experience of God. Like other religious emotions, guilt can come from sources that have little or no connection to anything divine. In some cases, people feel guilty when they shouldn't; they feel guilty even though they've done nothing wrong and someone else has wronged *them*. This is especially common in cases of abuse, and in particular sexual abuse. Every human faculty is capable of being manipulated; every faculty is capable of error. People's eyes and ears play tricks on them; people seem to remember things that never really happened, and so on. The faculty of moral perception—conscience—is no exception: it too can be tricked; it too can be mistaken. The discussion in the main text should be understood to be about *paradigm* cases: that is, cases where everything is working as it should, cases where the experience of personal conviction is genuinely *truth-revealing*.

seeks the forgiveness of God and others whom they have wronged, and—in whatever ways are possible—seeks to amend the damage of their wrongdoing. These are among the most important movements of faith, because they are the *proper* responses to the Holy Spirit's conviction.

But another reaction is possible, as well: the one the Bible calls **hardness of heart**. It's a natural human tendency to want to see oneself in the best possible light. The experience of conviction is a challenge to the self-image that each of us prefers. The recognition of personal guilt is intensely unpleasant: it's humiliating to have to admit that you've done something really wrong, something that was inexcusable, something that can't be morally justified. It's wounding to one's pride. Because of this, it's tempting to become defensive whenever someone confronts you with an ugly truth about yourself that you've tried to keep hidden—and this is the case even when that "someone" is God. The experience of being confronted with personal wrongdoing is one that often elicits reactions such as denial, anger, and resentment. The biblical term for this kind of reaction is *offense*.

Whenever a person responds to the conviction of the Holy Spirit by hardening their heart, they reject the truth that's been revealed to them; they try to escape the unpleasant feelings of guilt and shame through dishonest means. Instead of acknowledging that what God has revealed is true, they instead try to justify themselves: they conjure up and recite to themselves (and to God) reasons why everything they've done is in fact perfectly understandable, morally permissible, or even praiseworthy. If they manage to actually convince themselves by these reasons—if they come to *believe* that their actions are all justified, even though, on a deeper level, they know this really isn't true—they've engaged in **self-deception**. (We'll have much more to say about this strange but all-too-common phenomenon in the upcoming chapters.)

There are other ways of trying to escape the nagging voice of conscience, as well. Intentionally seeking out distractions—in work, entertainment, news, social media, etc.—is another common way of trying to escape feelings of guilt. Intoxication is yet another. Along with self-deception, these are dishonest ways of trying to deal with the problem.

We've noted that it's unpleasant to be confronted with an ugly truth about yourself that you've tried to keep hidden and don't want to acknowledge. Even when someone confronts you in private, it's tempting to feel offended and to get defensive. It's even more offensive if someone calls you out or exposes your wrongdoing in a very public way. In our present experience, the conviction of the Holy Spirit reveals the truth about a person only *to that person*. It's a private audience with God, so to speak. But in the divine presence model, part of the reason this revelation is private is that we presently exist in a state of partial divine hiddenness. God is a God of truth and the source of all truth, and when His presence is *fully manifested*, the truth is *fully revealed*.

This idea is the first expansion of the divine presence model. At the end of the age, when Christ is revealed in glory and God is finally all in all, the deepest moral and spiritual truths about everyone will be revealed *to everyone*. No longer will the experience of conviction be a private revelation; no longer will these truths be revealed only to the ones they're about. To be in the unmitigated presence of God is for the deepest truths about a person to be finally and fully disclosed for all to see. It's an experience of complete transparency, of utter exposure.

This feature of the divine presence model provides an answer to two of the questions we previously raised. First: Why is the revelation of Christ in glory an experience of *judgment*? It's a judgment because it's a *public declaration of the truth* about each person, an event in which all that was previously hidden is made manifest. But it's important to emphasize that in the divine presence model, the final judgment isn't a matter of God's *making* something true by declaring it; it's a revelation of *what's already true*.[2] It's a public disclosure of the state of each person's soul—a revelation of the truth about everything a person has done and the kind of person each one has become. We could aptly call this a **judgment of transparency**.

Jesus repeatedly describes himself as "the light of the world."[3] In the book of Revelation, he's depicted as an eternal light that shines in the new

---

2. It should perhaps be noted that this view stands in stark contrast to one that some Christians hold: the view that salvation is a kind of legal fiction. In this type of view—an extreme version of the view that theologians call *forensic justification*—a person is *made* righteous, despite all of their sins, simply by God's *declaring* them to be righteous, much like a person who committed a crime is rendered "innocent in the eyes of the law" by a judge or jury declaring them to be innocent. Forensic justification of this type is incompatible with the divine presence model for multiple reasons. The primary reason is that this forensic model assumes damnation to be an artificial punishment. This is why it's thought that salvation can be secured for the sinner through divine declaration: insofar as the punishment of damnation is artificially imposed by God, and salvation is a matter of being delivered from eternal punishment, all it takes for the sinner to be saved is for God to declare the sinner acquitted. The divine presence model rejects the assumption that damnation is an artificial punishment, and so is incompatible with this forensic understanding of justification. The secondary reason this model of justification is incompatible with the divine presence model is the one under discussion in the main text: that final judgment is a not a matter of God's *making* something true through declaration; it's instead a revelation of what's *already true* about each person. The final judgment is the separation of the righteous and the wicked, not the wicked-who've-been-declared-righteous from the wicked-who-haven't.

3. John 8:12 and 9:5.

creation; a parallel prophesy is found in the Old Testament as well.[4] On the divine presence model, it is this light—the light of Christ, the glory of the Son of God—that reveals the deepest moral and spiritual truths about everyone. The revelation of Christ (the apocalypse) *is* the revelation of truth. It is in this way that "God judges the secrets of men by Christ Jesus" (Romans 2:16).

But which truths about a person, exactly, are revealed at the final judgment? First and foremost, the light of Christ illuminates *the record of each person's conscience*, revealing its contents for all to see. According to a fairly common interpretation of Revelation 20:12—"The dead were judged according to what they had done as recorded in the books"—the records of individual consciences will be "read" like open books at the final judgment. Certainly, the teaching that each person will be judged according to their works is a pervasive theme in Scripture.[5] But the Apostle Paul clarifies that each person will be judged not *simply* on the basis of their works, but rather on the basis of their works *in light of their own understanding of right and wrong*.[6] Thus each person's conscience will serve as his or her own judge. This idea is memorably expressed by the nineteenth-century Christian philosopher Søren Kierkegaard:

> [T]he person sitting in a showcase is not as embarrassed as every human being is in his transparency before God. This is the relationship of conscience. The arrangement is such that through the conscience the report promptly follows each guilt, and the guilty one himself must write it. But it is written with invisible ink and therefore first becomes clearly legible only when it is held up to the light in eternity while eternity is auditing the consciences. Essentially, everyone arrives in eternity bringing along with him and delivering his own absolutely accurate record of every least trifle he has committed or omitted. Thus a child could hold court in eternity; there is really nothing for a third party to do, everything down to the most insignificant word spoken is in order.[7]

Beyond these facts about individual works recorded in each person's conscience, other truths may be revealed at the final judgment as well:

---

4. See Revelation 21:23–25 and 22:5; Isaiah 60:19–20.

5. See, for example, Psalm 62:12; Proverbs 24:12; Jeremiah 17:10 and 32:19; Matthew 16:27; Romans 2:6 and 14:12; 1 Corinthians 3:8; 2 Corinthians 5:10; Colossians 3:25; 1 Peter 1:17; Revelation 2:23 and 22:12.

6. Romans 2:12–16.

7. Kierkegaard, *The Sickness unto Death*, 124.

each person's thoughts and deepest desires, whether acted upon or suppressed. Each one's tendencies, habits, and character. The consequences of all the sins each person committed—both the full extent of the harm caused to others and the damage it did to the sinner's own soul. The degree to which a person realized God's calling on their life, becoming—or failing to become—the unique individual that God called them to be. The final judgment is an event that lays bare the soul, exposing its contents, including its deepest secrets, for all to behold.

This feature of the divine presence model allows it to give a more developed answer to another question we previously raised: Why is the presence of God a source of *suffering* to the wicked? We've already discussed the first part of the answer: the presence of God, who is Love, is experienced as threatening and opposing to those who are incapable of true love and whose vicious natures have been forged in opposition to God. But we're now in a position to expand on this account and to cite a further reason why the presence of God is a source of suffering to the damned. The presence of God is truth-revealing. For those who've persisted in their sins all the way up to the day of judgment, the experience of exposure in the presence of God produces tormenting guilt and shame, because the truths that are revealed at this point are disgraceful, humiliating truths.[8]

The prophet Daniel prophesies in the Old Testament that "multitudes who sleep in the dust of the earth will awake: some to everlasting life, others to shame and everlasting contempt" (Daniel 12:2). The damned are those who've refused to become transparent to themselves, who have instead habitually engaged in denial and self-deception, and who have hardened their hearts against all attempts of the Holy Spirit to lead them to repentance. When transparency is finally forced upon them, against their wills, the effect of the exposure is crushing and embittering. This, on the divine presence model, is the reason Jesus repeatedly describes hell as a place of "weeping and gnashing of teeth."[9]

The idea of a judgment of transparency also explains why Jesus describes hell as a place "where their worm does not die and the fire is not quenched" (Mark 9:43–48).[10] According to a traditional interpretation, the phrase "their worm" refers to a gnawing conscience. Because the presence of God is inescapable in the new creation, the worm of conscience gnaws unceasingly, which is why there is "no rest day or night" for the damned (Revelation 14:11). This, too, is a source of profound suffering. In hell, the

---

8. C. S. Lewis briefly develops a similar idea; see Lewis, *The Problem of Pain*, 55.
9. Matthew 8:12; 13:42, 50; 22:13; Luke 13:28.
10. In this description of hell, Jesus is quoting the prophet Isaiah; see Isaiah 66:24.

methods that the damned used in their earthly lives for quieting their consciences are either no longer available (self-distraction, intoxication) or no longer effective in providing relief (denial, self-deception).

When the presence of God becomes inescapable, the voice of God within a person can no longer be quieted or ignored. For those in hell, the truths spoken by this voice are subjectively experienced as accusations, as personal rejections, as eternal judgments.[11] And yet, the damned persist in their habitual responses of denial, self-justification, and self-deception, refusing even in hell to accept the truth about themselves that God has finally and fully revealed. Even though the methods of self-deception no longer function as an effective means of *escaping* the truth, they are nevertheless deployed by the damned as a *defense* against the truth. Because of this, the light of Christ is actually *blinding* to the damned, rather than illuminating them in self-understanding.[12] It intensifies their feelings of guilt and shame, thereby exacerbating their maniacal, desperate, and self-deceived attempts to justify themselves. Exposure to the presence of God has the natural psychological and spiritual effect of permanently solidifying the wicked in their state of self-deception. In this way, the encounter with the glorified Christ causes the wicked to be "thrown into the outer darkness," spiritually speaking, as Jesus himself prophesied (Matthew 8:12 ESV).[13]

## The presence of God as life

We've seen the ways that the first expansion of the divine presence model—the inclusion of the claim that the presence of God reveals the inner truth about a person—gives the model greater explanatory power and allows it to answer certain pressing questions. But other questions remain, and perhaps the most difficult one is this: Why doesn't God simply annihilate the damned, mercifully putting them out of their misery?

The answer to this question is contained in a second expansion of the divine presence model: that *the very presence of God is life-giving*.

---

11. Note the way that Jesus reiterates and expounds upon Daniel's prophesy: "Do not marvel at this; for the hour is coming in which all who are in the graves will hear His voice and come forth—those who have done good, to the resurrection of life, and those who have done evil, to *the resurrection of condemnation*" (John 5:28–29 NKJV; cf. Daniel 12:2).

12. St. Basil remarks that there are "two capacities in fire, one of burning and the other of illuminating..." ("Homily on Psalms," 28:6, quoted in Puhalo, *On the Nature of Heaven and Hell according to the Holy Fathers*, 9). The dual experiences of being blinded by the light of Christ and burned by the fire of God go together.

13. See also Matthew 22:13 and 25:30.

To understand this idea, we need to first consider something that has been a working assumption of the divine presence model all along, though it hasn't yet been stated explicitly. The assumption is that the presence of God can be manifested to greater or lesser degrees. Put differently, God can be more or less *present to* a certain individual or group of people at a certain time and place.

In one sense, this is a strange idea, especially in light of the doctrine of divine **omnipresence**: the doctrine that God is everywhere present. It's not entirely easy to explain what we mean in saying that God is everywhere present, since God isn't a physical being and so isn't *physically* present anywhere. One common analysis of omnipresence tries to reduce it to divine knowledge and power: to say that God is everywhere present is to say that His knowledge and power immediately extends to everything in creation at every time. But there's a prominent idea in the Bible that this analysis doesn't quite capture: the idea that God is capable of manifesting His presence to varying degrees. God is said to "hide His face" from certain people at certain times, and to "dwell" with others. The term from rabbinic literature used to refer to the glory of the Lord manifested at certain times and places is *Shekinah*, which literally means "dwelling" or "settling."

One example of this in Scripture is the "pillar of cloud" and the "pillar of fire" that go before the Israelites as they wander in the wilderness following their exodus from Egypt.[14] Another example is the fire that descends from heaven and fills Solomon's temple as a "cloud."[15] Even if the theological content conveyed by these terms is difficult to analyze precisely, they clearly seem to indicate a sense in which the presence of God can be *especially* located or manifested at a certain time and place. We might struggle to make metaphysical sense of this, but the sacred literature of the Judeo-Christian tradition seems clearly committed to the idea that God is capable of varying the degree to which He is present or absent to different people at different times and places.

Given this assumption, let's now consider what would be—in theory at least—the possible upper and lower limits of these manifestations of the divine presence. At the extreme lower end would be a state of complete divine absence. Because nothing can exist entirely apart from God and His sustaining power, this would be a state of nonbeing. A world completely devoid of God's presence would be a world in which nothing exists. At the extreme upper end would be a state in which the presence of God is

---

14. Exodus 13:21–22; 14:20; 4:34–38, Numbers 14:10–14; Deuteronomy 1:33; Nehemiah 9:12–19.

15. 1 Kings 8:10–13; 2 Chronicles 5:13–14; 7:1–3.

manifested completely in an entirely unmitigated form, a state in which God is "all in all." This is the state of the new creation, according to the divine presence model.

On the expansion of the model we're now developing, death is absent to the degree that the divine presence is manifested. This is what it means to say that the very presence of God is life-giving. Our present, earthly existence is a state between the two extremes we just described. God is not entirely absent, but He's also not yet fully revealed. This in-between state is the one that we previously labeled a state of partial "divine hiddenness."[16]

In this world, where God is partially hidden, we find an abundance of both life *and* death. On the divine presence model, what makes this combination of life and death possible is that we presently exist in a state between complete divine absence and full manifestation of the divine presence. (The question of *why* God presently wills this combination is one that we'll save for chapter 17.) In the new creation, the presence of God will fill the universe; divine omnipresence will be fully manifested. This is the reason there's no death in the new creation, the reason the "curse of death" is abolished when Christ returns in glory.[17]

---

16. It's important to notice that divine hiddenness is primarily a metaphysical category in the divine presence model: it's a way of describing *the way the world is* rather than merely *the way the world appears to us*. Put differently: divine hiddenness isn't simply an illusion, or a limitation of our knowledge, or an inability to perceive the full reality of the world around us. The manifestation of God's presence is *actually* greater or lesser to different people at different times and places. This metaphysical difference has epistemological effects, however: that is, it affects *our ability to perceive and to know* certain things. Consider the following analogy. A floodlight is hidden behind a thick blackout curtain. A person standing in front of the curtain can't see the light; perhaps they can't see anything else, either, because they're in total darkness. If the curtain is pulled back, they now can see the light—and everything it illuminates. Now imagine that this person has a severe sensitivity to light; exposure to it burns them, even as it also illuminates them and everything around them. Here we have a convergence of the metaphysical (the effect of the light on the person's body) and the epistemological (the effect of the light on the person's ability to see). Returning to the divine presence model: to say that God remains partially hidden in this life is to say that He somehow mitigates our exposure to His presence; He shields us from it to a large degree. And He does so *for our sakes*. (Shielding the light-sensitive person from the floodlight is a benevolent thing to do.) But this shielding has epistemological consequences: it makes it harder for us to discern His existence. It also makes it harder for us to discern other moral and spiritual truths, including truths about ourselves. We'll return to these points in later chapters, especially chapter 17, to develop them in greater detail and to draw out the implications.

17. Some readers might be concerned that the divine presence model fails to account for the language of "the second death" in the book of Revelation: "The lake of fire is the second death. Anyone whose name was not found written in the book of life was thrown into the lake of fire" (Revelation 20:14b–15). But the first part of verse 14,

Nevertheless, there is also a sense in which the fate of the damned is accurately described as a kind of "living death." This is clearest if we add a further detail to our second expansion of the model: the divine presence is life-giving to all creation, but at an individual level, it confers life *to the extent that a being is capable of receiving it*. A person is a soul-body composite. The bodies of the damned are fully receptive to the life-giving presence of God in just the ways that bodies can be alive, but the souls of the damned are not fully receptive to the life-giving presence of God in all the ways that souls can be alive. Bodies are alive in the sense of being animated, capable of sensation, etc. Souls are capable of life in a much deeper sense, but this deeper sense is one that requires union with God. Hence the damned are eternally alive in one sense (they are sentient) but dead in another (devoid of participation in the life of God).[18]

We're now in a position to answer the question we previously raised about annihilation. If the presence of God is inherently life-giving, then it follows that the only way God could completely annihilate the damned would be to withdraw His presence completely from them. But we've already discussed the reasons God has for willing, instead, that Christ be revealed in glory at the end of the age. The apocalypse is the point when heaven comes to earth, when the presence of God fills all of creation—a reality exactly opposite of God's withdrawing His presence from the world.

Therefore, the summary answer to the question of why God will not annihilate the damned is that doing so is logically incompatible with the reality of the new creation. The action of God's withdrawing His presence from some people in order to annihilate them, and the action of God's filling all of creation with His presence, are incompatible alternatives. Trying to will them both would be like trying to draw a figure that's both a circle and a square. In the new creation, everyone will be fully in the presence of God, regardless of their individual preferences. It follows that no one will die, much less will anyone be annihilated—again, regardless of what any particular person or group might prefer.

There's a further consequence of this expansion of the divine presence model that's important to notice. Because the presence of God is life-conferring, when Christ returns in glory, his very presence on earth will bring about the resurrection of the dead. In other words, the second

---

omitted from the previous quote, is crucial: "Then *death and Hades* were thrown into the lake of fire." In other words, the second death is *the death of death*. It's the event in which death itself is destroyed, swallowed up in "the lake of fire"—a symbol of the presence of God, as I'll argue in chapter 20.

18. The understanding of salvation as participation in the life of God—a doctrine called *theosis*—will be developed in chapters 17 and 18.

coming of Christ and the resurrection of the dead are not two separate events; they are one and the same. This singular event is likewise identical to the event of God's abolishing the curse of death. As the Apostle Paul puts it, "For since death came through a man, the resurrection of the dead comes also through a man. For as in Adam all die, *so in Christ all will be made alive*" (1 Corinthians 15:21–22).

## Separation of the righteous and the wicked

There's one final question that we raised in chapter 9 but haven't yet fully answered: Does it follow from the divine presence model that everyone—both the saints and the damned—will be *in the same place*? In one sense, the answer is yes: everyone will exist in the new creation. But there's no reason to assume that everyone will be in the same place in the new creation, and there are several reasons to think otherwise.

One reason is biblical: the final chapters of Revelation describe a scene in which the enemies of God are *outside the gates* of the city that comes down from heaven, the city where the righteous will abide in the new creation.[19] Also, the language from Jesus' parables that we've repeatedly highlighted—regarding the wicked being "shut out" of the heavenly banquet, "thrown" into the outer darkness, and so on—suggests that there's a final separation of the righteous and the wicked. This could, perhaps, be construed entirely in spiritual terms: one could interpret it to mean simply that the damned will have no communion with either God or the saints. But when we consider it in combination with the imagery of Revelation and the fact that both the righteous and the wicked exist *in resurrected, bodily form*, it seems entirely likely that the physical places in which the saints and the damned reside are not the same.

There's also a principled reason for this conclusion that follows from the logic of the divine presence model. The Bible tells us that part of the process of salvation is being "conformed to the image" of Christ (Romans 8:29). Paul tells the believers at Corinth that "we all, with unveiled face, beholding the glory of the Lord, are being transformed into the same image from one degree of glory to another" (2 Corinthians 3:8); in the ESV translation, it's noted that "beholding the glory of the Lord" may also be rendered "*reflecting* the glory of the Lord." Moreover, Paul speaks of the church in the new creation as "a radiant church," and Jesus says that

---

19. "Outside are the dogs and sorcerers and the sexually immoral and murderers and idolaters, and everyone who loves and practices falsehood" (Revelation 22:15).

"the righteous will shine like the sun in the kingdom of their Father."[20] Interpreted through the lens of the divine presence model, these passages suggests that *the presence of the saints* will be a source of torment to the damned. Insofar as the righteous have been formed into the image of Christ and fully reflect his glory in the new creation, their presence intensifies the suffering of the wicked. Moreover, it's a common part of human experience that whenever we feel guilty or ashamed of ourselves, we want to avoid the company of others, in particular those whom we recognize (on some level) to be morally superior and whose judgment we dread.

We noted previously the prophesy from Daniel that at the resurrection, some will "awake . . . to shame and everlasting contempt." Insofar as it's possible for the damned to escape the presence of the saints, it seems altogether likely that they would do so. The imagery of the new creation in Scripture suggests that the way into the city of God remains forever open—"On no day will its gates ever be shut, for there will be no night there"—and yet "Nothing impure will ever enter it, nor will anyone who does what is shameful or deceitful, but only those whose names are written in the Lamb's book of life."[21] The combination suggests that those who remain outside the city do so of their own choosing—or at the very least, that the city of God is not a place where they could find happiness, given the kind of people they are. The separation of the righteous and the wicked is a natural effect of the radically different ways that each experiences the presence of God in the new creation.

---

20. Ephesians 5:27 and Matthew 13:43. Note the way that the prophesy of Daniel 12:2 continues in the verse that follows: "Multitudes who sleep in the dust of the earth will awake: some to everlasting life, others to shame and everlasting contempt. *Those who are wise will shine like the brightness of the heavens, and those who lead many to righteousness, like the stars for ever and ever.*"

21. Revelation 21:25, 27.

# Soul-Making and Self-Deception

(The Philosophical Case for the Divine Presence Model, Part I)

## Chapter 11

# The problem of evil and the soul-making theodicy

IN THE PREVIOUS TWO chapters, we introduced the basic elements of the divine presence model. At a number of key points in the discussion, we encountered ideas that were in need of further development—in particular, ideas that made use of the concepts of human free will and self-deception. In the upcoming chapters, we'll develop the philosophical basis of these ideas further. We'll also begin to situate the divine presence model in relation to two well-known philosophical problems: the problem of evil (which we'll discuss in this chapter) and the problem of divine hiddenness (which we'll discuss in chapters 15–17). Understanding the model's relationship to these problems will not only help to clarify key conceptual issues, but also to underscore the depth and explanatory power of the model.

### The soul-making theodicy

To begin, we need to bring together several points from discussions spread throughout the book so far. Early on, we introduced the problem of evil: the question of why an all-powerful, all-knowing, and all-good God would allow any evil and suffering to exist in the world. We later discussed the concept of *theodicy*. A theodicy attempts to give a plausible explanation of God's reasons for allowing evil and suffering. Natural consequence models of hell, in particular the choice model and the divine presence model, are best understood as expansions of a more basic theodicy. We will now develop this theodicy, which forms the philosophical foundation of the divine presence model.

A natural consequence model of hell begins with a principle of human development: habits are formed by making repeated choices of a certain type, and these habits eventually produce character traits. The character that an individual forms has natural consequences for their happiness and wellbeing. Damnation is an extreme version of this principle: those who persist in sin long enough eventually form an incorrigibly wicked character, which alienates them from God and from other people, which, in turn, naturally makes them miserable. (All of this was first introduced in our discussion of the choice model, in chapter 7.)

The more general type of theodicy that focuses on the developmental features of human nature to try to explain God's reasons for allowing evil and suffering in the world is called a **soul-making theodicy**. The basic idea is that God has designed the world not to be a hedonistic paradise (which it obviously isn't) but rather an environment that promotes moral and spiritual development.[1] We've noted repeatedly that the highest good of human beings is communion with God. On the soul-making theodicy, a deep and lasting communion with God requires one to have a certain kind of soul—one that is "well-ordered," to borrow a phrase from the ancient Greek philosopher Plato—and this requires a process of moral and spiritual development.

A well-ordered soul is, among other things, a soul that possesses the **virtues**. A virtue is a character trait: specifically, a character trait that disposes one to think, feel, and behave in ways that promote human flourishing. (**Vices** are also character traits, but ones that dispose a person to think, feel, and behave in ways that are contrary to human flourishing.) On a Christian understanding of matters, the virtues are all rooted in love, and many if not all of the virtues can be construed either as specific forms of love[2] or capacities that enable one to love well.[3] The main purpose of life is to be formed into the sort of person who is capable of eternal communion with God and

---

1. The most influential defense of this idea in the contemporary philosophical literature is John Hick's *Evil and the God of Love*. For a chapter-length excerpt from the book, which presents the main ideas of the theodicy, see Hick, "Soul-Making and Suffering." Hick adopts the phrase "soul-making" from the poet John Keats, but he argues that the foundational idea of the theodicy appears early in Christian thought, in the writings of the second-century church father Irenaeus.

2. For example, generosity—giving freely of one's own time, money, or possessions—is a way of loving other people by providing for their needs.

3. For example, courage is doing what's right in difficult or dangerous circumstances. The right thing to do, always, is to love God and to love other people. So courage is the capacity to love well even when it's difficult or dangerous.

other people—in short, to be made fit for heaven. Communion is the highest expression of agape love. So we could say, equivalently, that the purpose of life is to be formed into the sort of person who loves well. The Apostle Paul describes this as being "conformed to the image" of Christ, which makes sense, because Jesus is our model of what perfect love looks like in human form. To be conformed to the image of Christ is to be *perfected in love*.

For creatures who begin in a fallen state, however, this process of formation must include—or rather be a part of—a process of *salvation*. We are born with a deeply ingrained disposition toward pride and selfishness, which eventually expresses itself in countless sins of various types. Salvation includes not only being forgiven of our sins and reconciled to God (the theological term for this is **justification**), but also being completely delivered from the bondage of sin, a process that requires being morally and spiritually perfected (the theological term for this is **sanctification**).[4] This is key to understanding natural consequence models of heaven and hell, such as the divine presence model: the process of salvation includes sanctification, and sanctification is the process of being made perfect in love. As Jesus commands his disciples, rather shockingly, in the Sermon on the Mount: "Be perfect, therefore, as your heavenly Father is perfect" (Matthew 5:48).

This command initially seems impossible to fulfill. But it's crucial to understand that, in Christian theology, salvation is a process of spiritual transformation and renewal that happens not by human moral effort but rather by the grace of God through the atoning work of Jesus Christ and the inner working of the Holy Spirit. What Jesus requires of his disciples is that they remain in fellowship with him, continually receptive to his Spirit—that is, responsive to the Spirit's conviction and leading, open to the Spirit's renewing of their hearts and minds. This is the meaning of the repeated admonition Jesus gives to the apostles on the night that he was betrayed: "*Remain in me*" (John 15:1–17). By doing so, followers of Jesus are transformed by the power

---

4. Whether justification and sanctification can (or should) be sharply distinguished from one another is an issue that historically has separated Protestants from Catholic and Orthodox Christians. The divine presence model is capable of remaining neutral on this issue, so long as it's recognized that justification and sanctification are both essential to salvation. In some extreme versions of Protestant theology, salvation is reduced to justification alone, and justification is reduced to being forgiven by God, which in turn is reduced to being acquitted of sins and exempted from eternal punishment, which is understood in retributive (artificial) terms. In short, to be saved is nothing more than for God to decide not to punish one eternally in hell. The divine presence model is incompatible with this sort of theology, but this is hardly a liability of the model, since the view of salvation just described is thoroughly unbiblical.

of God at work within them, eventually being perfected in love and coming to "image" the Savior whom they follow.[5]

As we've developed it so far, it might not be clear why the soul-making theodicy is a *theodicy*: an explanation of God's allowance of evil and suffering in the world. It's one thing to say that the world has been carefully designed by God with the intention of facilitating the process of human moral and spiritual development; but how is this supposed to explain the presence of evil and suffering in the world?

We come now to the second key idea of the soul-making theodicy: God's allowance of evil and suffering in the world actually *promotes* human soul-making and its divinely intended end. The divinely intended end (goal, purpose) of soul-making is to perfect human beings in love, thereby making humans capable of entering into a state of eternal communion with God and with one another.

Initially, this might seem like a strange idea. Why should we think that an environment well-suited for soul-making must be one in which God allows evil and suffering—and in particular, evil and suffering of the types and quantities that we find in the actual world? To understand this idea, we'll need to think more about the process of human moral and spiritual development: both what it requires, and what it involves.

## Free will and moral agency

The soul-making theodicy is an elaboration of a more basic explanation of God's allowance of evil called the **free-will theodicy**. According to the free-will theodicy, the principal reason God allows evil in the world is that He must allow it in order for humans to have genuine free will. Free will is regarded by some as *intrinsically* valuable and good: that is, valuable and good in itself. More commonly, though, free will is regarded as something that's necessary for *something else* that's tremendously valuable and important: possible candidates for this "something else" include moral and spiritual development, love and worship of God, and salvation. The soul-making theodicy regards free will to be necessary for all of these. It's required for moral

---

5. Since it's apparent that few, if any, followers of Jesus attain this state by the end of their earthly lives, the process of sanctification must continue beyond death and come to completion at some point in the afterlife. Traditionally, this has been understood to occur in the **intermediate state,** between a person's death and their resurrection on the day of judgment. Different versions of this view are widely accepted in Catholicism and Orthodoxy; an extensive Protestant argument for the view is developed by Walls in *Purgatory: The Logic of Total Transformation*. In the next chapter, we will return to the topic of the intermediate state to consider the role it might play in the process of damnation.

and spiritual development, which in turn is required for the especially deep and permanent sort of love and worship of God that the saints experience in heaven, which is the culmination of human salvation. In short, the soul-making theodicy regards human free will to be a logically necessary condition of our achieving the highest end for which we were created: a state of eternal communion with God and other people.

Let's explore this idea in more detail. In order for God to create humans with the capacity for moral and spiritual development, He must create humans as **moral agents**, which in turn requires that God create humans with the capacity for moral choice. To be a moral agent is to have the capacity to form moral judgments and to perform actions of moral significance. This requires that one has the ability to choose between right and wrong. In order for this moral freedom to be genuine, God must not interfere whenever humans opt to misuse their free will by choosing to do something evil. Both good and evil must be *genuine* options for our choices and actions. If one of these options were an illusion—if, for example, God had created the world in such a way that it *seemed* like we could do something evil, but for some reason we couldn't *actually* do anything evil—then we wouldn't be moral agents at all, regardless of what we believed about ourselves.[6] Likewise, if God intervened every time someone was about to misuse their free will and *caused* them instead to will what is morally good, then no one would actually have moral freedom.

So far, we've briefly sketched a number of key ideas that could be considered fundamental principles of the soul-making theodicy. Let's state them baldly. First, the highest human good is eternal communion with God. Second, achieving this end requires a process of moral and spiritual formation. Third, moral and spiritual formation requires moral agency. Fourth, moral agency requires moral freedom.

A further principle that's fundamental to the soul-making theodicy is that moral freedom requires the capacity to cause harm. To appreciate the plausibility of this claim, imagine a world where we had the ability to choose among various trivial options—such as what to wear, which shoe to put on first, what to have for breakfast—but we had no ability to inflict any harm whatsoever on any conscious being, including ourselves. If someone

---

6. Note that this provides a plausible explanation for why God includes the "tree of the knowledge of good and evil" in His creation of the garden of Eden in the opening chapters of Genesis. In order for Adam and Eve to have moral freedom and to be moral agents, there must be *something* that's within their ability to do that would count as a morally wrong action. So God creates the tree and commands Adam and Eve not to eat of its fruit. In this way, He creates the opportunity for disobedience, and thus the possibility of wrongdoing, without which there could be no moral freedom for human beings.

attempted to kick a dog, their foot would always miraculously miss; if someone attempted to insult another person, their words would miraculously be silenced; if someone attempted suicide, their efforts would miraculously be thwarted; and so on. In such a world, humans would possess a trivial sort of free will, perhaps, but we wouldn't have *moral* freedom. Moral freedom requires the ability to make choices that are morally significant, and choices lack moral significance wherever there's no potential whatsoever for any sort of harm to result from any available option.[7] So the reason God has given human beings the power to inflict harm on themselves and others is that this is a necessary condition of soul-making.

There's a further claim I wish to make, which is not a standard part of the soul-making theodicy but which significantly improves the theodicy if it's added to it: namely, that *the extent of human moral freedom is directly proportional to the amount of harm humans are capable of causing.* This proportionality principle, which we'll call the **freedom-harm principle**, helps to explain why God allows humans to cause such *horrendous* evil and suffering. The capacity for the worst kinds of evil that we observe in the world—actions such as kidnapping, rape, torture, murder, and genocide—is not required for humans to possess moral freedom. In a world where we had the ability to lie, insult, and steal from one another, but not the ability to rape, torture, or murder one another, we would still possess moral freedom. But we wouldn't have *as much* moral freedom as we have in the actual world. In general, for creatures who possess moral agency, the capacity for causing *worse types* of harm and *greater quantities* of harm is reflective of the degree of moral freedom possessed. This is part of the reason that God has equipped humankind with the capacity to cause such tremendous harm with our wrongful choices: in creating us this way, God has given us tremendous moral freedom.

But this doesn't yet fully explain why God has given us the ability to cause so much harm and suffering. After all, one might think it would be a *good* thing if humans didn't have so much moral freedom. God certainly could have put much stricter limits on our capacity for inflicting harm. And wouldn't the world have been significantly better if He had done so? God would thereby have prevented the most horrendous evils that we observe in

---

7. It might seem that there's an exception to this. There appear to be some actions that wrong God but harm no human being: silently hating God in one's heart, for example. Since God cannot be harmed, it might seem that this is an example of an action that is wrong but causes no harm whatsoever. But in fact, this action does cause harm—to the one who does it. It damages both one's soul and one's relationship to God, thereby moving one in the direction opposite human flourishing.

the actual world. And wouldn't a world without even the *possibility* of such things as torture and genocide be a better world?

It certainly seems so, at least initially. But perhaps a world like this wouldn't actually be better. There's another proportionality principle that's worth considering: namely, that *the extent of human moral freedom is directly proportional to the human capacity for spiritual communion*. We'll call this the **freedom-communion principle**. Spiritual communion includes both communion with God and communion with other people. It includes the highest form of love: agape love. Unlike some other kinds of love, agape is possible only for moral agents, because it's an expression of moral freedom. (Note that its highest expression is God's love.) And it seems quite plausible that the capacity for agape love increases as moral freedom increases.[8] If this is correct, then it helps to explain why God creates human beings with so much moral freedom, and hence with the capacity for causing so much harm: this is what's required to create beings who are capable of the extraordinarily deep and lasting communion with God that is constitutive of existence in heaven.

In this way, the soul-making theodicy is capable of explaining not only God's allowance of mundane evils, but also horrendous evils. The human capacity for willing horrendous evil and inflicting tremendous harm is *required* in this life in order for the highest human good of eternal communion with God to be possible in the next. And it's for this reason that God creates humans with this capacity.

It's important to head off a potential confusion at this point. On the soul-making theodicy, the *existence* of evils resulting from misuses of creaturely freedom is not required to achieve the highest human good. What's required is the *potential* for such evils, the human *capacity* for causing tremendous harm and inflicting horrendous suffering. Whether or not this potential is actualized is entirely up to human beings. In order to create us as moral agents with significant freedom, God must give us this capacity and permit us to actualize it *if we so choose*. God *permits* evil for this reason, but He is not the author of evil in any way.

There's another part of the soul-making theodicy that we'll only briefly mention, because it's not as central for present purposes. The soul-making theodicy is usually intended to be an explanation not only of *moral*

---

8. To see this, imagine a world in which it was possible for human beings to give away their money and possessions to help others in need, but no greater sacrifice was possible. Compare this imaginary world to the actual world, in which it's possible for people to sacrifice their lives to save the lives of others. Note that humans have greater moral freedom in the actual world—and also, correspondingly, a greater capacity for self-sacrificial love (agape).

*evil*—evil whose cause is traceable to misuses of creaturely free will—but also *natural evil*. Natural evil is pain, suffering, and other kinds of harm that are *not* traceable to misuses of free will, but rather are caused by natural processes. Examples of natural evil include the pain, suffering, and death caused by diseases, natural disasters, and mental illnesses.[9] Natural evil extends beyond considerations of human wellbeing to animals as well. (Perhaps surprisingly, animal suffering is one of the most difficult types of natural evil for a theodicy to explain.)

A full-fledged soul-making theodicy attempts to explain natural evil in terms of the way that it promotes human moral and spiritual development. Perhaps the reason God allows people to suffer terrible diseases is to encourage their development of virtues such as fortitude. Perhaps the experience of watching loved ones suffer through mental illness is intended to encourage the development of compassion and charity. Perhaps the fear of death is meant to force us to look beyond earthly comforts and concerns to more lasting matters, such as our relationship to God. Perhaps the purpose of all natural evil, including animal suffering, is to promote greater human trust in God and dependence upon Him, and thereby to increase our faith. We'll put to the side the question of whether any such explanation of natural evil is fully adequate.[10] These matters are crucial to a full consideration of the soul-making theodicy, but peripheral to our discussion of the problem of hell. For present purposes, what's important to understand is the way that the divine presence model is an extension of the basic logic of the soul-making theodicy, and in particular its account of moral freedom as it relates to the moral and spiritual development of each person.

9. Those who are new to the discussion of the problem of evil are often initially puzzled by the term "natural evil." Why would pain and suffering be considered a type of *evil*? One way to understand this is by considering a thought experiment. Imagine a world that contained no moral evil of any kind, but which was nonetheless filled with death, diseases, natural disasters, and so on. Would there be a problem of evil in such a world? There would be, because we'd still reasonably wonder why a perfectly good and all-powerful being would allow such things. This thought experiment doesn't help to explain the origin of the term "natural evil," but it helps to clarify why the topic of pain and suffering resulting from natural causes is properly considered a part of the problem of evil.

10. One important objection is that natural evil seems unnecessary to achieve the intended goals of the soul-making process. Moral evil is a source of all kinds of pain, suffering, and death, and thus provides more than ample opportunity for acquiring and practicing all of the various virtues. Why, then, does God include natural evil in the world as well as moral evil, and in such unfathomably large quantities and terrifying types? And why, moreover, does He allow animal suffering? Presumably, animals don't suffer for their own sakes—they're incapable of moral and spiritual development—and their suffering seems to make no *essential* contribution to human soul-making: any benefit that we derive from observing their suffering could, it seems, be acquired in other ways.

# Chapter 12
# Developing a natural consequence model of hell

IN THE WAY WE'VE developed it so far, the soul-making theodicy is just a few steps away from becoming a natural consequence model of hell. The most important claim still needed is that *salvation and damnation are the two possible terminating points of the soul-making process*. This is the idea we'll develop in this chapter.

### Soul-making gone awry

In order for the soul-making theodicy to uphold the doctrines of God's perfect goodness and love, it must be maintained that the environment God creates to facilitate human soul-making is designed in such a way as to maximize the likelihood of positive outcomes. In other words, it must be held that God desires that all would be saved, and that He's created an environment that is maximally conducive to the salvation of all, or at least as many as possible. In universalist versions of the soul-making theodicy, this intended purpose is destined to actually be realized: every human being's soul-making process will eventually be successful, terminating sooner or later in eternal communion with God.[1] The most natural development of the logic of the soul-making theodicy, however, leads to a more traditional view of hell.

---

1. The soul-making theodicy of John Hick is of this sort; see *Evil and the God of Love*.

We've seen that the soul-making theodicy is built on a non-deterministic account of human free will. On a view of this type, it would seem that it's impossible for God to ensure that everyone will use their free will in the way that's required to make the soul-making process proceed as divinely intended. As we discussed in chapter 4, it's logically impossible for God to *make* anyone repent, because a genuine act of repentance must be an expression of a creature's own free will. Repentance is essential to the process of salvation, which in turn includes a process of moral and spiritual formation. So if a person refuses to repent of their sins—if they instead use their free will to act in ways they know to be contrary to the moral law, persisting in sin and rebellion against God—the process of soul-making will not go as divinely intended, and no exercise of divine power can unilaterally correct its course. If a person stays on this wayward path, they'll eventually develop deeply ingrained character traits that are vicious: that is, a character marked by the moral and spiritual vices.

Several things are especially important to understand about this developmental process toward greater viciousness and depravity. The first is that it involves more than just a corruption of the will; it also involves a corruption of the mind, the emotions, and the desires. Second, it's a process that tends to gain *momentum* as it progresses. And finally, it's a process that reaches a terminal point—a point at which development in the opposite direction is no longer possible.

Consider this first in regard to the intellect. A person's mind is "darkened," as the Apostle Paul puts it, when they are "alienated from the life of God" (Ephesians 4:18)—and all the more so as they descend further and further into evil. The wicked person is increasingly unable to tell right from wrong, not because of an innocent ignorance, but because they have willfully and repeatedly hardened their heart to the conviction of the Holy Spirit and seared their conscience by repeatedly engaging in self-deception. Their perception of the world is twisted, because they continually employ their faculty of reasoning not to seek the truth, but rather to construct arguments and reasons that justify their selfish motives and wicked actions. Eventually, their entire system of beliefs is oriented to this end. In moral and spiritual matters, they are blind; they cannot perceive the moral and spiritual terrain as it really is. This is the corruption of a person's *cognitive* nature.

The descent into evil also involves a progressive corruption of a person's *affective* and *appetitive* natures: that is, their emotions and desires. The wicked person is characterized by emotional reactions and moods that are morally inappropriate: they may be amused by cruelty and violence, unmoved by the sufferings of others, depressed by news of others' success, delighted by the knowledge of others' misfortune, enraged by others' attempts to correct them, and so on. Even more importantly, their desires are warped and depraved. The objects of their desires include things that are morally bad, corrupting, perverse, or otherwise sinful—and as their descent into evil continues and gains momentum, they increasingly want nothing else. The satisfaction of these evil desires only increases their appetite for them even more, and also weakens their desires for things that are good and edifying. This is the momentum that eventually leads to the total corruption of the individual's appetitive nature.

There's more than one way in which a person's appetitive nature is an expression of their moral character. The first part, which we've just discussed, has to do with what a person finds desirable. The second part has to do with what they find satisfying or fulfilling. These two can come apart. Those who are neither fully sanctified nor incorrigibly wicked—the vast majority of people in their earthly lives—find certain things that are forbidden to be desirable, but when they give in to the temptation to satisfy these desires, they experience regret and remorse; the experience is not satisfying. The reverse is true as well: there are certain actions that are recognized to be morally good but also very onerous or personally costly, and thus an average person may have little or no desire to perform these actions. But if and when such a person actually makes the sacrifice to perform an action of this type, they experience a deep sense of personal satisfaction.

At the extreme upper end of character formation, when sanctification is complete, desire and satisfaction no longer come apart. The saints in heaven are not people who are constantly struggling with temptation but always overcoming it; they are, rather, people whose very desires have been sanctified and now perfectly coincide with their duty; they *want* to do what's right and *desire* what is good. And they experience deep satisfaction in the fulfillment of these desires—that is, in willing the good.

At the extreme opposite end of character formation, matters are importantly different, but there are at least two different forms that entrenchment in evil could take. The most wicked individuals are those who not only desire evil but also take satisfaction in willing it; they *delight* in evil. They find no satisfaction at all in submitting to God or in willing what's good; the depravity of their character makes them incapable of experiencing any enjoyment in such things. Instead, doing what's evil is a source of pleasure to them—and even happiness *of a sort*. The kind of happiness they experience in willing evil isn't a deep and lasting happiness, of course, but it's an experience of self-satisfaction, a feeling of having gotten their way, which they don't regret in the least. Nevertheless, all such evil actions and pursuits are *ultimately* self-destructive, and the satisfaction of all evil desires naturally leads, in the long run, to frustration, alienation, and misery. The only happiness of which the truly wicked are capable is limited and fleeting at best.

It may well be that some people who are thoroughly corrupted by evil are reflective enough to understand this principle, but powerless to escape it. This suggests a second possibility that entrenchment in evil could take: a deep sense of inner conflict between a person's *first-order desires* and *second-order desires*—that is, between what a person wants and what they *want* to want. It's clear that these two types of desires can come apart. Consider the self-loathing alcoholic, who craves alcohol and desperately wishes that they didn't. They have a first-order desire to drink, but a second-order desire to not want to drink. It's possible that even in hell, some of the damned experience a permanent form of this conflict between their first- and second-order desires. Perhaps, on some level, they wish they were good, but they find themselves unable to resist giving in to their wicked desires. They want what's evil, because their appetitive natures are corrupt, but they experience no satisfaction, only bitter regret, whenever they do something evil. They're addicted to sin—"enslaved," in the biblical idiom[2]—and they hate themselves for it. The net result is eternal frustration, misery, and self-loathing.

The explanation of why the damned might be unable to resist giving in to their wicked desires leads us to the final, and perhaps most important, facet of the descent into evil: the corruption of the will, the *volitional* nature. The principle of momentum applies here as well, and along several different lines. The first of these has to do with the issue of which actions are psychologically impossible for a person to perform.

In chapter 4, we illustrated the concept of psychological impossibility with a gruesome example: while it would be physically within your power to stab a loved one through the eye with an ice pick, you simply couldn't bring yourself to do such a horrible thing. Psychological impossibility is relative to individuals—what's impossible for one person is possible for another—and based upon the beliefs, desires, appetites, tolerances, values, commitments, character traits, etc. that each person possesses. But since humans are developmental beings, the range of actions that are psychologically possible for a person can change over time. As a general rule, each time a person does something morally wrong, it becomes a little easier for them to will an action of that same type the next time there's an opportunity. Eventually, the action may not produce any pangs of conscience at all and may no longer seem in any way objectionable to them. Moreover—and especially significant for the present discussion—this process can have the effect of moving certain types of actions from the category of psychologically

---

2. John 8:34; 2 Peter 2:19; and, especially, Romans 6.

impossible to the category of psychologically possible for a person. An action that, previously, a person truly could not bring themselves to do, becomes an action that seems *nearly* unthinkable, but not quite. And if this action is performed, even more depraved actions that were previously psychologically impossible may now become possible. This is part of what it is to descend into wickedness and depravity: as a person's will is corrupted, they become capable of ever more horrendous evils.

Second, there's the issue of *moral effort*: the moral and spiritual exertion that's required to resist temptation and to do what one believes to be the right thing. In the spiritual life, repentance is among the most important actions by which a person opens themselves up to the work of God in reorienting their soul toward the good. But repentance can be more or less difficult, depending on the individual and the circumstances. Each time a person gives in to temptation, it requires greater moral effort to resist the same temptation the next time it arises. Consequently, the longer a person persists in a certain sin, the more difficult it is to turn away from it. The sin eventually becomes habitual, then deeply ingrained in a person's character, and may even become incorporated into their sense of **self-identity**: that is, their sense of who they are as an individual. *Identifying with* one's sins—that is, ceasing to regard them as moral temptations to be resisted and instead coming to embrace and even to celebrate them as part of one's self-identity—is among the most dangerous actions of the spiritual life. As the "investment" in sin increases, it becomes increasingly difficult to turn back; the individual feels they have too much to lose in doing so.

On a natural consequence model of hell, the cumulative effect of this process is that, eventually, the wicked person reaches a point at which *repentance is psychologically impossible*. At this point, the sinner regards the prospect of turning from their sins to be unthinkable; it's something that they simply could not bring themselves to do. Perhaps it seems too painful (the spiritual equivalent of cutting off their own hand without anesthesia), or too humiliating (akin to debasing themselves before their most despised enemy), or too arduous (like the prospect of beginning a journey around the world on foot). Or perhaps it seems to them a betrayal of their deepest commitments and values, their personal history and experience, their very identity ("my truth"). Regardless of the particular combination of reasons and motives, the point at which repentance becomes psychologically impossible for an individual is the point at which their entrenchment in evil is permanent. There can be no coming back from a state of depravity apart from repentance; the very concept of repentance is that of turning away from one's sins and turning toward the good. It follows that if a person reaches the point that they cannot bring themselves to make even this first movement away from evil, there's no possibility of further moral improvement or conversion.[3]

It might seem doubtful that anyone actually reaches this point. Indeed, earlier in this chapter, we noted in passing that the vast majority of people seem to be neither fully sanctified nor incorrigibly wicked. We can now state this more precisely: hardly anyone seems to be, at the time of their death, either perfectly virtuous, such that sinning is psychologically impossible for them, or completely depraved, such that repentance is psychologically impossible for them.

However, on the usual way of working out a natural consequence model, the process of soul-making extends beyond death: more specifically, it continues into the **intermediate state**, the period between a person's death and resurrection.[4] This view offers a number of theoretical advantages to

---

3. Some readers might object to this account on the following grounds: "The grace of God *just is* the divine enabling power that makes repentance psychologically possible for a person when it would otherwise be impossible; this is an analysis of the very concept of divine grace. So it makes no sense to describe damnation as the *natural* endpoint of a soul-making process gone awry. It's always within God's power to give a person the grace that enables repentance, *if God so chooses*. Damnation is simply the state in which God refuses to give a person any more grace. The damned are those whom God has forsaken." This objection can be answered. The critic's analysis of grace—"the divine enabling power that makes repentance psychologically possible for a person when it would otherwise be impossible"—may well be an accurate description of the way that grace operates on those who haven't yet reached the state of damnation. But there's good reason to think that there's a point beyond which divine grace could no longer have this effect on a person. As an individual persists in sin, greater and greater amounts of grace are required to enable them to repent. The damned are those who have persisted in sin to the point that they've forged a character that is *solidified* in its orientation toward evil. For such persons, divine grace would not simply be a matter of enabling an action that would otherwise be impossible for them; it would instead require *undoing* the very character they've formed for themselves through their own exercises of free will. This would be equivalent to destroying their moral freedom. What this really means is that *no* amount of grace could make repentance psychologically possible for the damned, because a divine act that destroys creaturely freedom is one that also destroys the possibility of repentance, since repentance requires freedom. This is why, on a natural consequence model of hell, it's possible for a person to become *incorrigibly* wicked: that is, so entrenched in evil that not even omnipotence can rescue the individual from it. This is the reason that some could be damned despite God's doing *everything in His power* to save them.

4. The Bible tells us very little about the intermediate state, and disagreements about it have historically divided—sometimes sharply divided—the different branches of Christianity from one another. Most Christians hold the view that the intermediate state is one in which the soul, though disembodied, is nevertheless conscious and capable of experience, including experiences of joy, suffering, reflection, regret, anticipation, rest, and even communication and interaction with Jesus and perhaps with other persons. (Passages that arguably bear on this topic include Luke 16:19–31; 23:42–43; 2 Corinthians 5:8; Philippians 1:23; and Revelation 6:9–11.) There is no consensus,

proponents of natural consequence models. The process of soul-making is necessarily gradual, and it requires the free participation of those whose souls are being shaped: that is to say, it cannot happen all at once (for example, at the moment of death), and it cannot happen entirely by an outside force or agent (such as God) acting unilaterally on the soul to bring about significant changes. The logic of the soul-making theodicy thus suggests that the process of moral and spiritual formation continues into the intermediate state, and it continues for as long as it takes a person to reach one of the two possible terminating points. The damned are those who, at the time of the resurrection and final judgment—though not necessarily at the time of their deaths—have a character that is not only wicked, but *incorrigibly* wicked, because the process of soul-making has brought them to a point at which repentance is, for them, no longer possible.

We've now completed our sketch of the process of damnation on a natural consequence model of hell that's built on a soul-making theodicy. The trajectory of souls that are formed in this direction—increasingly away from God and toward evil—is one that terminates in a state of permanent disunion with God. This is what it is for the soul-making process to end in utter ruin and for its divinely intended purpose to be finally and completely thwarted.

## Further explanations of the impossibility of repentance in hell

The path to damnation as it's been described so far can be adopted by any natural consequence model of hell, including the choice model. But on the divine presence model, there are additional possible explanations as to why repentance becomes psychologically impossible after the final judgment. In this section, we'll briefly explore some of these possibilities, which highlight the greater explanatory resources of the divine presence model in comparison to other natural consequence models of hell.

In chapters 9–10, we discussed the various ways in which the presence of God is a source of suffering to the damned. The love of God—which seeks to conform every person to the image of Christ and to unite every

---

however, about whether the experiences that people have in the intermediate state could be morally and spiritually formative. Even more controversial is the question of whether changes in a person's fundamental trajectory, either toward or away from God, are possible in the intermediate state. According to the mainstream of Christian tradition, postmortem conversion is impossible, but some who defend a natural consequence model diverge from the mainstream on this point: see, for example, Walls, *Heaven, Hell, and Purgatory*, chapter 8.

person to God and to one another in a communion of agape love, thereby fulfilling every human being's true nature and highest good—is contrary to the will of those who are damned. The damned experience the love of God as an opposing force; the divine action whose intent is to bring all to glory is experienced as a hostile takeover. Likewise, the presence of God reveals the truth about everyone, and for the damned this is a source of humiliation and offense. This has the effect of entrenching the damned in their hardness of heart and self-deception. There are a number of different ways in which these effects of exposure to the presence of God could make repentance psychologically impossible for the damned.

One possibility is that the conditions of hell are unintentionally coercive. The intensity or type of suffering of those in hell might be such as to corrupt the motive of any possible attempt at repentance. In other words, it may well be impossible for the damned to perform an act of repentance for the right reasons—the kinds of reasons that would make the action *qualify* as an act of repentance.

To see this, notice, first, that there's a limited range of motives that are compatible with genuine repentance. A thought experiment helps to illustrate this point. Imagine a husband who offers his wife ten thousand dollars to stop cheating on him. If she promises to break off the affair in order to get the money, her action certainly doesn't qualify as an act of repentance of her adultery. Now imagine a different version of the thought experiment: suppose the husband tells his wife that he'll kill her if she doesn't stop cheating on him. If she promises to break off the affair in order to avoid being killed, it again doesn't qualify as an act of repentance. Now consider one more variation: suppose the husband tortures his wife until she promises to break off the affair. Under these circumstances, as well, her action doesn't qualify as an act of repentance. In fact, it's hard to imagine how *anything* the wife could do under these conditions, while she's actively being tortured, would count as genuine repentance. Only a free action can possibly count as a genuine act of repentance, and any action the woman performs under these circumstances will be coerced.

The thought experiment demonstrates the incompatibility of various motives with genuine repentance, and the final variation of the thought experiment is especially instructive for present purposes. It may well be that the suffering of hell is of such a type, or of such an intensity, that any attempt at repentance would count as coerced, and thus not free, and thus not a genuine act of repentance. This is one possible way that the revelation of Christ in glory—the apocalypse—could have the foreseen but unintended consequence of making repentance psychologically impossible for the wicked, thereby permanently entrenching them in evil.

## DEVELOPING A NATURAL CONSEQUENCE MODEL OF HELL

Other ways are possible, as well. It may be psychologically impossible for the damned to begin to love and trust God, because they experience His presence as a source of torment. Under these conditions, they can no more begin to love and trust God than a prisoner of war can begin to love and trust the captors who daily torture him. But trust is essential to faith (as we discussed in chapter 6), and love is essential to worship, and all four are components of salvation. So if these attitudes toward God become psychologically impossible for a person, salvation likewise becomes impossible.

The truth-revealing function of the divine presence raises further possibilities as to why consignment to hell is permanent. It's noteworthy that Jesus repeatedly admonishes his listeners, "Blessed is he who is not offended at me."[5] We noted in chapter 10 that it's humiliating and offensive when someone makes an ugly truth about oneself public. Insofar as the damned are inescapably in the presence of God, which reveals the shameful truths about them for everyone to behold, it's easy to imagine that the damned would be offended at God. And this offense would likely last for as long as the source of offense remains in place, which is for all eternity. It would seem, then, that *everlasting offense* may be a permanent barrier to repentance for the damned.

One more possibility is worth considering. Rarely if ever does a person realize the full extent of their own sin and depravity at the time of their conversion. As the prophet Jeremiah points out, "The heart is deceitful above all things, and desperately wicked: who can know it?" (Jeremiah 17:9 KJV). Part of the process of sanctification is coming to realize the true extent of one's own sinfulness. But this is a gradual process, as the Holy Spirit reveals these difficult truths, leads the believer deeper into repentance, and brings renewal and healing to these broken parts of a person's soul little by little. The gradual nature of this revelation is very likely needed to prevent the believer from being overwhelmed; a sudden realization of the full extent of one's own depravity would likely make one feel that the journey to complete healing was so long and difficult as to be impossible to complete, and thereby plunge one into despair. But, on the divine presence model, this would seem to be the very experience of unrepentant sinners at the final judgment, when they are suddenly and forcibly exposed to the unmitigated presence of God and the complete truth about themselves is made manifest all at once. The resulting feeling of hopelessness and despair is perhaps an experience that makes repentance thereafter psychologically impossible for the damned.[6]

---

5. Matthew 11:6 and Luke 7:23; cf. Matthew 15:12; Luke 2:34–35; Romans 9:32–33; 1 Corinthians 1:22–24; 1 Peter 2:7–8.

6. There's a certain feature of the doctrine of the return of Christ that, in combination with the possibilities discussed in this section, appears to create problems for the

It seems unlikely that we could *know* any of these possibilities to be true descriptions of those in hell. And yet, given the assumptions of the divine presence model, each of these scenarios seems to be not only possible but at least somewhat plausible. At the very least, there is no way to rule them out. And this is enough to undermine the confident universalist's claim that everyone must *sooner or later* turn from their sins and be reconciled to God. Judged solely on the basis of philosophical considerations, the most we can say is that, while it's possible that in the end all will be saved, it's also entirely possible that some—perhaps many—will not. Philosophical considerations alone are not sufficient to decide the issue one way or the other. But when, in addition to these philosophical considerations, the weight of tradition is taken into account—in particular, the tradition of interpreting the relevant passages of Scripture on the topic—the balance seems clearly to tilt away from universalism and back toward a more traditional view of hell.

---

divine presence model. It is the clear teaching of the New Testament that some people will still be alive at the time of Christ's return (see especially 1 Thessalonians 4:15–17 and 1 Corinthians 15:51–54), and the Christian tradition has always affirmed this. It follows that some people will not experience death, and thus some will not experience an intermediate state between death and final judgment. But given the logic of the divine presence model, this seems unfair—and perhaps even worse. The model seems to imply that the soul-making process of such individuals will be abruptly cut short. There will be no opportunity for the character of such persons to develop, naturally and gradually, to a terminating point of either perfect virtue or complete depravity. Those not yet in a right relationship with God will be instantly and irreversibly "thrown" into a state in which repentance is psychologically impossible. Whatever opportunities there might have been for postmortem repentance and conversion will be lost to them. Even more troubling, it appears to follow from the logic of the model that *believers* who have not yet progressed very far in their sanctification will be thrown into hell. An encounter with the glorified Christ at this point in their spiritual development will be an experience of torment, since they have not yet been adequately prepared for it. We can imagine some possible solutions to this problem. One possibility is that those still alive at Christ's return are consigned to a special place in the new creation, a place that—unlike the rest of the new creation—is somehow "shielded" from the full presence of God, a temporary holding place in which these individuals can continue their soul-making process to its completion. This solution might be implausible (it's certainly *ad hoc*). And perhaps *all* of the possible solutions that we can image are implausible. This by itself isn't fatal to the divine presence model. What matters is that there are possible solutions, and if we can imagine even one of these, there are likely others—and the actual solution is perhaps among this set of possibilities presently beyond our ken. Construed as a *defense* (as this term was defined in chapter 8), the divine presence model is not weakened by this problem so long as we can show that there is a *possible* solution. Construed as a *theodicy*, the divine presence model is incomplete until a *plausible* solution is formulated.

## Chapter 13
# Answering the universalist's objection, part I

HAVING DEVELOPED THE FIRST half of the philosophical basis of the divine presence model—its foundation in the soul-making theodicy—it's now time to consider some objections. In chapter 9, we briefly mentioned an objection to the understanding of free will that underlies natural consequence models of hell. It turns out to be one of the most popular and important objections to both the choice model and the divine presence model. In this chapter and the next, we'll develop this objection fully and address it in detail. In the process of doing so, a number of important facets of the divine presence model will be brought into sharper focus: most importantly, the crucial role that self-deception plays in bringing a person to the point of damnation.

### The universalist's objection

Some people—in particular, many universalists—find the idea that anyone could *freely* reject God forever to be incredible, perhaps even unintelligible.[1] The argument is developed as follows.[2] "Given that there's no true and

---

1. Thomas Talbott gives an especially clear presentation and powerful development of this type of objection in *The Inescapable Love of God*, chapter 11 ("God, Freedom, and Human Destiny").
2. The quotation marks around the passage that follows—and other such passages in the remainder of this chapter and the next—are meant to indicate the voice of an imaginary interlocutor. This device is used to give voice to the perspective of a critic: in this case, a critic who represents the perspective of a sophisticated Christian universalist.

lasting happiness apart from communion with God, there's no possible motive for anyone to finally reject God. More precisely, there's no *good* reason to do so, no motive that would make the choice *rational*. Consequently, those who choose to finally reject God, or who try to make such a choice, must do so either in ignorance, not really knowing what they're doing; or they must be completely irrational; or they must be 'enslaved to sin'—that is, in the grip of sinful passions and desires that they're powerless to resist. To the degree that their decision is motivated by ignorance, it's not one they're fully responsible for. (Recall, from the discussion of the problem of justice in chapter 2, that lack of understanding reduces culpability.) If God were to hold a person fully responsible for a decision they make in ignorance, He'd be treating them unjustly. On the other hand, if the decision is made by someone who's incapable of rational decision-making for any reason, such as mental incompetence or insanity, then that person is not a fully competent moral agent. And if they're not a fully competent moral agent, it would be unjust for God to treat them as if they were by holding them accountable to the full consequences of their choices. Finally, if a person's decision to reject God is motivated by sinful passions and desires to which they're enslaved, then it's not a *free* decision; their addiction to sin has destroyed their free will. But moral responsibility requires freedom, so in this case, once again, they wouldn't be fully responsible for their decision. These three motives—ignorance, irrationality, and enslavement to sin—are the only ones that could motivate a decision to finally reject God. Consequently, a decision to finally reject God is one for which no person could be fully responsible. And this is the case regardless of whether the decision is one that a person makes deliberately (rejecting God is what they *intend* to do) or whether final separation from God is the unintended but natural consequence of other free choices they make. In either case, the decision(s) could not possibly be fully informed, rational, and free, so the consequences of these decisions could not possibly be ones for which they're fully responsible and rightly held to account."

## The nature of self-deception

This is an important objection. In order to answer it, we'll eventually need to explore the concept of free will in more detail, and in particular its connection to the concept of self-deception. But let's start by simply noting the overall structure of the argument. It begins with the observation that rejecting God can lead only to misery; then infers that no decision to reject God could be truly informed, rational, and free; and concludes that a decision to reject

God couldn't be one for which a person is fully responsible. The driving assumption of the argument is that no sane, rational person would ever freely and intentionally do something that they knew would result in extreme and lasting pain, permanent unhappiness, or self-destruction.

The first thing to note about this argument is that its driving assumption is false, and it's easy to produce counterexamples to it. A rational person might intentionally put their hand into a fire in order to pull a loved one out of a burning building. (They might do so even in full awareness that their action will cause them permanent, painful scarring and disfiguration.) A rational person might throw themselves on a live grenade to prevent it from killing their comrades. A rational person might freely trade themselves to terrorist kidnappers, with no reasonable hope of future escape, in exchange for the release of their child. A rational person might freely undertake a hunger strike, even to the point of their own death, in order to bring to light a grave injustice. All that's required to motivate a sane, rational person to freely do something that they know will be extremely painful, result in their own unhappiness, or even their own destruction, is a firm belief that the action is necessary to accomplish a sufficiently worthy goal, plus the courage to do what they believe to be necessary.

The universalist critic is likely to respond that all of these examples are disanalogous to the case of someone who rejects God. "In each of the examples, the imagined person could have a *true belief* that the action in question is necessary to accomplish a sufficiently worthy goal. But no one could have a true belief that rejecting God is necessary to accomplish any worthy goal. So in every case where a person rejects God because they believe it to be necessary to accomplish a worthy goal, they're acting under the influence of a *false* belief, and consequently they're not fully responsible for their decision. Furthermore, any such belief is one that an omnipotent God could easily correct, and a perfectly good and loving God would *want* to correct it—at least eventually. So there's no possible scenario in which someone knowingly and freely decides to reject God forever and God allows them to do so."

This reply sounds convincing, until we consider carefully what self-deception really is and what it's capable of accomplishing. Self-deception is the ability to hide from oneself something that, on a deeper level, one knows to be true, for the simple reason that it conflicts with something else that one desperately *wants* to be true. It's the ability to suppress knowledge that conflicts with one's desires; it's an *unwillingness* to perceive the truth—or at least to admit the truth to oneself at a conscious level.

We're all familiar with this concept, and it's exemplified in a wide range of cases and can result in widely varying degrees of harm. Some examples seem nearly harmless: a person believes, against all objective evidence to the contrary, that they're the smartest and most interesting person in the room. Or they convince themselves that all the experts are wrong about some complex issue and that their own pet theory is obviously right. Other examples are not so benign: a person convinces themselves that their spouse isn't cheating on them, or that their spouse isn't abusing the kids, despite obvious evidence to the contrary. The *most* destructive examples, however, involve a person's relationship to God, because here there arises the potential for literally infinite harm and irreparable damage.

The language most commonly used in the Bible to describe self-deception is that of a person or a group of people "hardening their heart." It's suggested in Scripture that self-deception is the single most destructive activity of which any person is capable, because of its moral and spiritual consequences.[3] The reason it's so destructive is that it can be deployed to cut oneself off from the conviction and correction of God. Self-deception is the principal mechanism that people use to defend themselves against unpleasant, unwelcome, and unflattering truths—and in particular, moral and spiritual truths revealed through the inner conviction of the Holy Spirit.

Significantly, however, the attempt to deflect or evade hard truths is not always an attempt to escape discomfort or pain. As we've already noted, it's fairly common for people to willingly subject themselves to significant pain and danger if they believe they have a sufficient motive for it. And one of the most common and powerful motives is the belief that one is *in the right*, and that a certain action—even an extremely painful or personally costly action—is necessary to prove it. Self-deception can play a crucial role in motivating self-destructive behavior whenever it's deployed to rationalize and maintain the belief that one is morally justified.

This insight has important consequences for the universalist's argument. What it demonstrates is that a person can be highly culpable for the false beliefs they hold. In the moral and spiritual realms, at least, the process of forming beliefs is not entirely passive. Sometimes the reason a person fails

---

3. Although it's never stated explicitly, this principle is a subtext running throughout Scripture. Consider, for example, an otherwise perplexing feature of the Gospels: Jesus' sharp chastisement of the Jewish Pharisees and relative leniency toward the Roman pagans of his day, despite the fact that the Romans engaged in routine brutality and sexual immorality (at least by Jewish standards), whereas the Pharisees observed strict moral principles. The Pharisees viewed themselves as epitomes of human righteousness. But Jesus perceived their actual state to be one of false self-righteousness. Those who recognized themselves as sinners were drawn to Jesus, and (in many cases) his message of forgiveness and reconciliation to God was warmly welcomed and received. But those who viewed themselves as righteous and in no need of a personal Savior were offended at Jesus; they judged his message to be blasphemous and dangerous.

to perceive a certain truth is that they don't want to perceive it; they're *unwilling* to accept something that should be obvious, something that would be obvious to them if it weren't for the fact that it conflicts with their strong preferences and desires. Because of this principle, not every case of ignorance is innocent. Sometimes a person is blameworthy for failing to believe the truth, or for believing something false. When the belief that one is in the right is based on self-deception, and when this belief motivates self-destructive behavior, the self-destructive behavior is both intelligible—that is, perfectly understandable in its motive—and fully culpable.

It's also important to appreciate that there are *cumulative* effects of repeatedly engaging in self-deception. This brings us back to the topic of soul-making. If a person engages in self-deception on a regular basis, it becomes a habit—the most dangerous type of habitual lying. If a person persists in this long enough, they eventually develop a certain kind of character. We've already discussed the way that the descent into evil has a corrupting effect on a person's intellectual faculties. The wicked person is increasingly unable to tell right from wrong because, by repeatedly hardening their heart, they have cauterized their conscience. In rejecting the Holy Spirit's conviction, they have cut themselves off from the only truly reliable source of moral and spiritual discernment. They've employed their rational faculties not to pursue truth, but to construct self-justifying rationalizations of their evil pursuits. The result is that their perception of the moral and spiritual terrain is skewed and distorted. They're spiritually blind.[4]

It's crucial to understand that the *reason* the wicked person is spiritually blind is that their character is vicious. This is one of the most important "laws" of the spiritual life: *a person's ability to perceive moral and spiritual truth is a function of their character.* The more virtuous a person is, the clearer their moral perception and the greater their understanding of the deepest spiritual truths. The more wicked a person is, the more distorted their moral perception and the greater their misunderstanding of the deepest spiritual truths. The universalist critic imagines that anyone who engages in the foolish and wicked action of rejecting God must be in the grip of some delusion. But the critic has gotten things backward:

---

4. In Dostoevsky's masterpiece *The Brothers Karamazov*, the elder monk Father Zosima makes a similar point about self-deception when he advises the dissolute Fyodor Pavlovich: "Above all, don't lie to yourself. The man who lies to himself and listens to his own lie comes to such a pass that he cannot distinguish the truth within him, or around him, and so loses all respect for himself and for others. And having no respect he ceases to love, and in order to occupy and distract himself without love he gives way to passions and coarse pleasures, and sinks to bestiality in his vices, all from continual lying to other men and to himself. The man who lies to himself can be more easily offended than any one" (Dostoevsky, *The Brothers Karamazov*, 40).

the evil person isn't wicked because they're blind; the evil person is blind because they're wicked.

## Could God save the lost by presenting them with compelling evidence?

At this point, we should anticipate a different counterargument from the universalist critic: "It may well be that, in this life, God has good reasons for allowing us to form our moral and spiritual beliefs freely. But it's always within God's power to *forcibly dispel* the false beliefs that motivate people to reject Him. If God applied this method to those who are in hell, He would clearly be advancing their own happiness and wellbeing. A perfectly good and loving God would *want* to advance the happiness and wellbeing of those in hell, and an omnipotent God would be *able* to do so. It follows that, wherever necessary, God *will in fact* forcibly dispel the false beliefs that have led certain individuals to try to finally reject Him—including those in hell."

Once again, the problem with the critic's reply is that it either ignores or misunderstands the nature of self-deception. It fails to recognize both the extent of its capacity for deflecting truth and the extent to which it can be tied to someone's identity as a person. The reason that self-deception is so powerful in its capacity to deflect truth has to do with the nature of the way that humans form certain complex beliefs.

One of the interesting things about the way we learn from our experience is that it can force us to admit that we're wrong about *something*, but it can't always lead us to identify *which* "something"—which presently held belief—is the false one. And the reason it cannot do so is that we have to *interpret* our experience. This feature of human experience has a very important consequence.

Whenever a person interprets something, they're not just passively forming beliefs; their will is involved in the process. They're really engaged in a kind of decision-making process, even if it's a decision that's happening mostly at a subconscious level. Because of this, if a person is *determined* to retain a certain belief, they can always find a way to do so. Of course, the simplest way they could do so would be to simply retain the old belief alongside a new belief (formed on the basis of newly acquired evidence) that contradicts it; that is, they could just willfully believe a contradiction. But this would be blatantly irrational. The more interesting—and far more likely—tactic that a person could employ is to retain the old belief and restore coherence in their overall system of beliefs by rejecting or modifying *other* beliefs in order to accommodate the new belief.

To appreciate how this works, let's make the example concrete. Consider the proposition that God exists. Surely God could *force* someone—say, a militant atheist—to believe this proposition. Couldn't He? It would certainly seem so, given that God is omnipotent. But the important follow-up question to consider is this: *How* might God do so? The possible ways would seem to fall into two categories: those that operate through the individual's normal belief-forming mechanisms, and those that override them. In the former case, God would provide a person with *compelling evidence* of His existence and allow the individual to draw the obvious, rational conclusion. In the latter case, God would *directly cause* the individual to have a certain belief. This process would completely bypass the individual's free will in the belief-forming process. We'll consider each of these strategies in turn.

It's clear that God could give a person powerful evidence of His existence—evidence that would be absolutely compelling to any honest, objective, and rational person. Consider the way that Jesus appeared to Saul on the road to Damascus (Acts 9:1–19). Suppose that God gave an imaginary, militant atheist—we'll call him Bertie—some sort of evidence that was comparable to this, evidence that was overwhelming and seemingly undeniable. In fact, many Christians believe that everyone will have just such an experience after death. Let's consider this possibility. Suppose Bertie has a memory of having just died and is now having an experience of standing before God. Surely this would *force* him to finally concede that God exists. Wouldn't it?

In fact, it wouldn't. The reason it wouldn't compel Bertie's belief is that this method—presenting him with powerful evidence of God's existence—leaves Bertie's power of self-deception intact. Specifically, it leaves in place his ability to *interpret* the experience he's now having. And there are many different ways that Bertie could do so. He *could* interpret his experience as being *veridical*—that is, truth-revealing (not illusory). In other words, Bertie could conclude that things are just as they seem to be: that he has just died and that he's now standing before God. If he interprets his experience this way, he gives up his former belief that there's no God; he's now a convinced theist.

But this is not the only possible response Bertie could have. The crucial thing to notice is that he wouldn't *have* to interpret things this way; he wouldn't have to assume that his memory of dying and his present experience of standing before God are veridical experiences. He could conclude, instead, that he's in the grip of some sort of powerful delusion.[5] He might

---

5. C. S. Lewis suggests a similar idea in *The Great Divorce*: "There were materialistic Ghosts who informed the immortals that they were deluded: there was no life after death, and this whole country was a hallucination" (chapter 9). The Ghosts are those who come from the "gray town" (hell); the immortals are the saints who come down

tell himself that this is all a bad dream—albeit an unusually vivid one. Or he might decide that someone has slipped him a powerful psychoactive drug. Or that he's in the midst of a near-death experience (understood in purely naturalistic terms, such as neurochemical events in his brain going haywire). Or he could resort to more exotic explanations. He could decide that he's in a virtual reality simulation, like "the Matrix." He could conclude that he's been abducted by aliens who are presently experimenting on him with some unknown technology that induces powerful hallucinations. And so on.

When you stop and think about it, there's really no end to the possible explanations Bertie could give, and all of these explanations are really just different ways of interpreting his present experience. ("It's a dream experience"; "It's a near-death experience"; "It's a virtual reality experience"; etc.) There are endless ways of avoiding the obvious conclusion, if one is so inclined. And that's what self-deception is all about: an unwillingness to draw the conclusion best supported by the evidence, because one is *strongly motivated* not to do so.

Our example of Bertie the militant atheist shows that even the most seemingly compelling evidence can be resisted. Consider now how much easier it is to resist conclusions that are unwelcome but don't require outlandish explanations to avoid: conclusions like "What I did was wrong"; "I've been selfish"; "The way I conduct my business is unethical"; "I haven't been doing the things I know I ought to be doing"; "I need to make some major changes to the way I've been living my life"; "God is telling me that I must repent of my sins to be saved." So long as a person is allowed to retain their freedom to interpret the evidence of their own experience, they can *always* find a way to avoid the conclusions that they don't want—that they're *unwilling*—to accept. Of course, if they're forced to accept an outlandish explanation ("I'm in the Matrix") in order to retain some cherished belief or avoid an unwelcome conclusion, it will be obvious that they're being irrational. But in the vast majority of cases, a certain belief can be retained (or avoided) without resorting to anything so extreme. Self-deception is always irrational, because it's a way of rejecting the conclusion that the evidence clearly supports, a way of hiding from oneself something that, on a deeper level, one *knows* to be true. But the irrationality doesn't have to be blatant. In particular, it doesn't have to be obvious to the person who's exercising it—even if it's quite obvious to those observing it from the outside. This is, in fact, one of the most distinguishing—as well

---

from the mountains (heaven) to try to help the Ghosts understand and move past the spiritual problems that are posing barriers to their salvation. The resulting conversations depict the many forms that self-deception can take.

terrifying—characteristics of self-deception: it's usually easy to recognize when others engage in it, but difficult to detect in yourself.

There's another way of putting the point that we've been developing. So far, we've been focusing on the way that no amount of evidence from miraculous signs could compel a person to accept a conclusion that they're determined to avoid, so long as their free will is left intact. But there's a different kind of evidence that might be more effective in converting those in hell. According to many universalists, it's the evidence of *natural consequences* that ensures God has a fail-safe way of bringing all to repentance. The argument goes like this: "If all else fails, God need only allow those who are stubbornly rebellious to simply experience the full natural consequences of their own sin. The eventual but inevitable outcome will be an experience of abject misery for each sinner. God can allow the process to go on as long as necessary. Each and every person in hell will eventually turn to God *of their own free will*, because no one can continue forever on a path that yields nothing but suffering and unhappiness. Misery is a hard teacher, but an incredibly effective one in driving home the lesson."

The problem with this universalist argument is the same as before: it overlooks the crucial point that humans have to *interpret* the evidence of their experience—and it's always possible to *misinterpret* it. Just because someone finds themselves utterly miserable, it in no way follows that they'll eventually turn from the behaviors that are bringing them such misery. The reason is simple: knowing *that* you're miserable doesn't by itself tell you *why* you're miserable. Those who are in hell may continually misidentify the source of their misery. They could blame their unhappiness on others (the ways they've been mistreated, the injustices they've suffered). They could blame it on the unfair lot they had in life (the bad parenting they experienced in their formative years, the way the deck was stacked against them). They could blame it on God. And on, and on, and on.

The universalist might again object: "In all such cases, the person we're imagining is still operating on some false belief. And God could easily clear up the confusion: He could simply inform the damned, in no uncertain terms, that the source of their misery is not something external to themselves, but simply their own behavior and the character they've formed by it." Of course, God could do this. But why think it would be successful in leading those in hell to repentance? The damned could always tell themselves that God was lying to them—that He was trying to multiply their torment by getting them to blame themselves for their own suffering. Or they could convince themselves that it wasn't God, after all, who was giving them this message, but rather Satan who "disguises himself as an angel of light" (2 Corinthians

11:14). It's the same principle as before: there's *always* a way to explain away an experience, if one is so inclined.

Likewise, there's *always* a way to preserve a treasured belief that one is unwilling to relinquish. And among the most treasured beliefs that people naturally tend to hold are these: "I'm a good person"; "I haven't done anything really bad"; "I'm not the one to blame for this"; "What I did was perfectly justified"; "I'm *in the right*." These are the very kinds of beliefs that forestall repentance. And there's no limit to the ways that people can interpret and construe the evidence of their own experience to accommodate such beliefs, if they're determined to do so.

It would certainly be a mistake to underestimate how powerful the motive can be to engage in self-deception of this type. We see it all the time this side of the grave. God has, after all, *already* informed people, in no uncertain terms, that sin is a source of misery and that there's no true happiness apart from submission to Him. He's informed people of this through sacred Scripture, through Christian tradition, and through individual conscience. And yet many people still refuse to accept it, spending their entire lives in endless and fruitless pursuit of happiness in all manner of things, even some things that are obviously (to an outside observer) unhealthy or destructive, wondering at every turn why they're still miserable, blaming everything and everyone but themselves for their pitiful plight. Why assume that either death or endless duration of existence in the afterlife must change matters in *this* regard?[6]

---

6. For scriptural support of this principle, see Jesus' parable of Lazarus and the rich man (Luke 16:19–31), noting in particular the "punchline" of the parable in the final verse.

# Chapter 14
# Answering the universalist's objection, part II

IN THE LAST CHAPTER, we explored an important principle about the nature of evidence: it has to be interpreted, and so long as a person's free will is left intact, they are capable of engaging in self-deception, willfully misinterpreting the evidence in order to retain some cherished false belief or avoid accepting some unwelcome truth. But it seems that there's another, obvious way that God could compel people to believe the truth: He could simply override their free will. We'll now explore this possibility and its prospects for bringing recalcitrant sinners to repentance and eventual salvation.

### Could God save the lost by overriding their free will?

Let's return to our example of Bertie, the militant atheist, introduced in the previous chapter. We've seen that, so long as God tries to induce Bertie to give up his belief in atheism through the normal human belief-forming processes, there's always a way for him to resist. Likewise for divine efforts to bring a person to adopt the kinds of beliefs that are a necessary part of repentance. The only way that God could *force* Bertie to accept that theism is true, or to accept that he's a sinner in need of a Savior, would be to bypass the usual belief-forming processes and instead *directly cause* Bertie to form these beliefs. God would have to override Bertie's free will altogether with respect to forming these beliefs.

Many universalists hold the view that if this is what's required to get certain people to relinquish their unbelief and to accept the truth of their own guilt and need for a Savior—the minimal but essential first steps on the long path toward salvation—then God should do it. "Freedom may be important, but it's not *sacrosanct*. Perhaps it's best for people to believe in God of their own free will, but forced belief is better than no belief at all. If temporarily overriding or even destroying a person's freedom is the price of putting them on the path to salvation, it's well worth the cost."

Unfortunately, things are not so simple as this. Recall from chapter 11 the first four fundamental principles of the soul-making theodicy: the highest human good is eternal communion with God; achieving this end requires a prior process of moral and spiritual formation; moral and spiritual formation requires moral agency; and moral agency requires moral freedom. The problem with God's overriding someone's free will, and in particular their capacity for self-deception, is this: depending on how extensive the interference was, it would either have no positive effect or it would destroy the very conditions of soul-making and thereby make the individual's salvation *impossible*. The former would be pointless, and the latter would be completely counterproductive.

Let's consider each of these possibilities in order. Suppose that God's interference in Bertie's system of beliefs was minimal: suppose God directly caused Bertie to form the single belief that there's a God, but nothing beyond this. Almost certainly, this wouldn't be enough to accomplish anything lasting or worthwhile. As soon as the belief was formed, Bertie could employ his capacity for self-deception to try to dislodge it—that is, to begin casting doubt on his newly acquired belief. To avoid this, God would have to go further: He would have to completely override not only Bertie's normal belief-*forming* mechanism, but also his belief-*maintaining* and belief-*revising* mechanisms. In other words, God would not only have to bypass Bertie's free will in His first act of causing Bertie to believe that God exists; He would have to go on to destroy Bertie's free will with respect to maintaining, revising, or abandoning this belief. In short, God would have to take away Bertie's capacity for self-deception altogether—at least with respect to the belief that there's a God.

But in fact, God couldn't stop even here, at least not if He wanted to ensure any sort of change that was significant for soul-making. At this point, Bertie simply has a belief that God exists, nothing more. Our imagined, newly minted theist is not yet a *believer*, in the true sense of the term. Bertie doesn't yet *believe in* God, in the sense of trusting Him, having faith in Him, recognizing Him as Lord of his life, and so on. These complex states would require a much larger change to his overall beliefs, as well as changes to his attitudes, emotions, passions, commitments, and so on. Even limiting our focus to just the cognitive dimension of the needed changes, the list is extensive. In order to put Bertie on the road to salvation, God would have to forcibly dispel all kinds of beliefs that Bertie has acquired through self-deception, and replace these with true beliefs. God would have to dispel Bertie of his illusion that he's "a basically good person"; He'd have to cause him to believe that he's a sinner. He'd have to forcibly dispel Bertie's self-deceived rationalizations and cause him to believe that he needs to repent of his sins. He'd have to cause him to believe that God stands ready to forgive and restore him. That God loves him so much that He sent His Son into the world to die for his sins. That he should accept Jesus Christ as his Lord and Savior. And so on. Moreover, all of these beliefs would have to be not only directly caused by God—thereby overriding Bertie's free will on a certain occasion—but also *maintained* by God, which would involve a *continual* overriding of his free will.

It should be clear at this point that the process we're imagining is one that would undermine Bertie's free will in a very significant way. More specifically, it would undermine his free will to an extent that is incompatible with the very process of soul-making. And this would be all the more obvious the longer God maintained Bertie's newfound religious beliefs by force. To the extent that these beliefs had a profound effect on the rest of Bertie's subsequent spiritual formation—which they would *have* to, in order for the process of rehabilitation to be successful—it would be doubtful that the person thereby formed was the *same* person as the one whose initial beliefs were dispelled by force.

It's crucial to understand the reason it's doubtful that it would be the same person on the other side of this imagined divine intervention. The reason is that *the process of soul-making is formative of a person's self-identity*.

The beliefs, emotions, desires, values, commitments, habits, and character that a person has formed through their past free choices is partially constitutive of who that person is. So, in fact, the process we're imagining would not be one of rehabilitation at all. It would actually be a process of *annihilating* Bertie and creating another person in his place. This is the reason there's no prospect of God's saving Bertie—or any other recalcitrant sinner—by overriding his free will and *forcing* him to accept a set of true beliefs.

## Could God save the lost by restoring their freedom to repent?

These same considerations about the formation of beliefs (the *cognitive* aspect of the soul-making process) apply, with only minor modification, to the will (the *volitional* aspect of the soul-making process). Just as God cannot save a person by unilaterally correcting their errant beliefs, so God cannot save a person by unilaterally correcting their errant will.

To see this, let's consider a case where the process of soul-making for a certain individual has reached the point that the person no longer possesses the power to repent. In such a case, it might seem that God could restore this person's power to repent without taking away any of their freedom, since, after all, by hypothesis they've already lost their freedom. In fact, this is a common argument made by universalists: "God's action in this case would be freedom-restoring, not freedom-destroying. So even on the logic of a free-will model of hell, where human moral freedom is taken to be of utmost importance, there's no reason for God not to intervene and save a person by force once they've reached this point."

Let's grant, for a moment, that God could easily restore the moral freedom of someone who has reached the point of having lost the ability to repent of their sins. The crucial question is, what's supposed to happen next? The universalist assumes that things would immediately begin to improve: that the individual would use their newly restored power of free will to repent, to open themselves up to the inner working of the Holy Spirit—in short, that the process of regeneration and sanctification would immediately begin. But this assumption ignores one of the fundamental principles of the soul-making theodicy: the principle of *spiritual momentum*.

We'll use an extended metaphor to illustrate this point. Imagine the process of spiritual formation as a ball rolling down an inclined plane, with a drop-off at the end. The ball is the soul, its movement down the inclined plane is the soul's spiritual development, and the velocity of the ball is the rate of the soul's progression in a certain direction (toward salvation or damnation). The drop-off at the end of the inclined plane is the point at which the soul's character is so solidified that a certain type of action becomes psychologically impossible. When used to model the process of damnation, the drop-off is the point at which *repentance* becomes psychologically impossible. (When used to model the process of salvation, the drop-off is the point at which *sinning* becomes psychologically impossible.) If a ball is released at the top of the plane, it begins to roll down slowly at first, but its velocity increases the further down it goes; likewise for the soul's momentum in the process of soul-making. Now add one more detail to the illustration. Suppose the ball has some sort of built-in mechanism of self-momentum, analogous to the soul's moral freedom in cooperation with the enabling power of the Holy Spirit. The mechanism is powerful enough to slow down, and then reverse, the direction the ball is rolling in, so long as it's traveling less than a certain velocity. Once it reaches this "terminal" velocity, however, the maximum upward force that the mechanism can provide is less than the downward force of gravity, and the ball cannot be stopped. The exact point that it reaches this velocity, let's suppose, is the drop-off.

This illustration is helpful in responding to the universalist's suggestion that God should interfere to restore the soul's moral freedom whenever a person reaches the point of being unable to repent. Put in terms of the illustration, the universalist's suggestion is that God should "unwind" the soul-making process to some point before the drop-off—that is, before the point in the soul-making process where the freedom to repent was lost. But which point should God return the soul to? If it's a point close to the drop-off, the soul will have all the characteristics that gave it so much momentum in the direction of damnation. What would almost certainly happen next is simply a repeat of what happened the first time the soul was at this point: it would immediately begin speeding toward the drop-off, soon losing its moral freedom once again. In short, if the "unwinding" of the soul-making process were minimal, it would prove to be fruitless. In order to give the soul a real chance of progressing in a new direction, God would have to undo its soul-making process *significantly*. He would have to take it back to a point before it gained so much momentum in the direction of damnation.

But if God were to do this, a different problem would arise. The divine action we're imagining wouldn't actually restore the soul—the *very same soul*—to an earlier point in its soul-making process; it would instead destroy that soul and create a different one in its place. This is so because, as we noted previously, the process of soul-making is formative of a person's self-identity. If God reformed the soul all at once in a way that immediately removed the negative characteristics (the tendencies that gave the soul momentum toward evil) and replaced them with positive ones (tendencies that gave the soul momentum toward good), God would thereby destroy the soul's identity. So this isn't a possible way of restoring a person; it would instead be a way of annihilating a person.

Nor would it help if God reversed the soul-making process gradually, placing the soul at the point just before the drop-off and then pushing it slowly backward up the incline, so to speak. It might seem that this way of reforming a soul would preserve personal identity, because it avoids bringing about too much change in too short a time. But the fundamental problem would remain: a process of reforming a soul without any contribution of its free will would not be a process of soul-making—at least, not of the type that's required for human salvation. The process of God's "unwinding" the soul-making process would still be a change that was made *to* the soul, unilaterally, by an outside force, regardless of how gradually the process might be carried out. But it's a basic principle of the soul-making theodicy that the process of soul-making must involve the individual's free will. At worst, the process of unwinding would slowly destroy the individual. At best, it would bring about a type of soul-making that was incompatible with human salvation. Either way, it wouldn't accomplish the goal that the universalist is hoping for.

This completes our rebuttal of the universalist's critique. To summarize: the central inference of the universalist's argument is that a decision to finally reject God couldn't be truly informed, rational, and free, and thus it couldn't be one for which a person is fully responsible and justly held to account. By analyzing the concept of self-deception, we've seen that this inference is invalid. The moral and spiritual beliefs of the damned are admittedly rife with falsehoods, but these false beliefs are not acquired innocently, but rather through willful acts of self-deception. False beliefs formed through self-deception are blameworthy, and the decisions they inform are likewise culpable. The decision to reject God and persist in sin isn't rational, because it works at cross-purposes to a person's highest good and eternal happiness, but it *is* intelligible: it's certainly possible to understand and appreciate the motives at work. It's the decision a person makes to continue satisfying their immediate, selfish desires rather than to pursue the things they know to be right but do not (yet) desire. It's a willful irrationality for which the individual is fully culpable. And the decisions involved in this process are free, up to the point that moral freedom is lost altogether. But even beyond this point, the individual is responsible both for the state they're in and the decisions they make in this state, because both are natural consequences of their own past misuses of free will.

## The capacity for self-damnation as essential to human nature

We've seen that there's no easy fix to the problem of what God should do if a person's soul-making process goes badly awry, increasingly gaining momentum toward evil and finally terminating in a state in which repentance is no longer possible. But one question remains: Why does God allow for this possibility in the first place? More specifically, why did God create humans with the capacity for *so much* self-deception—so much that it can result in an individual's own eternal ruin? Isn't this reckless, akin to giving a child a loaded handgun?[1]

---

1. This is a variation of the objection that we raised, but did not answer, at the end of chapter 9.

To answer this question, we need to return to the two proportionality principles we discussed in chapter 11. We saw that the logic of the soul-making theodicy leads to an important conclusion: God gives human beings the capacity to cause great harm because this capacity is required for moral freedom, and moral freedom is required for humans to develop into the kinds of beings who can love and commune with God in eternity. We further explored the reasons for thinking that, in general, the capacity for inflicting harm is *proportional* to the degree of moral freedom possessed, which in turn is proportional to the capacity for communion with God. (The precise formulations of these ideas were labeled "the freedom-harm principle" and "the freedom-communion principle," respectively.) These principles supplied the initial answer to the question of why God creates human beings with the capacity for perpetrating *horrendous* evils. The answer is that humans *must* be created this way in order to be capable of eternal communion with God.

We're now in a position to develop this argument one step further. It follows from the freedom-harm principle that a capacity for inflicting the *greatest possible* harm would be required for a creature to have the greatest possible amount of moral freedom. Damnation is the worst possible harm that could befall any creature. So the greatest possible freedom that a creature could have would be *the power to consign someone to hell*. But it would be horribly unjust if one creature could bring about another's damnation. So the greatest harm that a creature could inflict that's compatible with divine justice is *self*-damnation. This is a power to cause literally infinite harm, but it's entirely self-directed. According to natural consequence models of hell, this power is one that human beings actually possess.

By itself, the freedom-harm principle doesn't explain why God creates creatures with the power of self-damnation. It specifies the connection between moral freedom and the capacity for harm, but it doesn't explain why God creates creatures with so much moral freedom. The freedom-communion principle supplies the remaining part of the answer. To be capable of an infinite form of communion—eternal communion with God—a creature must possess an infinite form of moral freedom.[2]

---

2. The basic logic of the freedom-communion principle can be put more generally: higher degrees of freedom are required to will greater goods; the two are directly proportional. Stated in this way, we can demonstrate that infinite freedom is required not only for eternal communion with God, but also for loving one's neighbors. A limited form of freedom is sufficient to will a finite good for another person: small children, and perhaps even some animals, are capable of this. An example is a three-year-old's willing/desiring the happiness of their friend at a birthday party, where "happiness" is conceived in terms of getting cake and presents. There are greater goods than this, of course, but these require higher forms of freedom to will. The three-year-old is

In short, the highest creaturely good is possible only for creatures who possess the power of self-damnation.

This highest possible good is the very purpose for which humans are created. We are *made for* eternal communion with God and with other human beings. But the very features of human nature that make it possible for us to achieve this highest good also make it possible for us to bring about our own damnation. The capacity for eternal joy and the capacity for eternal misery are logically inseparable, like two sides of the same coin.

On the divine presence model, this is what it is to be human: to be a creature who is *made for* eternal communion with God, a creature who is *divinely intended* for this end, but who also possesses the power to thwart this end. This is both the unfathomable dignity and the terrifying responsibility of being human, and it's built into our very nature.

Is it good for God to create beings with such a nature as this? It is, insofar as possessing such a nature is necessary for communion with God, and God fully intends every such creature to achieve this end.[3] It's especially clear that this act of divine creation is good insofar as God does *everything in His power* to guide every such creature to its appointed end. Not only does God have a justifying reason to create human beings with the capacity for self-damnation, it is, on the divine presence model, an expression of His perfect goodness and love for us.

It's a common objection of universalists that natural consequence models of hell place too high a value on human freedom. According to universalists, freedom is not as valuable as these models assume, and God would be reckless to give human beings the capacity for self-damnation. We've now found good reasons to think this objection is confused. The capacity for salvation appears to be inseparable from the capacity for damnation. A creature capable of experiencing heaven must also be capable of bringing about its own eternal ruin. And there is no way, even for an omnipotent being, to

---

incapable of willing the moral and spiritual perfection of their friend; their own rationality and freedom is not yet sufficiently developed for this. Jesus commands his disciples to love (*agape*) one another, and this requires willing one another's *highest* good. But the highest good of every human being is an *infinite* good: the good of eternal communion with God and other people. Since the ability to will higher goods requires the possession of higher degrees of freedom, it follows that loving God and loving other people requires an infinite form of freedom. It's important to note, however, that "infinite" does not always mean "unlimited." To take a mathematical example: the series of even numbers is infinite, but it's limited to those numbers evenly divisible by two. Likewise, there's an important sense in which human freedom is infinite, despite the fact that it's also limited in many ways.

3. The logic of this argument applies to angels, as well—and to any other possible creatures who are capable of damnation.

*ensure* that every human being will use their free will in the divinely intended way. God can, and does, provide sufficient grace to everyone to enable their salvation. On the divine presence model, He goes further, doing everything in His power to save everyone. But the intended purpose of human nature is, of logical necessity, one that cannot be realized without the free cooperation of the human will. Divine providence is neither the meticulous orchestration of all events, as Calvinists imagine, nor the power to bring every created nature to its divinely intended end, as universalists contend. It is, rather, the ability and intention to cause "all things to work together for good to those who love God" (Romans 8:28 NASB).

# Divine Hiddenness and Divine Disclosure

(The Philosophical Case for the Divine Presence Model, Part II)

## Chapter 15

# The interconnected problems of divine hiddenness and hell

In the previous chapters, we saw that the divine presence model is built on the foundation of a soul-making theodicy, with salvation and damnation being understood as the two possible terminating points of the soul-making process. We've explored the way that the process of soul-making involves the development of a person's cognitive, emotional, appetitive, and volitional capacities, and the way these capacities become corrupted as a person persists in sin. We've explored the principle of spiritual momentum in this process, and the crucial roles that are played by free will and self-deception. Most of the philosophical case for the divine presence model developed in chapters 11–14 could be applied equally well in defense of other natural consequence models of hell, such as the choice model. In this chapter and the ones that immediately follow, we'll explore a set of philosophical issues that distinguishes the divine presence model from these close neighbors.

### Divine omnipresence

We'll begin with an observation: there's a fundamental feature of certain standard views of hell, such as traditionalism and the choice model, that doesn't seem to fit with the rest of Christian theology. According to these views, damnation involves being eternally *separated* from God. For traditionalists, this is a matter of being forcibly cast out of the presence of God, whereas for proponents of the choice model, the separation is a self-exile. In our initial development of the divine presence model in chapter 9, we mentioned the doctrine of divine *omnipresence*: the doctrine that God is everywhere present. This doctrine immediately raises an awkward question for proponents of traditionalism and the choice model. How could anyone be eternally separated—or separated even for a moment, for that matter—from the presence of a God who is *omnipresent*?

It's a standard part of Christian orthodoxy that not only is God the Creator of everything that exists, but God must actively *sustain* everything in order for it to continue to exist from one moment to the next.[1] No created thing has the power to sustain its own existence; the maintenance of the universe requires a kind of continual creation. This is known as the doctrine of *divine conservation*. The significance of this doctrine for the present discussion is that it rules out the possibility of certain kinds of separation from God. Even those in hell couldn't be separated from God's creative and sustaining power; otherwise they would cease to exist.

Because of this constraint, when traditionalists and proponents of the choice model claim that hell is a matter of eternal separation from God, they must construe this separation in purely *relational* terms. They must simply mean that there's no communication, no experience of "being together," no *interaction* of any kind between God and the damned. Perhaps "separation" is meant to be a description of the way that the damned *experience* their existence in hell. To those in hell, it *feels like* they've been altogether excluded from the presence of God; it's *as if* God is completely absent.

And yet, even this restricted interpretation of the idea of hell as eternal separation from God is difficult to square with Scripture. Consider the words of the psalmist:

> Where shall I go from your Spirit?
> 
> Or where shall I flee from your presence?
> 
> If I ascend to heaven, you are there!
> 
> *If I make my bed in Sheol, you are there!* (Psalm 139:7–8 ESV)[2]

"Sheol" is the Hebrew term for the realm of the dead; it's equivalent to the Greek term "Hades." The idea of Sheol is the precursor, we might say, to the concept of hell.[3] (Notice the way it's juxtaposed with heaven in the

---

1. See, for example, Acts 17:24–28, and in particular the striking line from verse 28: "For in him we live and move and have our being."

2. See also Jeremiah 23:24.

3. Things are more complicated than this, because Sheol was regarded in the Old Testament as the destiny of *all* the dead—the righteous and the wicked alike. There seems to be some further development of this idea in the Second Temple period (roughly 515 BC to AD 70). In one of Jesus' parables, the parable of Lazarus and the rich man, it seems to be suggested that Sheol/Hades has something like separate compartments:

psalm.) In claiming that God is in Sheol, the psalmist is clearly suggesting that God is *everywhere*, without exception. Even in Sheol, there is no escape from the divine presence.

These are not the only scriptures that are difficult to reconcile with the idea of eternal separation from God. The Bible speaks of the resurrected Christ as "him who fills everything in every way," and as "the very one who ascended higher than all the heavens, in order to fill the whole universe."[4] This feature of Christ will become manifest at his return: the glory of the Lord will be fully revealed and God will be "all in all." The apocalypse, when Christ is fully revealed in glory, is the dramatic and definitive end of the phenomenon that we previously termed *divine hiddenness*.

In light of these biblical teachings about the day of judgment, traditionalism and the choice model appear to be theologically conflicted. No sooner has God put an end to divine hiddenness than He turns around and again imposes this very same condition upon the damned, eternally separating them from Himself by casting them into hell (traditionalism) or allowing them to separate themselves (the choice model). This is puzzling, at the very least. Is it not part of the very point of the revelation of Christ at the end of the age that it is witnessed by *all creation*? And wouldn't this revelation be more momentous, more consequential, more exalting and glorifying to Christ, if it were witnessed by all creation *for all eternity*? In fact, this way of understanding the apocalypse is not only theologically preferable, it is—as we'll see later—a more *scriptural* way of understanding events at the end of the age.

## The problem of divine hiddenness

The philosophical and theological advantages of the divine presence model extend far beyond its ability to fully accommodate the doctrine of divine omnipresence. The more significant advantages emerge when we reflect further on the phenomenon of divine hiddenness. When we briefly introduced this concept in chapter 10, in our initial development of the divine presence model, we noted that most people don't experience God in the same clear or straightforward way that they experience other beings. God isn't perceived fully by anyone, and the especially vivid experiences

---

a place of torment for the wicked, and a place of comfort (called "Abraham's bosom" in the parable) for the righteous. See Luke 16:19–31, especially verses 22–26. Note also Jesus' words to the "good thief" on the cross: "Truly I tell you, today you will be with me in paradise" (Luke 23:43).

4. Ephesians 1:23 and 4:10.

of God that some people report—like the one Saul famously experienced on his journey to Damascus—are relatively rare. In fact, many people claim that they've never experienced God at all, including some who, in all apparent sincerity, earnestly desire to experience God and have taken the usual measures to try to do so (seeking God in prayer or meditation; reading and studying sacred Scripture; participating in religious rituals, liturgies, or worship services; and so on).

This facet of human existence gives rise to a theological difficulty known as the **problem of divine hiddenness.**

The phenomenon of divine hiddenness is problematic in numerous ways. It's a source of distress to those who desperately want to experience God and to be reassured of their relationship to Him. This is particularly the case for those who are in the midst of extreme or prolonged suffering—those who, in crying out to God and failing to feel His reassurance, feel abandoned by God. In this version of the problem, divine hiddenness is a species of the problem of evil, because it involves an experience of suffering.

A different and more common form of the problem, however, concerns the implications of divine hiddenness with respect to the consequences of failing to believe in God. The individual and collective experiences of divine hiddenness would seem to make it much more likely that many people will fail to believe in God, and it also seems to make such unbelief more reasonable and rational. And yet, orthodox Christianity regards the failure to believe in God as not just lamentable, but *blameworthy*. On the face of it, it seems unjust and unloving for God to remain hidden if there are serious consequences for failing to believe in Him. This would be true even if the only consequence of unbelief were that of missing out on something extremely good (eternal life, communion with God in heaven); but according to orthodox Christianity, it also leads to something infinitely bad (eternal punishment, consignment to hell).

Clearly, the problem of divine hiddenness and the problem of hell are closely interconnected. Yet the standard views of hell have a hard time explaining divine hiddenness. If the stakes are so high, why doesn't God reveal Himself clearly to every person in the course of their earthly lives, so that no one would miss out on a relationship with God due to doubts about His existence? In order for a view of hell to be adequate, it needs to have a *principled* answer to this question. That is to say, there must be an explanation of divine hiddenness that logically follows from its account of damnation. In fact, even more than this is required: an adequate view of hell needs to demonstrate that divine hiddenness is somehow *required* for human salvation. Otherwise, God's perfect goodness and love are brought into question by His hiddenness.

To begin to see why this is the case, let's consider another thought experiment. Imagine a janitor who mops a tile floor and then deliberately places a caution sign in some obscure location, one that virtually guarantees the sign will be overlooked by most people as they approach the slick area, making it much more likely that some people will slip and fall. Clearly, those approaching the area need to know the information conveyed by the sign in order to avoid harm. Let's further suppose that there's no good reason to obscure the sign; nothing good is accomplished by its being hidden. Suppose, finally, that the janitor understands all of these things. Given all these factors, we would judge that the janitor has acted maliciously.

We can generalize the point. It seems clearly bad to intentionally obscure or withhold information from someone in a situation where you know they need the information to avoid harm. Just *how* bad it is to withhold such information depends on how much harm is likely to result from it. These two factors—the badness of the action and the harm that's likely to be caused by it—increase in direct proportion to one another. (Thus a doctor who withheld a cancer diagnosis from a patient, thereby preventing the patient from seeking treatment, would be doing something even worse than our imagined janitor.)

There are, however, possible circumstances in which a person could be justified in withholding such information. Two sorts of circumstances are possible. In the first, a person knows that something *even worse* would happen if they disclosed the information. In the second, a person knows that something very good can be accomplished *only* by their withholding the information—something whose goodness outweighs the badness of the harm that's likely to be caused by withholding it. In general, the greater the harm that's risked by withholding the information, the greater the good that it must serve; otherwise, failure to disclose the information is blameworthy.

These points have a direct application to the problem of divine hiddenness. The greatest harm that any person could possibly suffer is eternal damnation. And according to orthodox Christianity, one must believe in God in order to avoid damnation. Belief in God involves much more than simply believing that God exists, but it *includes* this. So anyone who lacks the knowledge that God exists is at risk of damnation. God surely has it within His power to convey the knowledge of His existence to anyone He chooses.[5] He could give everyone a Damascus Road experience if He wanted. And yet He doesn't; to most people, God remains at least partially hidden.

---

5. More precisely, God surely has it within His power to provide everyone with such compelling evidence of His existence that *anyone who is not in the grip of self-deception* would believe that God exists.

Based on what we've just discussed, God's failure to disclose Himself fully to everyone is evidence that He's not perfectly good and loving *unless* His doing so is necessary to achieve some greater good or avoid some worse evil. But we've already concluded that there's no evil that could possibly befall a person that is any worse than damnation. So the only way divine hiddenness could be justified is if it's necessary to achieve something very good—something *so* good that it's even worth risking some people's damnation to achieve it. And the only way this could be *loving* on God's part is if those put at risk by divine hiddenness are the very ones who stand to benefit from it. The only good that meets all these conditions is human salvation.

We've reached a very important conclusion. For some reason, the possibility of human salvation *must* require God to remain partially hidden in this life.

But why? The argument we've just constructed explains the theological *need* for such a connection. It doesn't yet explain *why* it should be the case that divine hiddenness is a necessary condition of human salvation. One of the requirements of an adequate view of hell is that *it must explain this*.

In the next chapter, we'll explore the most important standard explanations of divine hiddenness that are directly connected to various ways of thinking about hell. The conclusion we'll eventually reach is that the standard explanations of hiddenness each get *something* right, but they also turn out to be incomplete or problematic in some significant way. To construct a fully satisfying account, we're going to need the resources of the divine presence model.

# Chapter 16

# The usual explanations of divine hiddenness—and their inadequacy

IN THIS CHAPTER, WE'LL explore the standard explanations of divine hiddenness. For many readers, this will be the most challenging chapter of the book. Those who have not previously considered the problem of divine hiddenness, or who have no investment in any of the standard ways of trying to solve it, may wish to skip ahead to chapter 17. However, many of the views discussed in this chapter are philosophical versions of popular ideas, and it's important to understand why these ideas about divine hiddenness turn out to be problematic. As we've already seen, the theological stakes surrounding the problem of divine hiddenness are high. The consequences of misguided solutions can extend beyond theoretical concerns to practical matters of spiritual devotion and practice.

The standard explanations of divine hiddenness fall into two broad types. The first type focuses on what's required to safeguard human freedom. The second type focuses on the consequences of human sin. We'll consider each of these in turn. Throughout this discussion, it will be helpful to have a term that we can use to refer to a state in which the presence of God is fully revealed. We'll call this **divine disclosure**.

### Divine hiddenness as a safeguard of human freedom

In the first broad type of explanation, divine hiddenness is thought to be a necessary condition of human freedom. We'll call this *the preservation-of-freedom explanation*. Its characteristic claim is that divine hiddenness is a feature of human experience without which we would be incapable of making a certain important kind of free choice (or choices). The choices in question are not only important, but crucially connected to human salvation. There are various possible candidates as to what these free choices might be. The three most popular candidates are (1) the choice to accept the gospel, (2) the choice to love God, and (3) the moral choices that play a crucial role in the soul-making process. Because of these three options, the preservation-of-freedom explanation of divine hiddenness comes in three different forms. However, all of these forms share in common the underlying assumption that there would be something *coercive* about a situation of divine disclosure.

In the first form, divine hiddenness is considered necessary for a free response to the gospel. This way of explaining divine hiddenness is most attractive to traditionalists, who think of hell in retributive terms. To understand the argument, we need to return to the problem of coercion that we developed in chapter 4. Recall the thought experiment of the desperate lover who threatens his beloved at gunpoint, demanding that she reciprocate his love. We noted that the revelation of hell on the traditionalist account seems to function like the gun at this woman's head. Just as the element of coercion makes it impossible for the woman to respond in the way that's demanded of her (a response of *genuine* love), so it seems that no one who truly believes the traditionalist doctrine of hell, with its implicit threat, can respond freely to the gospel.

Some traditionalists imagine that divine hiddenness provides the solution to this problem. The logic is as follows. If people *knew* the doctrine of hell to be true, their response would be coerced. By remaining partially hidden, God makes His existence ambiguous, which in turn makes it uncertain whether the doctrine of hell is true. This lowers the level of threat that the doctrine of hell poses, to the point that it's no longer coercive, which allows people to make a free choice about whether to accept the gospel. This is the reason God remains hidden: it enables people to make a free decision about whether to place their faith in Christ. Divine hiddenness isn't a problem; it's a solution!

Unfortunately for traditionalists, this is not a good explanation of divine hiddenness. It depicts God as deploying a bumbling solution to try to solve a problem of His own making. God threatens humans with the artificial and arbitrary punishment of hell, and then tries to backpedal by obscuring His own existence, hoping the combination will somehow elicit from humans a positive response to the gospel. (To fully appreciate how misguided this explanation is, imagine a variation on the desperate lover thought experiment in which the man suddenly realizes that his beloved cannot possibly begin to reciprocate his love in response to a threat of being killed, so he tells her that his gun *might* be unloaded. This is a depiction of blundering foolishness and incompetence rather than wisdom and power.)[1] It seems much more sensible to reject the retribution thesis—the proposition that generates the problem of coercion—than to try to double down on traditionalism by assigning this function to divine hiddenness.

There are, however, much better ways of developing the idea that divine hiddenness is required to safeguard human freedom. The other two forms of the preservation-of-freedom account don't assume that hell is an arbitrary or artificial punishment. These strategies of explanation are preferable to those who advocate non-retributive views of hell.

The most important such strategy claims that divine hiddenness is necessary for the soul-making process—more specifically, that it's necessary for humans to develop moral agency. The basic idea is that, in a situation of divine disclosure, humans would feel so threatened that we wouldn't dare to make a choice that we believed to be contrary to God's will. In this kind of scenario, our every moral decision—every occasion where we made a choice to do the right thing—would be coerced rather than free. But moral decisions must be free decisions; any choice that's coerced doesn't count as a moral choice at all. So in a world of divine disclosure, moral choice would be altogether impossible for human beings. We wouldn't be moral agents under such circumstances. But moral agency is required for the developmental process—such as the forging of a character—that's constitutive of soul-making. We discussed in chapter 11 the reasons for thinking that soul-making is required for human salvation. These reasons complete the explanation for why divine hiddenness is necessary for human salvation.

This is a more interesting explanation of divine hiddenness. But it has a weakness. To reveal it, we need to ask why it should be thought that humans would necessarily feel threatened in a situation of divine disclosure. There's a suppressed premise that's driving the argument: namely, that a fully revealed God would *have* to punish human wrongdoing, and with such an immediacy and severity as to make disobedience an irrational option. But why should we assume this? Why couldn't God adopt a policy toward human beings similar to the one that parents often adopt toward their adult children: allowing them to make their own decisions without interference—and in particular without attempting to punish them for

---

1. One might object: "The revised thought experiment is disanalogous, because God—unlike the desperate lover—hides *His very existence*." Very well; let the revised thought experiment be one in which the desperate lover hides in the shadows, whispering, nearly inaudibly, "I'll kill you if you don't love me"—so softly that the woman wonders whether it might just be the wind and her imagination. This too is foolishness.

bad behavior or reward them for good behavior? If it's even possible for God to treat humans this way—and apart from the characteristic claims of the divine presence model, it's hard to see why it wouldn't be possible—there's no good reason to assume that divine disclosure *itself* poses a coercive threat to human moral development or decision-making. This is the problem with the standard way of trying to explain divine hiddenness as necessary for the soul-making process: it rests on the assumption that a revealed God would *have* to punish human wrongdoing, but it lacks the conceptual resources to support this assumption.

There's one remaining form of the preservation-of-freedom explanation that we need to consider. Here the key claim is that God must be hidden in order for human beings to be free to choose whether they will love Him. All of the strategies we've discussed have the crucial feature of connecting divine hiddenness with the conditions of human salvation. (In this respect, they're the right *kinds* of explanation.) In this case, the connection is that a choice to love God is required for salvation because heaven involves an eternal *communion* with God, and communion is a kind of love.

Why might it be thought that God must remain hidden in order for humans to love Him? We've already considered the type of view in which the human ability to love God is hampered by a fear of divine punishment, a fear that God aims to lessen by obscuring His presence. We found this view lacking. But there are other, better lines of reasoning to consider. The most interesting versions of this view make no reference to divine punishment; yet they still insist there's something about divine disclosure that would imperil a free and loving response from humans. At first, this seems to be an odd claim. Other, more familiar types of loving relationships don't have any such constraint. Obviously, it's not required of parents that they hide from their children in order for their children to come to love them! So what is it about our relationship to God that's supposed to make matters so different?

There are two different types of answer, and both require us to reconsider the concept of coercion. Up to this point, we've been assuming that a coercive influence must be some sort of *threat*. But it's also possible that something could be coercive in a "positive" rather than a negative way. To see this, let's consider one more variation on the desperate lover thought experiment. Imagine the man offers his beloved a million dollars in exchange for loving him. The offer isn't threatening, but it still has the effect of making it impossible for his beloved to give him what he wants. The offer of a million dollars introduces a motive that works at cross purposes to his goal of eliciting a response of *genuine* love from her, because any love that's given for the sake of securing a payoff isn't genuine.

Some philosophers have worried that the revelation of the doctrine of heaven might have this sort of coercive effect. Since our concern in this book is with problems having to do with the doctrine of hell, rather than the doctrine of heaven, we'll put this worry to the side.[2]

There remains, however, a different sort of "positive coercion" that we need to consider. Perhaps divine disclosure would compel a certain human response entirely apart from any offer of artificial rewards. Some philosophers have contended that the very presence of God, fully revealed, would be so overwhelming to human beings that the only possible response—the only response of which humans would be psychologically capable—would be to love Him in return. An experience of divine disclosure would eliminate every other option. But what God wants is for human beings to love Him *freely*, and this requires that we have an alternative option available to us. This is the reason God remains hidden: He wants to create the conditions under which human beings are capable of freely choosing to love Him in return.

There are two questions we need to ask in response to this argument. Is it really true that an experience of divine disclosure would compel a loving response from human beings? And if so, why would this be undesirable? We'll take these questions in reverse order.

Suppose it's true that anyone who had an experience of divine disclosure would be compelled to love God in return. In this case, the person's love for God would not be a *free* response. But why would this be such a bad thing? There are other kinds of loving relationships in which one or both members lack the ability to do otherwise. Consider the love that young children have for their parents. This is (in normal cases) a deep and genuine love, and yet it develops long before there's any ability on the child's part to make a decision to do otherwise. Romantic relationships are often described in similar terms. The first onset of love is often described as an experience of being overcome, of being consumed, of being helpless to resist, and so

---

2. It's worth noting, however, that this worry is not baseless. Depending on the way one understands the doctrine of heaven, it could be a very serious problem. The worry is that the revelation of the doctrine of heaven potentially undermines the ability of anyone to come to love God in the right way. (This type of argument is most directly concerned with threats to our ability to love God *genuinely* rather than *freely*.) Some philosophers think divine hiddenness is the solution to this problem: God remains hidden in order to make it uncertain that there will be a big "payoff" for those who love Him, thereby restoring the possibility of a *genuine* human love for God. It's crucial to notice that the logic of the argument requires the assumption that the rewards of heaven are *artificial*, just like the traditionalist assumes that the punishments of hell are artificial. The divine presence model rejects *both* of these assumptions, and thus neither problem of coercion arises for it.

on—and it's rarely assumed that this feature of the experience makes the love any less real. Furthermore, it seems that divine love, the very highest form of love—both God's love for humans and the love exchanged among the Persons of the Trinity—is not a love that could be withheld, since God is *of His very nature* perfectly loving. Apparently, then, genuine love, even in its highest form, doesn't require the ability to do otherwise, and the absence of this ability doesn't make the love coerced. Upon reflection, the ability to withhold love doesn't even seem to be an especially desirable feature of loving relationships. But these conclusions appear fatal to the explanation of divine hiddenness under discussion, which seemed to assume that genuine love must be love that's given freely.

There is, however, a possible response to this critique. It could be that, even though certain kinds of love don't require freedom, the *highest love that is possible for human beings* is one that requires freedom. This response is actually implicit in the logic of the soul-making theodicy. In its explanation of why God allows evil and suffering in the world, the soul-making theodicy assumes that God *cannot* bypass the painful process of human moral and spiritual development. There's no possibility of creating human beings in an *initial* state of perfect communion with God; He can't just skip to the end of the process.[3] If He could, then the whole travail of soul-making would be pointless. Requiring humans to undergo it would be an exercise in Tom Sawyer-like mischief: a matter of going to elaborate and (for us) painful lengths to accomplish something that was (for God) readily and easily obtainable without them. The soul-making theodicy is plausible only if the outcome at which the process of soul-making aims—a final state of loving communion between God and human beings—is one that requires human freedom. In short, it must be that the kind of love exchanged in heaven is a love that is freely given. And within Christian theology, this is the kind of love that constitutes the highest human good. So for anyone who accepts the soul-making theodicy, it looks like there are good reasons, after all, for concluding that freedom is required for humans to be able to love God—at least, to be able to love God in the particular sort of way that constitutes the highest human good.

We raised two questions in response to the freedom-to-love explanation of divine hiddenness, and we've now answered one of these. Let's turn to the other: Is it really true that an experience of divine disclosure would compel a loving response from human beings? We might reasonably think

---

3. If these descriptions of what God "can't do" sound like a denial of divine omnipotence, recall a point that we discussed in chapter 9: *omnipotence is not the ability to do the logically impossible*. On the soul-making theodicy, the actions being described here are ones that are logically impossible.

so—*if* there were no record of anyone's ever having such an experience and we were forced to answer the question using only the resources of philosophical and theological speculation. But Christians have another source of information about the matter: the revelation of Scripture. And the scriptural record of human encounters with God paints a starkly different picture. Whenever humans come "face to face" with God in the Bible, the result is nothing like the soothing encounter of newborn and mother, or the pleasant "buzz" of first love. In most cases, the characteristic feature of these encounters is, on the human side, an experience of sheer terror and an intense self-awareness of sinfulness or uncleanness. We'll return to this topic in chapter 18, where we'll explore the biblical accounts of these events in more detail. For now, suffice it to say that any explanation of divine hiddenness that cannot accommodate this feature of the scriptural record is flawed, or at best incomplete.

## Divine hiddenness as a consequence of sin

Now that we've developed the first broad type of explanation of divine hiddenness and found it lacking in all its major forms, let's turn to the second. The characteristic claim of the second broad type of explanation is that the human experience of divine hiddenness is a consequence of sin. It's not something that God intends or imposes on us, and it's not due to any failure on God's part to reveal Himself. The failure is entirely on our side of things. It's a failure of perception whose cause is a deeper moral and spiritual failure. The ultimate cause traces all the way back to the first sin, and to the fall of humankind. Divine hiddenness, in this account, is one of the *noetic effects of sin*: that is, an effect of sin upon the human mind. Much like a hard blow to the head could cause one's sight to become impaired, the consequence of the first sin was to plunge humanity into a partial moral and spiritual blindness.

There's a sophisticated framework in which these ideas have been worked out by contemporary philosophers called *Reformed epistemology*. We don't need to get bogged down in the technical details here, but the basic idea is that, were it not for sin, we would have no more difficulty perceiving God than we have in perceiving any other person. Human beings in their original state had an *immediate sense of the divine* that was as clear as any visual perception or rational intuition[4] or memory that any of us might have

---

4. A rational intuition is the sort of experience you have when you perceive the sum of 1 + 1 to be 2, or the shortest distance between two points to be a straight line. It's the kind of experience you might describe by saying, "Anyone can see that's true just by

today. It's because of an impairment or malfunction in our present cognitive capacities, an *unnatural* condition that's contrary to God's original design for us, that we presently fail to perceive God clearly or easily. And this unnatural state is one for which we are ourselves responsible.

This is a very different sort of explanation of divine hiddenness than the one we discussed in the previous section. One of the most important things to notice about it is that it understands divine hiddenness to be a *natural* consequence of human action rather than a condition that God artificially imposes on us. In the preservation-of-freedom explanation of divine hiddenness, God hides Himself or causes us to be unable to perceive Him (the two are perhaps equivalent) in order to safeguard human freedom. Divine hiddenness is a *good* thing, in this account, because it enables something important (a free response to the gospel, or soul-making, or love for God) that would otherwise be impossible. On the present account, by contrast, divine hiddenness is a bad thing, a dangerous effect of a cognitive malfunction.

This difference, however, raises a potentially troublesome question for the defender of the view. If the human experience of divine hiddenness is the result of a malfunction that's contrary to God's design for us, why doesn't God simply repair it? It's surely within God's power to restore our cognitive and spiritual faculties to their original state. And given that this malfunction poses a threat to our salvation (since it makes unbelief much more likely), it seems that a loving God would *want* to fix it. So why doesn't He? It's not at all clear that the Reformed account has any good explanation of this.

One might at first think that the explanation is obvious: God is allowing us to reap what we've sown. We brought the problem on our own heads through our own sinfulness and rebellion, and it's not God's responsibility to bail us out. In fact, it's *good* that God does not do so. In allowing us to experience the full natural consequences of our own free choices, God is satisfying the demands of justice, as well as showing respect for human moral agency.

Considered more carefully, however, this type of response loses credibility because of the degree to which it conflicts with ordinary sensibilities about the way we should treat our loved ones. It might be good to allow a loved one to experience the natural consequences of a bad choice on some occasions or in some circumstances, but there are limits to this. It wouldn't be good to allow an obviously intoxicated loved one to drive

---

stopping and thinking about it."

home, for example, even if it were somehow known that he posed no danger to anyone but himself.

A more elaborate thought experiment can be used to map the view under discussion more closely, and to bring out the relevant moral intuition more clearly. Imagine a father who strictly forbids his twin boys from fighting or roughhousing. The boys have terrible eyesight and are nearly blind without their prescription glasses, and the rule against fighting is partially due to the likelihood that such behavior would result in their glasses being broken. The boys disobey the rule against fighting on a certain occasion, with predictable results: both of their glasses are damaged beyond further use. Later in the day, the father observes from a distance his sons walking close to a high cliff, which he knows they can't see because they no longer have their glasses. What would we expect the father to do in this scenario? Would we expect him to stand idly by, allowing his boys to fall to their deaths, on the grounds that they willfully defied his command against fighting and must now be allowed to reap the natural consequences of their disobedience? Or would we expect him to intervene to try to prevent this horrible outcome? The analogues of the various elements of the thought experiment (disobedience = the fall of humankind; glasses = the faculties by which we perceive God; seeing the edge of the cliff = perceiving God; falling off the cliff = damnation) are meant to bring the relevant moral intuition into sharp focus. A loving father might allow his sons to experience *some* natural consequences of disobedience—the inconvenience of having to go for a certain time without being able to see well, or the expense of having to use their own money to buy replacement glasses—but he would surely try to prevent his sons from experiencing a natural consequence as severe as death. Likewise, if humans are at risk of damnation because of an inability to perceive God, and if God has it within His power to eliminate this risk simply by repairing a certain damage to our spiritual faculties, we would expect that a perfectly good and loving God would do so, even if this damage was a natural consequence of human disobedience.

There's a second problem for this account of divine hiddenness, as well. It's at best incomplete insofar as it doesn't explain *why* sin has the particular effect upon our minds that this account claims. Such an explanation is needed, because it's certainly not obvious why sin should have this effect. Think of it this way. Human sinfulness, and the fall of mankind, apparently left other human faculties intact. We can still see and hear things in our immediate vicinity, we can still reason through math problems, we can still remember what we had for breakfast, and so forth. Why, then, did sin bring about a malfunction in our faculties of spiritual perception? Remember that on the present account, divine hiddenness is held to be a *natural* consequence of human sinfulness, not something that God artificially or arbitrarily imposes on us. The challenge for the defender of this view is to explain how sin is supposed to have as one of its natural effects the impairment of our ability to perceive God. The mechanism of this supposed malfunction—the *way* that it's supposed to come about—is not at all clear.

It might be suggested that the mechanism is self-deception. But this won't do, for several reasons. First, there are limits to how far self-deception can blind a person. There may be no upper limit on how far self-deception can be used to retain (or to avoid) certain *beliefs*. But perception is a different matter. No amount of self-deception alone can make you unable to see the person sitting right across the table from you, no matter how much you might want to not see them there. So how is self-deception supposed to make us unable to perceive God? Second, even if self-deception *could* bring about such perceptual blindness, this wouldn't explain why some people who desperately *want* to perceive God find themselves unable to do so. One of the most famous examples of this in modern times is the case of Mother Teresa.[5] If the cause of divine hiddenness were self-deception, why would it be experienced even by some of the most devout believers?

In light of these problems, the conclusion we're finally driven to reach is that, like the preservation-of-freedom explanation of divine hiddenness, the explanation of divine hiddenness offered by Reformed epistemology is at best incomplete.

It's important not to learn the wrong lessons from the discussion we've just completed. As we'll see in the next chapter, several of the ideas about divine hiddenness that we've been discussing—that it's required for soul-making, and that it's a consequence of human sin—will turn out to be a part of the divine presence model's explanation as well. It hasn't been the purpose of our discussion in this chapter to refute these ideas, but rather to demonstrate that they're not adequately supported or developed in the right way in the standard explanations of divine hiddenness. We'll now explore the way that the resources of the divine presence model can be used to provide a more coherent and complete explanation of divine hiddenness.

---

5. See *Mother Teresa: Come Be My Light*.

## Chapter 17
# Hiddenness on the divine presence model

WE'VE SEEN THAT THE phenomenon of divine hiddenness is the source of numerous problems, and the standard explanations of divine hiddenness are at best incomplete. In this chapter, we'll introduce a distinction that will help us to understand one of these problems more clearly. We'll then draw upon the resources of the divine presence model to address the problem of divine hiddenness in a way that's more satisfying and complete than any proposed solution we've discussed so far. By the end, it should be clear that one of the strengths of the divine presence model is its ability to make significant headway on one of the most challenging problems in philosophical theology.

### Two problems of divine hiddenness as a source of unbelief

In chapter 15, we noted that one of the problems of divine hiddenness is connected to the problem of evil (divine hiddenness as a source of suffering) and another is connected to the problem of hell (divine hiddenness as a source of unbelief). We now need to make a further distinction that will subdivide the latter problem. There are two different types of knowledge of God, and these correspond to two different problems of divine hiddenness as a source of unbelief.

The first type is called **propositional knowledge**. This includes all the things that can be known *about* God. Propositional knowledge is indicated by "that" clauses: knowledge *that* God exists, *that* He's the Creator of the universe, *that* Jesus is the Son of God, and so forth. Philosophical discussions of *epistemology*—the theory of knowledge—tend to focus on propositional knowledge. These discussions are usually preoccupied with questions about *evidence* and *justification* (or the lack of it) for various beliefs, including religious beliefs. The version of the problem of divine hiddenness that's concerned with propositional knowledge is expressed by the following question: *Why doesn't God provide everyone with compelling evidence of His existence?* (The question is stated more precisely, but less naturally, by using the phrase "compelling evidence for the proposition that God exists.") It's certainly within God's power to provide everyone with such evidence. Imagine if every night He rearranged the stars in the sky to spell out "Jesus is Lord" in a different language. Had God provided evidence like that, every rational person would believe there's a God. And since belief of this kind is needed (as a minimal requirement) for a person to be saved, the problem of divine hiddenness in this form is the challenge of explaining why God hasn't provided this kind of evidence.

Although propositional knowledge tends to be the type that's emphasized in philosophical discussions of divine hiddenness, it's not the only type of knowledge. There could also be an **experiential knowledge** of God. Christians believe that such knowledge is not only possible, but actually possessed by many people: in particular, by those who've had an unusually powerful or "close" encounter with God. Biblical examples of this include Moses, in his encounters with God on Mount Sinai; Isaiah and Ezekiel, in their visions of the Lord; Peter, James, and John, in their witnessing of Christ's transfiguration; and Paul, in his experience on the road to Damascus. The version of the problem of divine hiddenness that pertains to experiential knowledge is expressed by the question, *Why doesn't God cause everyone to have some sort of experience like this?* To use the terminology we introduced in chapter 16: Why doesn't God cause everyone to have at least one experience of divine disclosure during the course of their earthly lives?

Such an experience would surely remove any and all reasonable doubt that God exists. Like messages in the night sky, this kind of experience would provide ample justification for the belief that God exists. But it would seem to provide something much more valuable, as well. A personal encounter with God would almost certainly be a life-changing experience. Imagine if God were to give each person a temporary experience of what Christians have traditionally called the **beatific vision**: a direct perception of God, a clear apprehension of His infinite goodness and love, an experience of perfect communion with God, resulting in the greatest possible happiness and joy. An experience of the beatific vision in one's earthly life would be like a preview of heaven. Having this experience would seem to make it very likely—as likely as possible—that a person would not only come to believe in God, but also respond to Him with love, adoration, and worship, and to submit their lives fully to Him. Given that God desires the salvation of all and that He's capable of providing the beatific vision to everyone, why doesn't He do so?

The two versions of the problem of divine hiddenness that we've just developed are interconnected, but they're also different enough from one another that a solution to one type of problem might not be a solution to the other. We'll begin with the way that the divine presence model addresses the second version of the problem, since it's more directly connected to the core idea of the model. After that, we'll return to address the problem pertaining to propositional knowledge.

### The explanation of divine hiddenness on the divine presence model

On the divine presence model, the reason God doesn't give everyone a temporary experience of the beatific vision is that it's *impossible* to do so. If God revealed Himself fully to every person—that is to say, if the divine presence were manifested in all its glory to everyone in their earthly lives—the result would be, for most people, an experience not of rapture but of horrendous suffering. This follows straightforwardly from the core idea of the divine presence model. The experience of sinners in the presence of a loving God is damnation; to exist in this state is to be in hell. The beatific vision is the way that the presence of God is experienced by those whose sanctification is complete: those who have been perfected in love, fully conformed to the image of Christ. This is the reason it's not available to everyone, or even to the vast majority of people in their earthly lives. It's not a matter of what God is willing to give people. It's a matter of what they're capable of receiving.

This is also the reason that divine hiddenness is required for human salvation. According to the doctrine of *original sin*, humans begin their lives in a fallen state, a state of moral and spiritual disorder. We have an innate tendency toward selfishness and pride, a natural orientation away from God and toward self-gratification. Because of this, there must be an initial period of time in each person's life in which God remains at least partially hidden. Otherwise, human existence would begin in hell! The purpose of divine hiddenness is to provide one of the necessary conditions of soul-making, and thus one of the conditions of salvation. Everyone will experience divine disclosure in the end. It's an act of mercy on God's part to shield us from this, for a time, in order that human repentance, regeneration, and sanctification can first take place.¹ Divine hiddenness creates a "safe space" in which human beings can be prepared for the experience of divine disclosure that awaits them at the end of the age. It provides each of us an opportunity to be transformed into the kinds of beings who are *capable* of experiencing the presence of God as the beatific vision (heaven)—as God has always intended for us—rather than as an experience of horrendous suffering (hell), as most of us would experience it now.

Undergoing this transformation is the principal purpose of each person's earthly life, on the divine presence model. In Orthodox theology, it's called **theosis**:² the process whereby those who are united to God in Christ "become partakers of the divine nature" (2 Peter 1:4, ESV)—that is, increasingly conformed to the image of Christ, becoming more and more like Jesus in being wholly and perfectly loving, more and more filled with the Holy Spirit, increasingly participating in the life of the Trinity.³ This is the process of salvation—the process of being delivered from the corrupting bondage of sin and death, and of being renewed, in order that we might fulfill the divinely intended purpose of our lives—and the early stages of this process require divine hiddenness. It's not just that God is justified in remaining partially hidden in our earthly lives. Divine hiddenness is an expression of God's perfect love for us as fallen creatures.

In our initial development of the problem of divine hiddenness, we concluded that an adequate view of hell must have a *principled* answer to the question of why God remains partially hidden in this life. We can now see that the divine presence model meets this requirement. Or at least, it has the beginnings of such an answer. It has a principled explanation of why God isn't yet *fully* revealed. But this explanation of divine hiddenness is not yet complete. There's a lot of middle ground between being fully revealed and being fully hidden, and we might still wonder why God doesn't

---

1. See, for example, 2 Peter 3:3–13. This connection between divine hiddenness and the divine presence model finds expression in a remarkable passage in C. S. Lewis's *Mere Christianity*: "God will invade. But I wonder whether people who ask God to interfere openly and directly in our world quite realise what it will be like when He does.... For this time it will be God without disguise; *something so overwhelming that it will strike either irresistible love or irresistible horror into every creature*" (Book II, chapter 5, italics added).

2. The doctrine of theosis is especially emphasized in Orthodoxy, but it's also officially recognized in Catholicism (see *Catechism of the Catholic Church*, 2nd ed., paragraphs 1, 460, 1988, 1997, and 1999), and some Protestants accept it as well.

3. It was previously suggested (in chapter 11) that the principal purpose of life is to become the kind of person who loves well. This suggestion is consistent with—in fact equivalent to—the suggestion now being made in the main text. Becoming a "partaker of the divine nature" is equivalent to being perfected in love, because *the nature of God is love*.

reveal Himself to some greater degree than He does, and why He reveals Himself more to some people than to others.

Also, we haven't yet offered anything to explain why God doesn't provide everyone with compelling evidence of His existence: messages written in the stars, for example. There's nothing in the account we've sketched so far that suggests a miraculous sign of this sort would be overwhelming (as an experience of divine disclosure would be), or that witnessing it would be a painful experience, even to those who are presently in a sinful or rebellious state. But this kind of evidence would ensure that everyone has propositional knowledge of God's existence; even better, it would remove all room for rational doubt. What remains to be considered, then, is why God doesn't provide this kind of evidence.

The best answer to this question about the lack of compelling evidence for God's existence is one that's compatible with the divine presence model but not unique to it.[4] It seems possible, even likely, that the kind of evidence provided by messages written in the stars would not actually have the desired effect. Regardless of how true the content of the message was ("Jesus is Lord!"), humans would very likely draw the wrong conclusion from it. This is because, if God went to extravagant lengths to convey such propositional truths, humans would naturally infer that what God cares about most, and what He most wants from us, is that we *believe the right things* about Him. But this is not what God most wants from us at all. In fact, believing true propositions about God is *by itself* worth very little. (As the Apostle James put it to a group of early Christians: "You believe that there is one God. Good! *Even the demons believe that*—and shudder" [James 2:19].) What God most wants from us is a certain kind of *relationship*. He wants our trust, our allegiance, our love, our devotion, our worship. He wants sinners to repent, to turn away from paths that lead to misery and destruction. He wants us to be reconciled to Him, to be healed of the moral and spiritual disease of sin that alienates us from Him and from one another. Filling the world with miraculous signs and wonders could actually work at cross-purposes to these goals. Humans need to be encouraged to seek a right relationship with God, not merely to acquire propositional knowledge about Him.

On the divine presence model, God has created the world in such a way that propositional and experiential knowledge of God are *connected* in an important way. Everyone (of normal cognitive capacities, beyond a certain age) is capable of some propositional knowledge of God, and everyone is capable of experiencing God—and thus of knowing God on

---

4. The idea that's discussed in this paragraph is developed by Peter van Inwagen in *The Problem of Evil*, Lecture 8 ("The Hiddenness of God").

the basis of personal experience—to some degree as well. Both kinds of knowledge are fairly limited for most people. But they increase together, and this is by divine design.[5]

To understand why, we need to return to the important "law" of the spiritual life that we mentioned in chapter 13: *possessing moral and spiritual understanding requires a person to have a certain kind of character*. This is an initially surprising principle; it seems like all that would be required for moral and spiritual knowledge is sufficient intelligence. But common experience makes it clear that this is not so. There are many intelligent and even brilliant people who are utterly lacking in wisdom. And if we remember the larger discussion of the previous chapters, it's not too hard to see why. The problem, once again, is self-deception.

Many of the moral and spiritual truths that are most important for each of us to understand are facts about ourselves. For most people, these include a great many facts that are ugly, shameful, and offensive to pride. As we previously discussed, these unpleasant facts about our own moral and spiritual condition are the ones that it's most tempting to resist or suppress. But we can expand this point. There are many moral and spiritual truths that are *indirectly* convicting: for example, those expressing moral principles that we've failed to abide, or spiritual ideals we've failed to attain. ("Love your neighbor as yourself." "Love your enemies." "Forgive as the Lord forgave you." "Be perfect, as your heavenly Father is perfect.")[6] It's tempting to ignore these principles, or to pretend that our lives display them already, or to reinterpret them in a way that lessens the requirements to a level we've already attained. The deepest reason many of us fail to grasp the most important moral and spiritual truths is that we're *unwilling* to understand them. And this is why, in general, the degree to which one understands and accepts these truths is the degree to which one has a virtuous character, and a love of truth, and a desire to do the will of God. The attainment of moral and spiritual knowledge isn't simply a function of how smart a person is. It's more fundamentally connected to matters of the heart and the will.[7]

---

5. This is not to say that the two types of knowledge *always and immediately* increase together; it is not to deny that a particular individual, at a certain time in their lives, might possess more of one type of knowledge than the other. Rather, the claim being made here is that God intends for the two types of knowledge to increase proportionately in human beings, and He has designed the world in such a way that, *roughly* and *in general*, this is the way things go. (The upcoming paragraphs will explain why.)

6. Mark 12:31; Matthew 5:44; Colossians 3:13; and Matthew 5:48, respectively.

7. One of the most perceptive philosophers on this point is Søren Kierkegaard. For some helpful essays on this facet of Kierkegaard's writings, see Evans, *Kierkegaard on Faith and the Self: Collected Essays*, chapters 10, 11, and 17.

This is something important that proponents of Reformed epistemology get right. Human spiritual faculties function properly just to the extent that a person's heart and will are rightly ordered. It's *by design* that matters of character and matters of spiritual discernment are connected. The *ability* to bring about distortions of moral and spiritual perception through acts of self-deception is not itself a defect; it's simply a facet of moral freedom. But the exercise of this ability really does make it harder for a person to perceive God. The more one engages in self-deception, and the longer one persists in willful sin, the greater one's spiritual blindness becomes.

Conversely, growth in moral and spiritual maturity brings with it greater spiritual discernment—that is, it results in one's spiritual faculties functioning in a way that's closer to their design plan. "Blessed are the pure in heart, for they will see God" (Matthew 5:8). We're exhorted by Scripture and Christian tradition to seek out wisdom and righteousness, and encouraged that our efforts will be rewarded. "Seek, and you will find" (Matthew 7:7). "Blessed are those who hunger and thirst for righteousness, for they will be filled" (Matthew 5:6). Propositional knowledge of God, personal experience of God, and moral and spiritual development are all interconnected and designed to increase (or decrease) in proportionate degrees. Thus—in general, and other things being equal—an individual's ability to perceive God and their experience of doing so increases with their growth in moral and spiritual maturity, and their experience of divine hiddenness progressively diminishes.[8]

These points help to explain a number of otherwise puzzling features of the spiritual life: (1) why a person's free will must be involved in their experience of coming to know God, (2) why knowledge of God must develop gradually, (3) why God remains partially hidden even to those

---

8. The qualifiers ("in general, and other things being equal") are important. We mentioned previously the case of Mother Teresa, who struggled with discouragement because of a persistent experience of divine hiddenness throughout much of her life. It in no way follows from this that she was lacking in moral or spiritual maturity. In fact, there's a well-documented history of Christian saints who have struggled with similar experiences: spiritual crisis, struggles with doubt, feelings of being abandoned by God, the "dark night of the soul." And a similar theme can be found in Scripture; in fact, it's a recurring one in the Psalms and central to the book of Job. On some interpretations, it was even experienced by Jesus on the cross, expressed in his so-called cry of dereliction: "My God, my God, why have you forsaken me?" (Matthew 27:46). It's beyond the scope of this book to investigate these matters or try to offer an explanation of this phenomenon. Suffice it to say, the claim in the main text at this point is a claim about the *ordinary* manner of things in the spiritual life. The qualifier is thus meant to allow for the possibility (perhaps we should say "the established fact") of exceptions to this principle that God presumably wills for the sake of some greater good—a good that may or may not be known in any particular case.

who've already accepted the gospel and given their lives to Christ, and (4) why God does not reveal Himself to everyone in the same way or to the same degree. We'll take these in order.

If a person's experience of coming to know God is connected to matters of their moral and spiritual formation, as the divine presence model claims, then it's clear that a person's free will must be involved in the process. We've already seen that the soul-making process is one that requires the involvement of the individual's free will throughout. What we now see is that coming to know God is a part of the soul-making process, so it too must involve a person's free will at every stage.

Moreover, since knowledge of God is connected to the development of a person's character, and a person's character is part of their self-identity—that is, a part of who they are as an individual—it follows that a person's knowledge of God must develop gradually. Any changes that involve a person's self-identity must occur gradually in order for it to be the case that these are changes in one and the same person, rather than the destruction of one person and the creation of another. This is one of the reasons that sanctification cannot occur all at once, in an instant. The process must be gradual in order that a person can "survive" it.

Since knowledge of God is connected to self-knowledge, the process of attaining self-knowledge must also be gradual. A key part of the divine presence model, which we discussed in chapter 10, is that the presence of God is truth-revealing. The closer one comes to God, the more that the truth about oneself is revealed. Hence the process of coming to know God is also a process of coming to know the full truth about oneself. Because of this, an encounter with God is potentially fraught with danger, for a reason mentioned in chapter 12. For most of us, the sin that we consciously perceive in our own lives and souls is merely the tip of the iceberg. The human heart is "deceitful above all things, and desperately wicked: who can know it?"[9] If a person were faced with the full truth about themselves all at once, or even too much too quickly, it could easily plunge them into despair.

This, in turn, explains why God remains partially hidden even to those who've already freely accepted the gospel and pledged their allegiance to Christ as Lord. A gradual diminishment of the experience of divine hiddenness, rather than a sudden and total divine disclosure, is required in order for the soul-making process to continue progressing in the direction of sanctification, in a way that both preserves personal identity and does not lead a person to despair. The process of sanctification is a process of being completely delivered from sin. It's helpful to think of sin

---

9. Jeremiah 17:9 KJV.

as a spiritual disease, or perhaps a kind of addiction. In the treatment of many serious diseases and severe addictions, a treatment has to be sufficiently gradual in order to be effective. Too much at once could kill the patient. Matters are similar in the spiritual life. Again, sanctification must be gradual in order that a person can survive it.

The answer to the final question—*Why doesn't God reveal Himself to everyone in the same way or to the same degree?*—is contained in the points we've already made. God's interactions with each person are designed to facilitate each one's soul-making process, and to maximize the likelihood that the process will be successful. God meets each person where they are, revealing Himself in the way and to the degree that's best suited to their present condition, which is largely, though perhaps not entirely, determined by the present state of their character and their will. Of course, given our very limited perspective on the state of each person's soul and our very limited understanding of what is most needed to facilitate the soul-making process in each individual case, it's not surprising that many people's experiences of God (or lack thereof) don't always align with our expectations or assumptions about what would be best.

Let's end by summing up the main ideas of the account that we've developed, and by noting what the various standard accounts of divine hiddenness get right, despite their deficiencies. Proponents of Reformed epistemology are right that human spiritual faculties are affected by sin. But they struggle to explain how it is that sin brings about a malfunctioning of these spiritual faculties, and they exaggerate the extent to which human sin is the cause of the experience of divine hiddenness. The divine presence model provides the missing explanation and the needed correction. A person's ability (or inability) to perceive God is *partially* determined by the state of their character and their will. It's certainly true that the experience of divine hiddenness can be intensified by self-deception. But even though divine hiddenness is entirely a consequence of sin, it's only partially a *natural* consequence. For the most part, divine hiddenness is something that God freely and intentionally brings about in response to the fall of mankind, as an act of divine mercy.

Certain forms of the preservation-of-freedom account of divine hiddenness also get something right. It's true that divine hiddenness is necessary to enable the soul-making process and to safeguard the human power of free will that plays an essential role in it. But the required conditions of soul-making are not *by themselves* enough to explain divine hiddenness. The full explanation requires the fact that humans are presently in a fallen state, along with the description (provided by the divine presence model) of what an encounter with God would be like for creatures in this state. In addition to providing the missing piece of this explanation, the divine presence model also explains why God remains partially hidden even to those who have already come into a right relationship with Him—something that certain forms of the preservation-of-freedom account struggle to explain.

In summary: On the divine presence model, the overall reason that God remains partially hidden in this life is so that human beings can be saved. Divine hiddenness is one of the requirements of an environment in which soul-making can take place in a fallen world. By remaining partially hidden, God is creating the conditions that make it as likely as possible that all will be saved. God takes a personally tailored approach to each individual, however, which is why He doesn't reveal Himself to exactly the same degree or in exactly the same way to everyone. God reveals Himself gradually so as not to overwhelm human freedom or plunge anyone into despair. As an individual's sanctification progresses, they're enabled to perceive God more clearly and to commune with Him more deeply. Throughout the process, God is doing everything in His power to prepare each person for the event of Christ's return: the day of judgment, the apocalypse, the point when the Truth—including the complete truth about each and every person—is finally and fully revealed.

## Why not eternal divine hiddenness?

Throughout the discussion so far in this chapter, we've found that reflection on the problem of divine hiddenness has proven to be a significant source of philosophical support for the divine presence model. Before moving on, however, we need to address a potential way that the topic of divine hiddenness could also be problematic for the model.

The objection stems from the core idea of the model: that the experience of being in the presence of God is a torment to the wicked. We concluded in the previous section that the purpose of divine hiddenness is to shield sinners from this experience in their earthly lives, in order to give each person the opportunity to be saved. Those who persist in their sins all the way up to the day of judgment find themselves forcibly exposed to the presence of God when Christ is revealed in glory. This is damnation: to exist forever in the presence of God in an unregenerate state. But now a troubling question can be raised: Why doesn't God just remain hidden to the damned for all eternity? In doing so, He would spare the damned horrendous suffering. It seems vindictive for God to force the wicked to be forever in His presence. But it's been noted repeatedly that the divine presence model rejects the retribution thesis. It denies that the purpose of hell is to inflict suffering upon the wicked as recompense for their earthly wrongdoing. So why, then, doesn't God do what He can to reduce the suffering of the damned in eternity?

There doesn't seem to be anything impossible about the idea of God's remaining forever hidden to the damned. Presumably, He would just need to continue relating to these individuals in the afterlife the same way He related to them in their earthly lives. He could arrange the new creation in such a way that the saints experience eternal divine disclosure and the damned experience eternal divine hiddenness. And this would seem to be the *loving* thing for God to do. Granted, the state of the damned in the new creation would be infinitely worse than the state of the saints if God were to remain forever hidden to them, because they would be missing out on the highest good of eternal communion with Him. But the damned would be missing out on this highest good *in any case*. They've used their free will to thwart the end for which they were created, and thus the highest human good cannot be obtained for them, even by an omnipotent God. In a situation where the highest good is unobtainable for a person, the loving thing to do is to will for them the highest good that *is* obtainable. For the damned, this would be some kind of existence in which God is eternally hidden. But, in the divine presence model, God doesn't offer the damned this option. Consequently, the model seems not to account for the perfect goodness and love of God after all.

To answer this objection, we first need to remember why God allows *any* evil or suffering. Evil and suffering are bad things, and God allows a bad thing only if doing so is necessary to achieve some good thing. Furthermore, it must be that the good thing God is aiming to achieve outweighs the bad thing that He allows in order to achieve it. These points apply to divine hiddenness, because the experience of divine hiddenness is a source of suffering and doubt to many people. The reason God remains hidden, for a time, is that it's necessary to achieve the greater good of human salvation. Once divine hiddenness has served this purpose—that is, once everyone has had ample opportunity to repent of their sins, to be reconciled to God, in short, to be *saved*—then divine hiddenness no longer serves a greater good. At this point, it would become a *pointless* evil if it were allowed to continue, and God doesn't allow any pointless evil to exist in the world.

The likely response from the critic at this point is that divine hiddenness wouldn't be a pointless evil if it were extended into eternity, because it would serve the greater good of sparing the damned horrendous suffering. And sparing the damned horrendous suffering wouldn't diminish the happiness of the saints, since God could be fully revealed to them while remaining hidden to the damned. It seems, then, that something very good would be achieved by eternal divine hiddenness, and it wouldn't come at the cost of sacrificing anything else that's very good.

But in fact, this isn't true. There are at least *two* very good things that would be lost in a world in which God remained eternally hidden to the damned. The first is justice for the victims of horrendous evil. Remember that what causes the damned much of their suffering is that being in the presence of God reveals the truth about them. They're forcibly faced with the truth about themselves and what they've done, and this truth is somehow revealed for all to see. It's not at all obvious that it would be a good thing to shield the perpetrators of horrendous evil from the truth—or the pain that it causes them. The thing that victims of injustice often want more than anything else is for those who have wronged them to really know and appreciate the full extent of the harm and the pain that they caused, and to feel remorse for it. Because moral freedom requires the capacity for self-deception, it may be impossible to make the damned feel genuine remorse for what they've done. But they can be forced to face the truth. Being in the presence of God for all eternity accomplishes this, whereas eternal divine hiddenness would prevent it.

In giving this response, we're not going back and endorsing the retribution thesis. The *purpose* of hell isn't to make the damned suffer for all eternity; the purpose isn't retribution. Nevertheless, it's important that the design of the new creation does not *thwart* justice. Justice requires, minimally, that perpetrators of horrendous evil be forced to face the truth of what they've done. This is not only good, but more valuable and important—that is, a *greater* good to bring about—than the good of sparing the damned the pain of this experience. This is the first reason God will not remain hidden to the damned in eternity.

The second is that doing so would thwart something else of tremendous value. According to Scripture, Christ will return at the end of the age to finally and fully reclaim what is rightfully his as King of all creation. The earth will be "filled with the knowledge of the glory of the Lord," and God will finally "be all in all."[10] It's a very good thing for Christ to be revealed in *all* of his glory to *all* of creation in the age to come, to be exalted in the sight of *all* creatures for all eternity. It's supremely good for this to be so. More specifically, it's good to a degree that far outweighs the badness of the suffering that it causes to those who have stubbornly persisted in sin and rebellion against God, and thereby thwarted their own happiness.

Again, it's not the purpose of hell to bring suffering to the damned. The *purpose* of God's being fully revealed is to bring about the highest human

---

10. Habakkuk 2:14; 1 Corinthians 15:28.

good, to bring human nature—in fact, to bring all of creation—to its fulfillment. God fully *intends* this experience of divine disclosure to be the greatest possible happiness for all His creatures, even though He *foresees* that it will not be for some. It's important to understand that those who experience suffering in His presence are not being sacrificed for the sake of someone else's benefit. God isn't playing favorites. *Every* human being's highest good is one that can be realized only by being in the presence of God for all eternity. In bringing about the conditions of the new creation, God is thereby willing the highest good of every human being. God is love, and His will is always directed toward the highest good of those He loves. And God loves everyone—including the damned, whose experience of His love is hell.

# The Biblical Case for the Divine Presence Model

## Chapter 18

# The first and second unveilings

THROUGHOUT THE BOOK SO FAR, we've focused primarily on philosophical and theological matters, with only occasional mention of supporting scriptures. To complete our discussion, we'll now consider the biblical case for the divine presence model in detail.[1] What we'll see in these closing chapters is that, not only does the divine presence model find significant support in Scripture, it also allows us to make sense of some biblical passages that are otherwise confusing or even seem contradictory.

We'll begin by considering the biblical record of those who've had unusually "close" encounters with God, and then move on to consider various biblical themes and passages that lend further support either to the core idea of the divine presence model or its ancillary claims. Among these are the theme of unveiling, the theme of disclosure, the theme of light and darkness, and the descriptions of God as fire. We'll draw on a broad range of scriptures throughout the Old and New Testaments in our discussion, but special attention will be given to 2 Thessalonians 1:9, which provides the strongest support for the divine presence model of any single passage.

---

1. This section of the book ("The Biblical Case for the Divine Presence Model," chapters 18–20) directly incorporates large portions of the appendix of R. Zachary Manis, *Sinners in the Presence of a Loving God: An Essay on the Problem of Hell* (Oxford: Oxford University Press, 2019). This material is reprinted with generous permission of Oxford University Press. © Oxford University Press 2019. Reproduced with permission of the Licensor through PLSclear.

## Biblical descriptions of encounters with God

One of the most striking features of the biblical narratives are their accounts of religious experiences. The most remarkable of these are events in which God is manifested in such a vivid or dramatic way that it's as if a person has come "face to face" with God. This is the recorded experience of several of the Old Testament prophets, at least four of the apostles, and numerous other prominent biblical figures. What's especially notable about these encounters, for present purposes, are the reactions and emotions attributed to those who experience them. They aren't pleasant or comforting experiences, but rather distressing, overwhelming, and even terrifying experiences. They are, in short, exactly the kinds of experiences that we would expect people to have under the circumstances if the divine presence model is true.

Records of these kinds of encounters with God are spread throughout Scripture, with some of the most important found in the opening and closing chapters of the Bible. The creation story of Genesis 2 is especially instructive, because it's suggestive of the way that humans relate to God in a state of innocence. In the story of Adam and Eve in the garden of Eden, there's no indication that the first humans find the presence of God in any way disturbing prior to their disobedience. But as soon as they eat the forbidden fruit—the fall of humankind accounted in Genesis 3—something immediately changes:

> Then the eyes of both of them were opened, and they realized they were naked; so they sewed fig leaves together and made coverings for themselves. Then the man and his wife heard the sound of the Lord God as he was walking in the garden in the cool of the day, and they hid from the Lord God among the trees of the garden. (Genesis 3:7–8)

In the wake of their sin, Adam and Eve obtain a new kind of knowledge ("the eyes of both of them were opened"), an *experiential* knowledge of evil, which brings with it a feeling of exposure ("they realized they were naked") and an intense desire to avoid the presence of God ("they hid from the Lord God"). What was previously a source of joy—the fullness of God's presence—becomes for Adam and Eve in their fallen state the very thing that causes them to suffer.

This wretched state is inherited by the descendants of Adam and Eve; even the most righteous individuals become intensely self-aware of their relative unrighteousness when they find themselves in the presence of the most holy God. The prophets are in a way paradigmatic examples of this phenomenon, insofar as they are divinely chosen for some role (and thus presumably are favored by God in some sense), and yet they still often experience the presence of God as threatening. The Lord is recorded as saying of Job, "There is no one on earth like him; he is blameless and upright, a man who fears God and shuns evil" (Job 1:8). And yet, when Job finally comes face to face with God, he reacts with shame and self-loathing: "My ears had heard of you but now my eyes have seen you. Therefore I despise myself and repent in dust and ashes" (Job 42:5–6). Likewise, Isaiah's vision of God in the temple prompts him to cry out, "I am ruined! For I am a man of unclean lips, and I live among a people of unclean lips, and my eyes have seen the King, the LORD Almighty" (Isaiah 6:5). (Significantly, Isaiah is able to converse with the Lord once the seraphim touches his mouth with the live coal from the alter, declaring, "your guilt is taken away and your sin atoned for," suggesting that his experience of terror is connected to a state of guilt.) Moses' first encounter with God is likewise one of fear and trembling. When the Lord identifies Himself to Moses in the burning bush, Moses "hid his face, because he was afraid to look at God" (Exodus 3:6). Later prophets behave in a similar manner: when Ezekiel encounters "the appearance of the likeness of the glory of the LORD," he "fell facedown" (Ezekiel 1:28).

Turning to the New Testament, we find a number of accounts that parallel these Old Testament passages. Peter's reaction to Jesus after the miraculous haul of fish is reminiscent of Isaiah: he becomes immediately self-conscious of his own unworthiness, exclaiming, "Go away from me, Lord; I am a sinful man!" (Luke 5:8) The reaction of Moses and Ezekiel—falling facedown on the ground in terror—is paralleled in a number of key passages in the New Testament: Saul's encounter with the risen Lord on the road to Damascus ("suddenly a light flashed around him; and he fell to the ground . . ."); John's encounter with the Lord in a vision on the island of Patmos ("When I saw him, I fell at his feet as though dead"); and Peter, James, and John's experience on the mountain, seeing Jesus transfigured before them and hearing the voice from heaven ("they fell facedown to the ground, terrified").[2]

Such are the experiences and natural reactions of sinful persons coming into the presence of a holy God. And yet, although these are accounts of divine disclosure to an unusually high degree, the disclosure is still only partial and temporary. There are biblical suggestions that the experience of God *fully* revealed in all His glory—seeing "the face of God," as the idea sometimes is expressed—would be more than humans could bear in a fallen state. Thus in response to Moses' demand to "show me your glory," the Lord responds, "You cannot see my face, for no one may

---

2. Acts 9:3–4; Revelation 1:17; Matthew 17:6.

see me and live." The Lord then makes provision for Moses to experience His presence in a veiled form:

> "There is a place near me where you may stand on a rock. When my glory passes by, I will put you in a cleft in the rock and cover you with my hand until I have passed by. Then I will remove my hand and you will see my back; but my face must not be seen."
> (Exodus 33:18–23)

This passage explains, in anthropomorphic language, one of the central purposes of divine hiddenness: to shield human beings from an experience that would destroy us in our present, unregenerate state.

Likewise, the divine presence model makes intelligible the Lord's warning to Moses (earlier in the Exodus account) that the Israelites must not approach Mount Sinai, where the Lord is residing, lest the Lord "break out against them" (Exodus 19:12–15, 21–24). Construed volitionally, the statement seems a bit bizarre, as if God is warning about His bad temper and His tendency to suddenly "lose it" and lash out at those around Him. But construed metaphysically, the statement makes sense: God is telling Moses about the *kind* of being He is—not psychologically, but metaphysically. He's warning (not threatening) that the people will be destroyed if they draw too close to Him—not by His choice, but merely in virtue of the kind of creatures they (presently) are, and the kind of being God is.

Thus we find throughout Scripture a conspicuous pattern: the reactions of the biblical figures who experience God revealed to an usually high degree are those that the divine presence model predicts. Likewise, the way that God behaves in relation to humans on these occasions (exiling Adam and Eve, shielding Moses, warning the Israelites not to approach) seems to support the model.

However, there are also passages in Scripture that seem to diverge from this pattern, at least on a surface reading. The account of Cain's exchange with God following the murder of Abel is a striking example of an apparent outlier: rather than seeming terrified, Cain is brazen when God confronts him ("Am I my brother's keeper?" [Genesis 4:9–15]). In other passages, God interacts with various prophets without any of the aforementioned, characteristic elements (terror, intense self-consciousness of sin, etc.) being discernible: for example, in many of His later interactions with Moses, after the initial encounter at the burning bush.

There are possible ways of reconciling these passages with the divine presence model.[3] Nevertheless, these passages do demonstrate that the scrip-

---

3. For some possible suggestions, see Manis, *Sinners in the Presence of a Loving God*, 346.

tural record is mixed; the evidence from biblical accounts of encounters with God is not, by itself, either clear enough or consistent enough to make a compelling case for the divine presence model. There's a measure of indirect biblical support for the model to be found in many of these accounts. But in order for the model to meet the standard of finding *significant* support in Scripture, more is required; the biblical case for the divine presence model cannot rest entirely on its accounts of religious experiences.

In the remainder of this chapter and the ones that follow, the broader biblical case for the divine presence model will be developed by way of an analysis of various scriptural themes and central teachings about the nature of divine judgment. It is here that we find the strongest biblical support for the model. The teachings about judgment are understood most clearly in relation to the teachings about salvation: since damnation is the ultimate ruin of human nature, we can understand it only if we understand what it is for human nature to be fulfilled. For this reason, we will also review and further develop the meaning of salvation on the divine presence model.

## The first unveiling: overcoming "hardness of heart"

We've noted repeatedly that God's intention for every person is to deliver each one from the bondage of sin, to work a divine act of spiritual healing that will lead, ultimately, to a state of perfect loving communion with God and with other people. A person can resist these divine efforts, however. The principal obstacle to God's efforts to save human beings is the human ability and tendency to engage in self-deception, a grave type of misuse of creaturely free will. Engaging in self-deception on moral and spiritual matters results in what the Bible calls **hardness of heart**. To harden one's heart is to resist the conviction of the Holy Spirit, to stubbornly persist in error rather than turning to God in repentance, which has the effect of perpetuating one's state of spiritual blindness.

The initial personification of this idea in the Bible is Pharaoh, whose heart is repeatedly hardened against God's command, delivered through Moses, to let the Israelites go into the desert to worship. Pharaoh becomes increasingly irrational in his stubborn refusal to comply, even in the face of escalating consequences, ultimately leading to the death of all firstborn Egyptian males, the destruction of his army in the Red Sea, and even his own death.[4] Throughout the scriptures that follow, the Israelites are repeatedly charged with the same offense: hardness of heart, being "stiff-necked" in stubbornly refusing to submit to God and obey His law, whether in letter

4. Exodus chapters 5–14.

or in spirit. In the New Testament, the Pharisees serve as the quintessential example of the latter tendency. (More on this shortly.)

Because hardness of heart is a hindrance to the healing work of God in us, the process of delivering us from sin must begin with something that the Bible calls *circumcision of the heart*. The image conveys the removing of that which makes the heart insensitive, an exposing of one's heart to the divine presence, a receptivity to God's leading. The Israelites were given the command to "circumcise your hearts," but it's elsewhere made clear that this is actually a work of God in the inner person: "The LORD your God will circumcise your hearts and the hearts of your descendants, so that you may love him with all your heart and with all your soul, and live."[5] The phrase "so that" is important; it's by undergoing this spiritual transformation that an individual is enabled to fulfill the biblical commandment to "Love the LORD your God with all your heart, and with all your soul, and with all your strength" (Deuteronomy 6:5). The consummate fulfillment of this commandment is the experience of perfect communion with God: the experience of the saints in heaven. All who would be saved, then, must begin with the circumcision of the heart.

An interesting variation on this theme is developed in 2 Corinthians chapter 3, where the Apostle Paul writes of a "veil" that covers the hearts of unbelievers.[6] In this passage, Paul takes the idea of exposing our hearts to God and develops from it one of the most important claims of the New Testament concerning the doctrine of salvation. He recalls the story of God's giving the law to Moses, whose face was said to be so radiant upon his return from his meeting with God on Mt. Sinai that the people could not stand to behold it, prompting Moses to wear a veil (2 Corinthians 3:7–16).[7] Paul then remarks that "we are not like Moses," veiling the glory of God, but instead reflect it fully to the world, a glory that in Christ is even greater than the glory of the law of Moses. A veil remains, however, over the hearts of unbelievers:

> But their minds were made dull, for to this day the same veil remains when the old covenant is read. It has not been removed, because only in Christ is it taken away. Even to this day when

---

5. Deuteronomy 10:16 and 30:6.

6. Though the passage is a discussion of a more specific group (the ancient Israelites and Paul's Jewish contemporaries who have rejected Christ) and a more specific activity (reading and understanding the Mosaic law), I take the central theological point made in the passage to be applicable to all who are not rightly related to God, and I will develop the passage accordingly.

7. The passage from the Old Testament to which Paul is referring is Exodus 34:29–35.

> Moses is read, a veil covers their hearts. But whenever anyone turns to the Lord, the veil is taken away. (2 Corinthians 3:14–16)

When a person turns to God in repentance, the veil over their heart is lifted and spiritual renewal begins. This healing accrues to *all* who are in Christ ("whenever anyone turns to the Lord, the veil is taken away") and *only* to those who are in Christ ("only in Christ is it taken away"). The way of salvation is in Christ. By remaining in him, we are freed from the bondage of sin.[8]

The form that this spiritual renewal takes, and the end goal at which it aims, is rather astonishing: Paul concludes the above passage by claiming that "we all, with unveiled face, beholding [reflecting] the glory of the Lord, are being *changed into his likeness from one degree of glory to another*; for this comes from the Lord who is the Spirit" (2 Corinthians 3:18 RSV).[9] This is the essence of the Christian doctrine of *theosis*, briefly introduced in chapter 17. According to this doctrine, the end for which human beings are created is a state of eternal communion with God, understood more specifically (and astonishingly) as a *participation in the life of God*. The Bible teaches that believers "may become partakers of the divine nature" (2 Peter 1:4 ESV). The degree of this participation increases throughout the process of sanctification, as believers increasingly fulfill Jesus' command to "Be perfect, therefore, as your heavenly Father is perfect" (Matthew 5:48).[10] The remarkable idea of participation in the communion of the Trinity is suggested throughout the Pauline epistles, as believers are repeatedly described as being "in Christ." It is likewise found throughout the Fourth Gospel: Jesus instructs his disciples that as he is in the Father, and the Father is in him, so his disciples are in him, and they must remain ("abide") in him.[11] This teaching culminates in the high priestly prayer of Jesus: "I have given them the glory that you gave me, that they may be one

---

8. Compare 2 Corinthians 3:17: "Now the Lord is the Spirit, and where the Spirit of the Lord is, there is freedom."

9. A footnote on verse 18 in the RSV indicates that the term translated as "beholding" can also be translated as "reflecting." Similar notes appear in the NIV, ESV, and ASV, the latter of which suggests "reflecting as in a mirror" as an alternate translation.

10. Note the verses that immediately follow 2 Peter 1:4—the verse in which it is revealed that believers may become partakers of the divine nature: "For this very reason, *make every effort to supplement your faith with virtue,* and virtue with knowledge, and knowledge with self-control, and self-control with steadfastness, and steadfastness with godliness, and godliness with brotherly affection, and brotherly affection with love. For if these qualities are yours and are increasing, they keep you from being ineffective or unfruitful in the knowledge of our Lord Jesus Christ" (2 Peter 1:5–8 ESV).

11. John 14:20 and 15:1–17.

as we are one—I in them and you in me—so that they may be brought to complete unity" (John 17:22–23).

Especially important for the present discussion is Paul's claim that believers, in the process of being sanctified, are being "changed into his [the Lord's] likeness." Elsewhere, in his epistle to the Romans, Paul writes that those undergoing this process are "predestined to be conformed to the image of his Son" (Romans 8:29). He writes to the Galatians that "all of you who were baptized into Christ have *clothed yourselves with Christ*" [literally, "put on Christ"], and he tells them that he is "again in the pains of childbirth *until Christ is formed in you*."[12] This theme is not limited to the Pauline epistles. The Apostle John states that "what we will be has not yet appeared; but we know that *when he appears we shall be like him*, because we shall see him as he is" (1 John 3:2).

What is the nature of this "likeness"? It might be tempting to construe it entirely in terms of personal traits: that those who are sanctified exemplify the Christian virtues, are devoid of any vices, submit to God in perfect obedience, etc. But according to the doctrine of theosis, being formed into the image of Christ is more than this. One of the best glimpses of the final state of the blessed is suggested in the account of the transfiguration, in which Christ's glory is prefigured (Luke 9:28–36). The contrast between the living witnesses (Peter, James, and John) and the deceased (Moses and Elijah) is important. The disciples are overwhelmed and dismayed by the experience, unable to fully behold Christ revealed in his glory, but Moses and Elijah converse with the Lord, face to face. The passage from 1 John, above, offers a clue as to why the disciples experience the transfiguration so differently from the prophets. The word "because" is especially noteworthy: "when he appears we shall be like him, *because* we shall see him as he is." The state of being "like" Christ ("being changed into his likeness," as Paul puts it) is inseparable from the state of "see[ing] him as he is" ("with unveiled face, beholding the glory of the Lord," as Paul puts it). The prophets, but not (yet) the disciples, have been changed into the likeness of Christ, and accordingly are able to behold the Lord in truth.

In the new creation, when Christ is fully revealed, all of the blessed will be like Moses and Elijah in this respect: having been sanctified and perfected in holiness, they will manifest the image of God purely and without distortion; having been formed into the image of Christ, the blessed will behold the Lord in truth and—like Moses after his descent from Mt. Sinai—they will reflect his glory.[13] This is why, as Paul puts it, "[w]hen

---

12. Galatians 3:27 and 4:19.

13. This is one explanation of why the saints are depicted with halos—a glowing

Christ, who is our life, is revealed, then you also will be revealed with Him in glory" (Colossians 3:4 NASB).[14] Christ will "present her [the church] to himself as a radiant church, without stain or wrinkle or any other blemish, but holy and blameless" (Ephesians 5:27). At this point, the words of Jesus will be fulfilled: "the righteous will shine like the sun in the kingdom of their Father" (Matthew 13:43).

This is at least part of what it means that Christ is *the way* of salvation: by being "yoked" to him and "abiding" in him, believers are gradually—in a process that begins in this life and comes to completion in the next—"changed into his likeness."[15] By opening their hearts to the work of God within them, believers come to a knowledge of the truth of God's glory; this increasing knowledge of His glory is, in turn, a part of what forms them into the likeness of the Son.[16] As Paul states elsewhere, "For God, who said, 'Let light shine out of darkness,' made his light shine in our hearts to give us the light of the knowledge of God's glory displayed in the face of Christ" (2 Corinthians 4:6). The process that begins with conviction and turning to God in repentance, followed by the Lord's removing the veil of one's heart, ends in the state of eternal communion with God for which all humans are created: a beholding and reflecting of the divine glory by which the blessed participate in the life of God.

## The second unveiling: beholding "the face of God"

We've seen that the process of salvation requires an "unveiling" of a person's heart toward God in response to the conviction of the Holy Spirit. The alternative response that a person can take is to harden their heart—something Scripture repeatedly warns against. We'll now consider what the Bible says about those who refuse to heed this warning: those who persist in their rebellion, refusing to allow the Lord to circumcise their heart, so that the veil of their heart remains all the way up to the day of judgment.

---

light surrounding their heads, or in some cases even their entire bodies—in traditional Christian art and iconography.

14. Elsewhere, this shared/reflected glory is referred to as a "crown of righteousness" by Paul: "Henceforth there is laid up for me the crown of righteousness, which the Lord, the righteous judge, will award to me on that day, and not only to me but also *to all who have loved his appearing*" (2 Timothy 4:8 ESV).

15. John 14:6; Matthew 11:29–30; John 15:4; 2 Corinthians 3:18 (RSV). The reasons that this process must be gradual were discussed in chapter 17.

16. Recall, from chapter 17, that knowledge of God and spiritual transformation are connected, on the divine presence model.

The following words of the prophet Jeremiah, warning of the consequences of failing to heed the Lord's command to undergo the circumcision of the heart, offer a clue as to the fate of such individuals:

> "Circumcise yourselves to the LORD;
> *remove the foreskin of your hearts,*
> O men of Judah and inhabitants of Jerusalem;
> *lest my wrath go forth like fire,*
> and burn with none to quench it,
> because of the evil of your deeds." (Jeremiah 4:4 ESV)

The prophet Malachi gives a similar warning:

> "For behold, *the day is coming, burning like an oven*, when all the arrogant and all evildoers will be stubble. *The day that is coming shall set them ablaze*, says the LORD of hosts, so that it will leave them neither root nor branch. But for you who fear my name, the sun of righteousness shall rise with healing in its wings." (Malachi 4:1–2 ESV)

And from the prophet Isaiah:

> "Now I will arise," says the LORD,
> "*Now I will be exalted, now I will be lifted up.*
> You have conceived chaff, you will give birth to stubble;
> *My breath* [lit. spirit] *will consume you like a fire.*
> The peoples will be burned to lime,
> Like cut thorns which are burned in the fire." . . .
>
> Sinners in Zion are terrified;
> Trembling has seized the godless.
> "*Who among us can live with the consuming fire?*
> *Who among us can live with continual burning?*"
> (Isaiah 33:10–12, 14 NASB)

For those accustomed to thinking of divine wrath in volitional terms, these passages are read as the Lord's issuing threats. But the divine presence model suggests a different reading: these are warnings about the *natural* end of those who persist in evil. Such individuals are woefully unprepared for the encounter with the Lord on the day of judgment. Rather than "reflecting" his glory—the end for which they were made, and the end which God intends for them—their persistence in evil will result instead in their being "burned" by the glory of the Lord. For the wicked, exposure to God's presence is an experience of divine wrath, a "fire" that cannot be quenched. It is not a separate, divine act by which the unrighteous are punished; it is, rather, "the day that is coming" that "shall set them ablaze": that is, the very experience of being raised to life into the presence of the Lord, unveiled in glory.

On the divine presence model, this experience of the damned is understood in terms of beholding "the face of Christ." This is the very experience that is a source of blessedness to the saints; recall Paul's words that God has "made his light shine in our hearts to give us the light of the knowledge of God's glory *displayed in the face of Christ*" (2 Corinthians 4:6). But in the age to come, when, as Thomas Hopko puts it, "God's glorious love is revealed for *all* to behold in the face of Christ," some will experience the event as judgment.[17]

The idea of beholding the face of God is a prominent theme in the Bible, and worth careful consideration. Typically, it's an idea associated with blessing. The phrase is sometimes used to refer to the presence of God and communion with Him, including knowledge of His will; servants of the Lord are instructed to "seek his face always."[18] In the Old Testament, the Lord is said to "hide his face" from the wicked, and even from His own people as a punishment for disobedience.[19] Petitions for divine blessing regularly are put in terms of a request that the Lord cause His face to "shine upon" His people.[20] In the New Testament, Jesus remarks that there are angels who "always see the face of my Father in heaven" (Matthew 18:10), and the Apostle Paul instructs the believers at Corinth that in the age to come they will see God "face to face" (1 Corinthians 13:12)—traditionally understood to be a reference to the beatific vision.[21] Beholding the face of Christ is constitutive of the blessedness of heaven. The closing chapter of Revelation describes a return to paradise in which the servants of the Lamb "will see his face, and his name will be on their foreheads" (Revelation 22:4).

There are, however, other passages, initially more perplexing, in which the face of God is associated not with blessing, but rather with

---

17. Hopko, *The Orthodox Faith*, 196, italics added. The longer passage from which this line is taken was quoted in chapter 9.

18. 2 Samuel 21:1; 1 Chronicles 16:11; Psalm 119:135. A comparison of various translations of 1 Chronicles 16:11 is instructive: "Look to the Lord and his strength; seek his face always" (NIV); "Seek the Lord and his strength; seek his presence continually" (ESV). Isaiah 63:9 refers to "the angel of his presence," who saved the ancient Israelites in their distress (NIV). The Hebrew phrase can also be translated "the Angel of his face" (JUB).

19. See Deuteronomy 31:17–18; Ezekiel 39:23–29; Jeremiah 33:5; Psalms 13:1; 44:24; 88:14; Micah 3:4.

20. Numbers 6:25–26 (ESV); see also Psalms 4:6; 31:16; 67:1; 80:19; and 105:4.

21. See, for example, *Catechism of the Catholic Church*, 2nd ed., 163.

destruction or judgment. We previously noted the passage in which the Lord instructs Moses, "you cannot see my face, for no one may see me and live" (Exodus 33:20). In a different vein, the Psalmist declares that "the face of the LORD is against those who do evil"—divine wrath repeatedly is expressed in the Old Testament in these terms—and the same teaching is repeated in the New Testament.[22] In the account of the opening of the seven seals in Revelation, those still alive in the wake of the opening of the sixth seal are described as hiding in caves and crying out to the rocks and mountains, "Fall on us and hide us from the face of him who sits on the throne and from the wrath of the Lamb!" (Revelation 6:16).[23] On the divine presence model, these references to the face of God as experiences of both blessing and judgment are readily explained; in fact, they're central to the model's core claim that heaven and hell are the various ways that the righteous and the wicked experience the presence of God.

In the New Testament, the idea is presented in more explicitly Christological terms. We noted in chapter 9 that the *parousia*—literally, the arrival or appearing—is the event in which Jesus is revealed in all his glory, the event that inaugurates the final judgment, and that the Greek word "apocalypse," often translated as "revelation," has as its literal meaning "an unveiling." The theme of unveiling is one that we've already encountered, in Paul's discussion of the removing of the veil of the heart: a part of the process of salvation. But in his second letter to the church at Thessalonica, Paul discusses a very different kind of unveiling—the unveiling of Christ in glory—and he suggests that this event is identical to the consignment of the wicked to hell. The "righteous judgment of God" is coming, he tells the persecuted Thessalonians, a time when God will "repay with affliction those who afflict you . . . *when the Lord Jesus is revealed from heaven* with his mighty angels *in flaming fire*, inflicting vengeance on those who do not know God and on those who do not obey the gospel of our Lord Jesus" (2 Thessalonians 1:5–8 ESV).

Paul follows this statement with one of the most remarkable teachings on judgment in all of the New Testament, but it's one that's rendered very differently in various translations. In some, it's suggested that the damned will suffer the punishment of *exclusion* from the divine presence. Here's the passage in three of the most popular English translations:

> They will suffer the punishment of eternal destruction, *away from the presence of the Lord* and from the glory of his might, when he comes on that day to be glorified in his saints, and to

---

22. Psalm 34:16. Cf. Leviticus 17:10; 20:3; 26:17; Ezekiel 14:8; 15:7; 1 Peter 3:12.
23. Compare Isaiah 2:10–11, 19.

be marveled at among all who have believed, because our testimony to you was believed. (2 Thessalonians 1:9–10 ESV)

They shall suffer the punishment of eternal destruction and *exclusion from the presence of the Lord* and from the glory of his might.... (RSV)

They will be punished with everlasting destruction and *shut out from the presence of the Lord* and from the glory of his might.... (NIV)

In the English Standard Version, however, the phrase "away from" in verse 9 has a footnote attached to it which reads, "Or *destruction that comes from* . . . ," indicating an alternate interpretation of the Greek term (*apo*) that's used at this point. Substituting this interpretation, the verse reads, "They will suffer *the punishment of eternal destruction that comes from the presence of the Lord* and from the glory of his might." This rendering of the passage is found in several translations, including the New King James Version: "These shall be punished with everlasting destruction from the presence of the Lord and from the glory of His power." The translation in both the American Standard Version and the English Revised Version likewise lacks any connotation of separation from God; the eternal destruction is said to be "from the face of the Lord."[24]

There's very good reason to think that these latter ways of translating the passage are more accurate.[25] It's true that the Greek term *apo* can sometimes mean "away from." We previously cited one such verse, in Revelation: "Fall on us and hide us *from* the face of him who sits on the throne and *from* the wrath of the Lamb!" (Revelation 6:16). Another such verse is found in Isaiah: "Go into the rocks, hide in the ground *from* the fearful presence of the Lord and the splendor of his majesty!" (Isaiah 2:10). But whether or not *apo* has this connotation is determined by the context. In this regard, it's like the English word "from." There are some contexts in which "from" carries the implied meaning "away from," but there are other contexts in which it means "caused by." (Consider a sentence like, "The scar on his face is from a car accident.") The same is true of *apo*. The question, then, is which of these meanings is intended by the usage of this Greek term in 2 Thessalonians 1:9. Is the verse describing a punishment that's suffered *away from* the presence of God, or a punishment that is *caused by* the presence of God?

---

24. The verse reads: "who shall suffer punishment, even *eternal destruction from the face of the Lord* and from the glory of his might."

25. The argument that follows is developed by Thomas Talbott in *The Inescapable Love of God*, 89–90.

The best way to decide the matter is to compare this verse with other verses in the Bible that have a similar grammatical structure. The verses where *apo* is reasonably translated "away from" are those in which it modifies a verb that gives it this meaning: a verb like "hide" (as in the verses just mentioned). But there's no such verb in 2 Thessalonians 1:9. Moreover, the wording of the key phrase in this verse is identical to the one used in Acts 3:19: "Repent therefore, and turn again, that your sins may be blotted out, that times of refreshing may come *from the presence of the Lord*" (RSV).[26] Obviously, the verse isn't claiming that times of refreshing occur *away from* the presence of the Lord, and no respectable translation of the Bible renders the passage this way. Why, then, should the exact same phrase be translated in an entirely different way when it occurs in 2 Thessalonians 1:9? Clearly, it shouldn't. The best interpretations of the verse are those that make it clear that the destruction is one that's *effected by* the presence of the Lord. Thus translated, 2 Thessalonians 1:9 provides significant biblical support for the divine presence model.

It's crucial to notice that the punishment described in this passage is neither artificial nor arbitrary, contrary to the way that hell is understood in traditionalism. Nor is it a punishment of separation or self-exile, as hell is understood to be in the choice model. Rather, destruction comes from the experience of being in the presence of Christ, fully revealed in glory. Jesus' unveiling/appearing in glory *is* the punishment of the wicked. As Paul writes elsewhere, "the aroma of Christ" is, for some people, "an aroma that brings death" (2 Corinthians 2:15–16a).[27]

Putting these passages together, what we find in Paul's letters is a picture of two unveilings: the first taking place in this life, an event initiated by an individual act of human free will in response to the conviction of the Holy Spirit; the second taking place at the end of the age, an event brought about by an act of God without regard to human consent. The former is an unveiling of an individual's heart, an act in which a person voluntarily exposes themselves to the divine presence in this life, opening their heart to the Lord and allowing Him to begin the process of inner transformation and deliverance from the bondage of sin. The latter is the unveiling of Christ in glory, an experience that everyone will share, but which only those who have been born of the Spirit will be able to experience as God intends. For all others, it's an experience of wrath, an experience of "burning," an event that causes unrepentant sinners to suffer intensely, without end or relief.

26. In some translations, the key phrase occurs in verse 3:20 rather than 3:19.

27. The passage reads: "For we are to God the pleasing aroma of Christ among those who are being saved and those who are perishing. To the one we are an aroma that brings death; to the other, an aroma that brings life."

## Chapter 19
# The third unveiling (the judgment of transparency)

IN OUR INITIAL DEVELOPMENT of the divine presence model in chapters 9–10, we discussed the idea that the presence of God is *truth-revealing*. We noted that this idea goes beyond the core claim of the divine presence model, but we found it to be one that naturally fits with the core idea and expands the model in fruitful ways. The more important reason to accept this idea, however, is that it's a thoroughly biblical one. It's now time to explore this in more detail. As we'll see, the idea of a *judgment of transparency* that we introduced in chapter 10 is connected to the theme of unveiling that we discussed in the previous chapter. The judgment of transparency is a third type of unveiling that's closely connected to, but crucially different from, the first type. We'll begin to develop the biblical case for this idea by exploring the New Testament descriptions of Jesus' encounters with the scribes and Pharisees of his day.

### Jesus and the Pharisees

It's a fascinating feature of the Gospel narratives that Jesus' words and presence elicit such widely different reactions from those who encounter him. At one end of the spectrum are the "sinners" who are drawn to Jesus and whose encounters with him lead to repentance and even radical conversion. At the other extreme end are those who self-identify as "righteous," who are offended at Jesus, and whose encounters with him elicit indignation and even murderous rage.[1] The Gospels make it clear that those in the latter category—usually identified as "scribes and Pharisees"—are in fact every bit as sinful as the ones they condemn, and even more so. The crucial distinction between the two groups lies in the relationship that the members of each have to their own sin. When *confronted* with their sins, those in the former group are willing to acknowledge the truth about themselves, while those in the latter group are not. The former—if they're willing to go on to *repent* of their sins—experience God's forgiveness in Christ, eliciting from them expressions of gratitude and faith. The latter see themselves as having no need for spiritual regeneration or forgiveness in any deep sense—they are, after all, the "righteous" ones—so they take offense at Jesus.

This is the reaction of many of the Pharisees, who prefer to see themselves as righteous, favored by God, and morally and spiritually superior in every way to those who fail to keep the Mosaic law. A call to repentance is offensive to those who consider themselves righteous, and an offer of forgiveness is likewise offensive to those who believe they have nothing to be forgiven. But the offensiveness of Jesus to the Pharisees goes beyond this. What's most offensive about Jesus to the Pharisees is the way that he *exposes* them: their hypocrisy, their twisted and self-serving interpretations of the law, their wielding of the sacred for political gain. Insofar as a person is self-deceived about their own virtue, they will naturally feel resentment toward someone whom they recognize, on some level, to be superior to them. The Pharisees are offended by the very presence of Jesus, because the presence of such a genuinely righteous and loving person confronts them with the truth about their own moral status; it threatens to expose the lie.

*Offense*, in the biblical sense, is the reaction of those who seek to suppress the truth—in particular, the truth about themselves in relation to God. Paul describes such individuals in the opening chapter of his epistle to the Romans:

> The wrath of God is being revealed from heaven against all the godlessness and wickedness of people, *who suppress the truth by their wickedness, since what may be known about God is plain to them, because God has made it plain to them.* . . . For although

---

1. A third type of encounter that's relevant to the discussion of the divine presence model, but which we won't pursue here, are those occasions in which Jesus confronts evil spirits. The reaction of the two demon-possessed men "coming from the tombs" in a region near Gadarenes is instructive: "'What do you want with us, Son of God?' they shouted. 'Have you come here to torture us before the appointed time?'" (Matthew 8:29). The reaction of the demons to Jesus is understandable on the divine presence model: the presence of God is experienced as torment to the degree that a creature is given over to evil, and the uppermost limit of creaturely evil is the demonic.

> they knew God, they neither glorified him as God nor gave thanks to him, but *their thinking became futile and their foolish hearts were darkened.* . . . Therefore God gave them over in the sinful desires of their hearts. . . . They exchanged the truth about God for a lie. . . . Furthermore, just as they did not think it worthwhile to retain the knowledge of God, so *God gave them over to a depraved mind,* so that they do what ought not to be done. (Romans 1:18–28)

This passage gives a clear warning about the consequences of self-deception: those who "suppress the truth by their wickedness," even when the truth is "plain to them, because God has made it plain to them," become "darkened" in their hearts and "futile" in their thinking, until eventually, God *gives them over* to a "depraved mind." The language of "giving over" indicates that these are *natural* consequences of persistence in sin, a matter of reaping what one has sown. In giving oneself over to sin, and especially to self-deception, one eventually becomes unable to recognize or receive the truth, even when it's presented to one clearly. Jesus accuses his opponents of such when he says to them,

> "Why is my language not clear to you? Because you are unable to hear what I say. You belong to your father, the devil, and you want to carry out your father's desires. He was a murderer from the beginning, not holding to the truth, for there is no truth in him. When he lies, he speaks his native language, for he is a liar and the father of lies. . . . Whoever belongs to God hears what God says. *The reason you do not hear is that you do not belong to God.*" (John 8:43–47)

The last claim is especially important for our discussion: the *reason* certain people don't "hear"—that is, receive the truth about themselves when it's revealed to them by God—is that they don't "belong to God." This is the biblical expression of the idea that we discussed in chapters 13 and 17: that a person's ability to perceive moral and spiritual truth is a function of their character. Jesus says to Pilate, "For this purpose I was born and for this purpose I have come into the world—to bear witness to the truth. Everyone who is of the truth listens to my voice" (John 18:37). *All* who truly desire to know the truth will find it ("For everyone who asks receives, and the one who seeks finds, and to the one who knocks it will be opened" [Matthew 7:8]), and *only* those who truly desire to know the truth will find it. As long as a person's heart remains "veiled" or "uncircumcised," they are unable to receive the truth about themselves, because their hearts are hardened to it. As Paul puts it, "They are darkened in their understanding, alienated from the life of God because of the ignorance that is in them, due to their hardness of heart" (Ephesians 4:18).[2] When such a mind is *forcibly* exposed to the light of Truth—not through an act of repentance, but in a way that's against the individual's will—it elicits a response of offense and further entrenchment in self-deception.

This raises an important question: What would be the experience of such a person if they were exposed to the light of Truth *in full*, all at once, and in a way that was inescapable?

## Light and darkness

The answer to this question is found in one the most pervasive themes in Scripture: the contrast of light and darkness. It's an especially prominent motif in the gospel and epistles of John: "This is the message we have heard from him and declare to you: *God is light*; in him there is no darkness at all" (1 John 1:5). In his gospel, John describes Jesus as "[t]he true light that gives light to everyone," the light that "shines in the darkness."[3] These descriptions point to Christ's revelatory role: he is the *Logos* ("Word"), the living revelation of God to humankind; he is the embodiment of truth, the Truth incarnate ("The Word became flesh and made his dwelling among us" [John 1:14]). At the end of the age, Jesus is the light that shines in the New Jerusalem without ceasing: "The city does not need the sun or the moon to shine on it, for the glory of God gives it light, and the Lamb is its lamp. . . . On no day will its gates ever be shut, for there will be no night there" (Revelation 21:23–25).

The decision of how to relate to this light is the defining one of each person's life. Many who are in darkness avoid it; it's loathsome to the wicked because of the way that it exposes them:

> This is the verdict: Light has come into the world, but people loved darkness instead of light because their deeds were evil. Everyone who does evil hates the light, and will not come into the light for fear that their deeds will be exposed. But whoever lives by the truth comes into the light, so that it may be seen plainly that what they have done has been done in the sight of God. (John 3:19–21)

---

2. Paul writes this of "the gentiles," exhorting those at the church at Ephesus not to follow them "in the futility of their minds" (Ephesians 4:17).

3. John 1:9 and 1:5, respectively.

Paul instructs the believers at the church of Ephesus to have nothing to do with darkness, now that they've been delivered from it, and to seek to expose it:

> For you were once darkness, but now you are light in the Lord. Live as children of light.... Have nothing to do with the fruitless deeds of darkness, but rather expose them. It is shameful even to mention what the disobedient do in secret. But everything exposed by the light becomes visible—and everything that is illuminated becomes a light. This is why it is said:
>
> "Wake up, sleeper,
>    rise from the dead,
>    and Christ will shine on you." (Ephesians 5:8–14)

Those who are in Christ are filled with his light; indeed, Paul says that believers *are* light ("now you are light in the Lord"). Having themselves been "exposed by the light" which made the truth about them "visible," and having *received* this truth about themselves, however ugly or shameful, rather than suppressing it in self-denial, believers are "illuminated." But "everything that is illuminated becomes a light"—that is, having been filled with the light of Christ, believers now reflect this light to the world around them. This is the reason Jesus warns his disciples that the world will hate them and reject them, as it rejected him: because the light that shines within them is convicting to those who remain in darkness.

The theme of light and darkness is thus connected to another theme that's pervasive in Scripture: the theme of *disclosure*—in particular, that the secrets of the heart will be disclosed on the day of judgment. We find this teaching throughout the Old Testament: for example, in the closing of the book of Ecclesiastes ("For God will bring every deed into judgment, *including every hidden thing*, whether it is good or evil"); in the prayer of Psalm 90, traditionally ascribed to Moses ("You have set our iniquities before you, *our secret sins in the light of your presence*"); as well as in the book of Job ("He *reveals the deep things of darkness* and brings utter darkness into the light").[4] It is reiterated throughout the New Testament:

> Nothing in all creation is hidden from God's sight. *Everything is uncovered and laid bare* before the eyes of him to whom we must give account. (Hebrews 4:13)

---

4. Ecclesiastes 12:13–14; Psalm 90:8; Job 12:22. The phrase "utter darkness" in Job 12:22 is rendered "the shadow of death" in some translations.

> But the day of the Lord will come like a thief. The heavens will disappear with a roar; the elements will be destroyed by fire, and *the earth and everything done in it will be laid bare.* (2 Peter 3:10–12)

> Therefore do not pronounce judgment before the time, before the Lord comes, *who will bring to light the things now hidden in darkness and will disclose the purposes of the heart.* Then each one will receive his commendation from God. (1 Corinthians 4:5 ESV)

It's especially prominent in the teachings of Jesus:

> "For *there is nothing hidden that will not be disclosed, and nothing concealed that will not be known or brought out into the open.*" (Luke 8:17)

> "Be on your guard against the yeast of the Pharisees, which is hypocrisy. *There is nothing concealed that will not be disclosed, or hidden that will not be made known.* What you have said in the dark will be heard in the daylight, and what you have whispered in the ear in the inner rooms will be proclaimed from the roofs." (Luke 12:1–3)

Notably, Jesus immediately follows up the latter comment with a warning about hell:

> "I tell you, my friends, do not be afraid of those who kill the body and after that can do no more. But I will show you whom you should fear: Fear him who, after your body has been killed, has authority to throw you into hell. Yes, I tell you, fear him." (Luke 12:4–5)

It's clear from these passages that the disclosure motif is connected to judgment. And both are connected to the theme of light and darkness. The divine presence model brings all of these together: on the day of judgment, all are resurrected into the presence of the Lord, whose glory at his return is a radiant light that penetrates the darkness of each person's heart, exposing it for all to see. Whereas this life affords each person a choice between remaining in the darkness or coming into the light, there's no escaping the light in eternity. At the resurrection, when Christ is revealed in glory, his light will shine on both the righteous and the wicked ("Wake up, sleeper, rise from the dead, and Christ will shine on you").[5] The presence of God,

---

5. I take it that, in context, this quotation from Ephesians 5:14 has as its primary meaning the exhortation to accept the gospel: to "wake up" to the reality of sin in one's

who is light, reveals the deepest truths about every person. Every soul is laid bare before Christ, and the secrets of every heart thereby disclosed.[6] On the divine presence model, the central event of Revelation, the apocalypse, is thus a double reveal: the revealing ("unveiling") of Christ in glory, accompanied by the revealing of every hidden truth about every person. This is the final judgment: a judgment of transparency.

For those who've remained in their sins through persistence in self-deception and hardness of heart, the experience is bitter. Because these individuals were never transparent to themselves, the transparency that is now forced upon them results in "weeping and gnashing of teeth," a phrase that, as we previously noted, is used repeatedly by Jesus to describe hell. The opening chapter of Revelation connects this weeping with the event of peoples' beholding Christ at the second coming: "Behold, he is coming with the clouds, and every eye will see him, even those who pierced him, and all tribes of the earth will wail on account of him. Even so. Amen" (Revelation 1:7 ESV).[7] The experience of "beholding the face of Christ" results in tormenting shame for the unrighteous, because his presence reveals—and forces them to confront—the shameful truth about themselves.[8]

To those who haven't thought carefully about the nature of self-deception, it might seem that this forced transparency would cause sinners to finally accept the truth about themselves. Unfortunately, this isn't the case. To those whose hearts are hardened, a clearer revelation of the truth only leads to deeper entrenchment in self-deception.[9] Thus Jesus teaches, in the Sermon on the Mount,

---

life and to be delivered from its bondage through faith in Christ. In referencing the quotation here, I'm suggesting that in addition to its primary meaning it could also have a second meaning: one that applies to the day of judgment.

6. Compare *Catechism of the Catholic Church*, 2nd ed., 1039: "In the presence of Christ, who is Truth itself, the truth of each man's relationship with God will be laid bare. The Last Judgment will reveal even to its furthest consequences the good each person has done or failed to do during his earthly life."

7. Compare Zechariah 12:10.

8. Recall the prophesy of Daniel concerning the day of judgment: "Multitudes who sleep in the dust of the earth will awake: some to everlasting life, *others to shame and everlasting contempt*" (Daniel 12:2).

9. Jesus seems to cite this as one of the reasons he often teaches in parables. He tells his disciples,

> "This is why I speak to them in parables, because seeing they do not see, and hearing they do not hear, nor do they understand. Indeed, in their case the prophecy of Isaiah is fulfilled that says:
>
> 'You will indeed hear but never understand,
>     and you will indeed see but never perceive.

> "The eye is the lamp of the body. If your eyes are healthy, your whole body will be full of light. But if your eyes are unhealthy, your whole body will be full of darkness. If then the light within you is darkness, how great is that darkness!" (Matthew 6:22–23)

The "eyes" are a metaphor of moral and spiritual perception. Those who perceive themselves truthfully—those who are transparent to themselves—thereby open themselves up to the inner working of the Holy Spirit; they are filled with God's light. This, in turn, allows them to see Christ as he truly is, and (gradually) to be formed into his image, enabling them to reflect his glory and to "worship in the Spirit and in truth" (John 4:24). But those who harden their hearts to the inner conviction of the Spirit, deceiving themselves about their need for forgiveness and healing, remain in darkness. The experience of being forcibly exposed to the light on the day of judgment does not bring these individuals to repentance. Rather than illuminating the damned, the light of Christ serves only to blind them; rather than melting or "burning" their hearts,[10] it inflames their pride, setting them ablaze in self-righteous, self-deceived defensiveness. The experience of being in God's presence in a state of hardness of heart and spiritual blindness is thus an experience of great darkness. It is, for the damned, the greatest possible darkness: "the outer darkness," where shame ("weeping") and gnawing guilt ("their worm") is intermixed with anger, hatred, and resentment ("gnashing of teeth") toward God and those who reflect His light.[11]

> For this people's heart has grown dull,
>   and with their ears they can barely hear,
>   and their eyes they have closed,
> lest they should see with their eyes
>   and hear with their ears
> and understand with their heart
>   and turn, and I would heal them.'
> But blessed are your eyes, for they see, and your ears, for they hear."
> (Matthew 13:13–16 ESV)

The disciples' "eyes" are blessed, because they "see" (understand) the truth, and their "ears" are blessed, because they "hear" (receive) it. But those whose hearts are "dull"—those who have hardened their hearts—"never perceive," even when the truth is shown to them plainly. Jesus knows that presenting the truth plainly to such individuals would only result in their deeper entrenchment in self-deception—and thus even greater guilt. On this point, see also John 9:39–41.

10. This language is used in Luke's Gospel to describe an experience of illumination in the presence of God: following their encounter with the risen Christ on the road to Emmaus, two disciples "asked each other, 'Were not our hearts burning within us while he talked with us on the road and opened the Scriptures to us?'" (Luke 24:32).

11. See Matthew 8:12; Mark 9:48 ESV.

## Puzzling passages about Christ as judge

We've seen the way that the divine presence model elucidates the themes of *unveiling* and *revelation*, in their complex layers of meaning, which we find developed throughout Scripture. We'll now explore a further, significant advantage of this part of the model: namely, its capability of explaining a set of teachings about judgment in the New Testament that are otherwise very puzzling and even appear to be self-contradictory. In this section, we'll consider the most important of these passages and the way that the divine presence model can reconcile them.

The texts to be considered involve a set of claims concerning Jesus' relationship to judgment. These texts are scattered throughout the New Testament, but a number of the most prominent passages—that is, places where the "contradiction" seems most apparent—are found in the Gospel of John. On the one hand, several passages declare about Jesus (or record him as declaring about himself) that he has *not* come to judge:

> For God did not send his Son into the world to condemn the world, but to save the world through him. (John 3:17)[12]

> "If anyone hears my words but does not keep them, I do not judge that person. For I did not come to judge the world, but to save the world. There is a judge for the one who rejects me and does not accept my words; the very words I have spoken will condemn them at the last day." (John 12:47–48)

But many other passages seem to declare just the opposite:

> Jesus said, "For judgment I have come into this world, so that the blind will see and those who see will become blind." (John 9:39)

> "When the Son of Man comes in his glory and all his angels are with him, he will sit on his glorious throne. The people of every nation will be gathered in front of him. He will separate them as a shepherd separates the sheep from the goats." (Matthew 25:31–32)

> For we must all appear before the judgment seat of Christ, so that each of us may receive what is due us for the things done while in the body, whether good or bad. (2 Corinthians 5:10)[13]

---

12. It's unclear whether this verse should be interpreted as a quotation from Jesus. In some translations, the quotation ends at the previous verse; in others, it continues through verse 21.

13. Compare Matthew 16:27.

> For [God] has set a day when he will judge the world with justice by the man he has appointed. He has given proof of this to everyone by raising him from the dead. (Acts 17:31)
>
> And he commanded us to preach to the people and to testify that he is the one appointed by God to be judge of the living and the dead. (Acts 10:42)[14]
>
> I saw heaven standing open and there before me was a white horse, whose rider is called Faithful and True. With justice he judges and wages war . . . and his name is the Word of God. (Revelation 19:11–13)

In still other passages, Jesus seems to affirm about himself both that he does and does not judge—and in nearly the same breath:

> "You judge according to the flesh; I judge no one. Yet even if I do judge, my judgment is true, for it is not I alone who judge, but I and the Father who sent me." (John 8:15–16 ESV)
>
> "Moreover, the Father judges no one, but has entrusted all judgment to the Son. . . . And he has given him authority to judge because he is the Son of Man. . . . By myself I can do nothing; I judge only as I hear, and my judgment is just, for I seek not to please myself but him who sent me. . . . But do not think I will accuse you before the Father. Your accuser is Moses, on whom your hopes are set." (John 5:22, 27, 30, 45)

On the face of it, these passages seem to present a host of contradictory claims: Christ has *and* has not come to judge; he will *and* will not pass judgment, etc. But when these passages are read in the context of the divine presence model, in which the final judgment is a matter of *unveiling* the moral and spiritual truth about each person—holding each person's conscience up to the light of eternity to reveal its contents, so to speak—the various claims fit together to form a coherent picture. The judgment that's rendered by Christ is not like that of an earthly judge, who freely renders a verdict and decides upon a punishment to which the condemned will be sentenced. Christ's judgment is not a *decision* about a person's guilt or innocence; it's not something that's *made true* by declaration. As we discussed in chapter 10, the final judgment is a pronouncement of the existing truth about each individual ("I judge only as I hear"). It's a revealing of what is already the case, as recorded in a person's own conscience. This is why, to the Pharisees, whose understanding of right/wrong is that of upholding/failing to uphold

---

14. See also 2 Timothy 4:1.

the Mosaic law, Jesus declares, "Your accuser is Moses." For gentiles who don't know this law, the accuser is instead "the law . . . written on their hearts, their consciences also bearing witness" (Romans 2:15).

So in the ordinary, legal sense, with which we're all familiar, Christ does not judge. And yet, his presence is a judgment: the judgment of transparency, as we've called it. It's a punishment to the wicked for the truth about themselves to be disclosed. The truth hurts. The full revelation of the truth about those who are damned is so foul, in fact, that it's "loathsome" for others to behold. The prophet Isaiah reports in his vision of the apocalypse: "And they will go out and look on the dead bodies of those who rebelled against me; the worms that eat them will not die, the fire that burns them will not be quenched, and they will be loathsome to all mankind" (Isaiah 66:24). This is the fate of those who are never "made . . . alive with Christ": they are eternally "dead in transgressions" (Ephesians 2:5). What "slays" them, however, is *the word of God*—the truth. As Isaiah puts it elsewhere, "He will strike the earth with the rod of his mouth; with the breath of his lips he will slay the wicked" (Isaiah 11:4).[15] This is the reason Jesus is depicted throughout Revelation as having a sword coming out of his mouth.[16] The image of the word of God as a sword is not limited to apocalyptic literature; Paul identifies "the sword of the Spirit" as "the word of God" (Ephesians 6:17). The author of Hebrews elaborates on the same idea, explicitly connecting it to the theme of judgment as disclosure:

> For the word of God is alive and active. Sharper than any double-edged sword, it penetrates even to dividing soul and spirit, joints and marrow; it judges the thoughts and attitudes of the heart. Nothing in all creation is hidden from God's sight. Everything is uncovered and laid bare before the eyes of him to whom we must give account. (Hebrews 4:12–13)

So now we can see why Christ declares that he "did not come to judge the world, but to save the world," and yet, "[t]here is a judge for the one

---

15. Likewise, Paul states that the same fate awaits "the man of lawlessness" whose rebellion will precede the day of the Lord: "Then that lawless one will be revealed whom the Lord will slay with the breath of His mouth and bring to an end by the appearance of His coming" (2 Thessalonians 2:8 NASB). The final phrase can also be translated "the manifestation of his presence" (see YLT and footnote on the ASV translation).

16. Revelation 1:16; 2:16; 19:16, 21. Compare Isaiah 30:27:

> See, the Name of the LORD comes from afar,
>     with burning anger and dense clouds of smoke;
>   his lips are full of wrath,
>     and *his tongue is a consuming fire.*

who rejects me and does not accept my words; the very words I have spoken will condemn them at the last day." In the light of Christ's presence, "[e]verything is uncovered and laid bare," and it's "the word of God" that "judges the thoughts and attitudes of the heart"—that is, all are judged by their understanding of God's requirements, according to the records of their consciences.[17] Christ is the Truth, whose very presence to the wicked is eternal punishment, destruction, and judgment.

There's a further sense in which Christ does not come to judge, however: it is not his desire or intention to consign anyone to the punishment of eternal judgment on the last day. As already noted, God's intention for everyone is forgiveness, healing, and reconciliation; God does everything in His power to prevent anyone's arriving at the judgment seat of Christ still an unredeemed sinner. "For God did not send his Son into the world to condemn the world, but to save the world through him." And yet, "we must all appear before the Messiah's court of judgment, where everyone will receive the good or bad consequences of what he did while he was in the body" (2 Corinthians 5:10 CJB).[18] The judgment seat of Christ is his throne ("When the Son of Man comes in his glory and all his angels are with him, he will sit on his glorious throne"); his very presence there will "separate" the righteous from the wicked "as a shepherd separates the sheep from the goats." His word "penetrates even to dividing soul and spirit, joints and marrow." The "light of the world"—and the "light of life" to those who reflect it[19]—will "separate the light from the darkness" at the end of the age, as he did at the beginning.[20]

---

17. The judgment is both just and fitting, as it was the decision of Adam and Eve to partake of the fruit of *the tree of knowledge* that initiated the fall. The very thing obtained illicitly—the knowledge of good and evil—is that which judges mankind at the end of the age. The doctrines of original sin and final judgment are thus linked in a particularly strong way in the divine presence model.

18. The NIV renders this verse "*so that* each of us may receive what is due us"—similar to many other translations—which seems to imply an *intention* to pay back harm to evildoers at the final judgment. But many other translations, along with the CJB, do not carry this connotation: see, for example, the CEV, ERV, GNT, GW, MSG, NCV, NIRV, NLT, NLV, and NOG. In this particular verse, the divine presence model is most supported by the translation of The Living Bible (TLB): "For we must all stand before Christ to be judged *and have our lives laid bare—before him*. Each of us *will receive* whatever he deserves for the good or bad things he has done in his earthly body."

19. "I am the light of the world. Whoever follows me will never walk in darkness, but will have the light of life" (John 8:12).

20. In the opening passage of Genesis, the earth is described initially as being "formless and empty," with "darkness ... over the surface of the deep" (Genesis 1:2). The first act of creation is then recorded: "And God said, 'Let there be light,' and there was light. God saw that the light was good, and he separated the light from the darkness"

Even for believers, the presence of Christ on the day of judgment discloses the true worth, or worthlessness, of everything in a person's life (all that they've done, all that they've left undone), and everything in a person's soul (all that they are, all that they've failed to become). Paul hints at this in his warning to the believers at Corinth that they must "take care" how they "build on the foundation" of faith in Christ:

> Now if anyone builds on the foundation with gold, silver, precious stones, wood, hay, straw—*each one's work will become manifest, for the Day will disclose it, because it will be revealed by fire*, and the fire will test what sort of work each one has done. If the work that anyone has built on the foundation survives, he will receive a reward. If anyone's work is burned up, he will suffer loss, though *he himself will be saved, but only as through fire*. (1 Corinthians 3:12–15 ESV)

For some believers, it seems, the day of judgment will not be entirely without pain or regret. Perhaps the first exposure to the glorified Christ is a refining experience for these believers, the completion of their process of sanctification: in traditional terms, an experience of *purgatory*. But if so, then purgatory is merely a different way of experiencing the same reality that those already perfected experience as blessedness: it's the experience of the presence of Christ unveiled in glory, the light of the world, the consuming fire.[21]

---

(1:3). Notably, this is not the light of the celestial bodies, which are created later, on "the fourth day." The parallels between the opening verses of Genesis (1:1–5) and the opening verses of the Gospel of John (1:1–5) are striking, and clearly intentional.

21. On the divine presence model, the story from Daniel 3 of Shadrach, Meshach, and Abednego, consigned to the fiery furnace by Nebuchadnezzar, is a symbol of the experience of those who have been made holy: they stand within the fire of the divine presence but are not burned by it.

—— Chapter 20 ——

# Apocalyptic visions

It should be obvious even to casual readers of the Bible that the Christian scriptures are made up of books written in a variety of very different genres. We find, at the very least, historical narratives, poetry, legal codes, wisdom literature, prophesy, gospels, parables, epistles, and apocalyptic literature. Of all the scriptural genres, apocalyptic writing is the most foreign to modern readers, and the most commonly and easily misunderstood. The present work is not the place to go into a detailed discussion of right and wrong ways of interpreting apocalyptic literature. Suffice it to say, for present purposes, that these passages in Scripture are richly symbolic and generally should not be understood as giving literal descriptions of their subject matter. Nevertheless, we can reasonably draw some conclusions about the subjects that are symbolically depicted in these writings—and this is especially the case wherever a certain symbol is used repeatedly and employed in the same way in other, non-apocalyptic passages of Scripture.

### Depictions of God as fire

One of the most common symbols that we find in the Bible is the symbol of fire, and, significantly, fire is the primary way of symbolically depicting *both God and hell*. Most people are familiar with the idea of hell as a place of fire ("hellfire"). But the prevalence of the image of God as fire, in both the Old and New Testaments, is largely overlooked by many readers, who consequently fail to appreciate the theological significance of this overlapping imagery. The prevalence of this particular symbol and the ways in which it's used strongly suggest that there is a *singular reality* that's being depicted. To put the idea succinctly (albeit somewhat imprecisely): hell = fire = the presence of God. This connection is obviously important to making the biblical case for the divine presence model, so it's worth considering at least a representative sampling of the passages, beginning with those that connect God/the divine presence with fire. As it turns out, there are a great many such passages in the Bible.

We'll begin with some non-apocalyptic scriptures. In the Torah—the first five books of the Old Testament—God is repeatedly depicted either *as* fire or as being present *within* fire.

> For *the* LORD *your God is a consuming fire*, a jealous God. (Deuteronomy 4:24)[1]

> From heaven he made you hear his voice to discipline you. On earth *he showed you his great fire, and you heard his words from out of the fire.* (Deuteronomy 4:36)

> There *the angel of the* LORD *appeared to [Moses] in flames of fire* from within a bush. Moses saw that though the bush was on fire it did not burn up. (Exodus 3:2)

> By day the Lord went ahead of [the Israelites] in a pillar of cloud to guide them on their way and by night in *a pillar of fire* to give them light, so that they could travel by day or night. (Exodus 13:21)

In 2 Chronicles, one of the historical books of the Old Testament, the Lord's dramatic appearance in the dedication of Solomon's temple is described:

> When Solomon finished praying, *fire came down from heaven* and consumed the burnt offering and the sacrifices, *and the glory of the* LORD *filled the temple.* The priests could not enter the temple of the LORD because the glory of the LORD filled it. When all the Israelites saw the fire coming down and the glory of the LORD above the temple, they knelt on the pavement with their faces to the ground, and they worshiped and gave thanks to the LORD, saying,
>
> "He is good;
> his love endures forever." (2 Chronicles 7:1–3)

---

1. See also Hebrews 12:29, which references this verse, thereby highlighting the importance of the idea of God as a consuming fire in both Jewish and Christian thought.

Just as fire is a pervasive symbol of God in the Old Testament, so also is the image of fire *proceeding from* the Lord.[2] The following passage from Leviticus is an especially striking example:

> Aaron's sons Nadab and Abihu took their censers, put fire in them and added incense; and they offered unauthorized fire before the LORD, contrary to his command. So *fire came out from the presence of the* LORD and consumed them, and they died before the LORD. (Leviticus 10:1–2)

Turning to the prophetic writings, we find similar descriptions of God as fire throughout. The following is from the description of the inaugural vision of the prophet Ezekiel:

> In my thirtieth year, in the fourth month on the fifth day, while I was among the exiles by the Kebar River, the heavens were opened and I saw visions of God. . . .
>
> I looked, and I saw a windstorm coming out of the north—*an immense cloud with flashing lightning and surrounded by brilliant light. The center of the fire looked like glowing metal, and in the fire was what looked like four living creatures.* In appearance their form was human, but each of them had four faces and four wings.
>
> *The appearance of the living creatures was like burning coals of fire or like torches. Fire moved back and forth among the creatures; it was bright, and lightning flashed out of it.* The creatures sped back and forth like flashes of lightning.
>
> Above the vault over their heads was what looked like a throne of lapis lazuli, and *high above on the throne was a figure like that of a man. I saw that from what appeared to be his waist up he looked like glowing metal, as if full of fire, and that from there down he looked like fire; and brilliant light surrounded him.* Like the appearance of a rainbow in the clouds on a rainy day, so was the radiance around him.
>
> *This was the appearance of the likeness of the glory of the* LORD. When I saw it, I fell facedown, and I heard the voice of one speaking. (Ezekiel 1:1, 4–6, 13–14, 26–28)

The same imagery is found in the description of Ezekiel's second vision of God:

---

2. See, for example, Genesis 19:24–25; 1 Kings 18:38–39; 2 Kings 1:9–12; 1 Chronicles 21:26.

> In the sixth year, in the sixth month on the fifth day, while I was sitting in my house and the elders of Judah were sitting before me, the hand of the Sovereign LORD came on me there. I looked, and *I saw a figure like that of a man. From what appeared to be his waist down he was like fire, and from there up his appearance was as bright as glowing metal.* (Ezekiel 8:1–2)

Other prophets, including minor prophets, depict the Lord in similar terms:

> While the angel who was speaking to me was leaving, another angel came to meet him and said to him: "Run, tell that young man, 'Jerusalem will be a city without walls because of the great number of people and animals in it. And *I myself will be a wall of fire around it,*' declares the LORD, 'and I will be its glory within.'" (Zechariah 2:3–5)

> But who can endure the day of his coming? Who can stand when he appears? For *he will be like a refiner's fire* or a launderer's soap. (Malachi 3:2)

Clearly, the imagery of God as fire is prevalent even in the non-apocalyptic scriptures. The most dramatic depictions of God as fire, however, are found in apocalyptic passages in the Bible: most significantly in the book of Daniel, chapter 7, and in the book of Revelation, particularly chapters 19–22. One of the most important things to notice about the passages from Revelation are their depictions of Jesus:

> I turned around to see the voice that was speaking to me. And when I turned I saw seven golden lampstands, and among the lampstands was *someone like a son of man,* dressed in a robe reaching down to his feet and with a golden sash around his chest. *The hair on his head was white like wool, as white as snow, and his eyes were like blazing fire. His feet were like bronze glowing in a furnace, and his voice was like the sound of rushing waters.* In his right hand he held seven stars, and *coming out of his mouth was a sharp, double-edged sword. His face was like the sun shining in all its brilliance.* (Revelation 1:12–16)

> I saw heaven standing open and there before me was a white horse, whose rider is called Faithful and True. *With justice he judges and wages war. His eyes are like blazing fire, and on his head are many crowns.* He has a name written on him that no one knows but he himself. He is dressed in a robe dipped in blood, and *his name is the Word of God.* (Revelation 19:11–13)

> Then I saw *a great white throne and him who was seated on it. The earth and the heavens fled from his presence, and there was no place for them. And I saw the dead, great and small, standing before the throne, and books were opened*. Another book was opened, which is the book of life. *The dead were judged according to what they had done as recorded in the books*. The sea gave up the dead that were in it, and death and Hades gave up the dead that were in them, and each person was judged according to what they had done. *Then death and Hades were thrown into the lake of fire. The lake of fire is the second death. Anyone whose name was not found written in the book of life was thrown into the lake of fire*. (Revelation 20:11–15)[3]

These are striking images, to be sure. But to fully appreciate these passages, we need to read them together with the overlay of the apocalyptic vision from the prophet Daniel. We've already noted that the image of fire proceeding from the Lord is prevalent in the Old Testament. In Daniel's vision, the Lord is seen as having a *river of fire* coming forth from his throne:

> "As I looked,
>   thrones were set in place,
>     and the Ancient of Days took his seat.
> His clothing was as white as snow;
>   the hair of his head was white like wool.
> His throne was flaming with fire,
>   and its wheels were all ablaze.
> *A river of fire was flowing,*
>   *coming out from before him.*
> Thousands upon thousands attended him;
>   ten thousand times ten thousand stood before him.
> The court was seated,
>   and *the books were opened.*" (Daniel 7:9–10)

How are we to make sense of these apocalyptic visions? In the divine presence model, these are symbolic depictions of the experience of being in the unmitigated presence of God on the day of judgment: more specifically, the experience of being resurrected into the presence of Christ, revealed in his full glory. The opening of the books marks the beginning

---

3. As noted in chapter 10, in the divine presence model, the meaning of the expression that "death and Hades" will be "thrown into the lake of fire" is that death itself will be utterly destroyed by the presence of God at the final judgment. For further development of this idea, see *Sinners in the Presence of a Loving God*, 382–85.

of the judgment of transparency. Recall from chapter 10 that in the divine presence model, the meaning of Revelation 20:12 ("The dead were judged according to what they had done as recorded in the books") is that the records of individual consciences will be "read" like open books at the final judgment. The river of fire in Daniel's vision is understood to be identical to the lake of fire described in the closing chapters of Revelation (which in turn is identical to the "sea of glass glowing with fire" mentioned earlier in the book):[4] these are all references to the divine presence. As Jesus says in the Gospel of Luke, "I have come to bring fire on the earth, and how I wish it were already kindled!" (Luke 12:49). The presence of God is a consuming fire, and for some people, the experience of being fully exposed to it at the final judgment will be an experience of being "cast into hell," depicted variously in Scripture as a river of fire, lake of fire, or sea of fire.[5]

It's worth emphasizing that these apocalyptic visions should not be understood as *merely* symbolic. The descriptions of the visions of Ezekiel, Daniel, and John are remarkably similar to the description of what was witnessed in person by Peter, James, and John on the Mount of Transfiguration:

> About eight days after Jesus said this, he took Peter, John and James with him and went up onto a mountain to pray. As he was praying, *the appearance of his face changed, and his clothes became as bright as a flash of lightning.* (Luke 9:28–29)

This, in turn, is strikingly similar to what Saul experienced in his vision of Jesus on the road to Damascus:

> As he neared Damascus on his journey, *suddenly a light from heaven flashed around him.* He fell to the ground and heard a voice say to him, "Saul, Saul, why do you persecute me?"
>
> "Who are you, Lord?" Saul asked.
>
> "I am Jesus, whom you are persecuting," he replied. (Acts 9:3–5)

---

4. Revelation 15:2; cf. Ezekiel 1:22.

5. In our initial critique of the choice model of hell, in chapter 7, we noted that the idea of hell as separation from God is unbiblical. A key verse from Revelation, describing the punishment of the damned, was used to support this verdict: "They will be tormented with burning sulfur in the presence of the holy angels and of the Lamb" (Revelation 14:10b). We're now in a position to fully appreciate the significance of this verse. Sulfur was a substance known to the ancient world for its incendiary qualities: the very word "brimstone" means "burning stone." Burning sulfur is repeatedly used as an image of divine wrath and destruction in the Bible (see, for example, Genesis 19:24; Deuteronomy 29:22–23; Psalm 11:4–7; Isaiah 30:33; Ezekiel 38:17–23). Once we understand it to be an image of the divine presence—more specifically, the way that the presence of God is experienced by the wicked—we can understand why the torment of "burning sulfur" occurs *in the presence of Christ and the angels.*

Throughout Scripture, in apocalyptic and non-apocalyptic passages alike, the glory of the Lord is described as a fire or a flashing, blinding light[6]—and these are further revealed in the New Testament to be descriptions of Jesus as he will appear at the end of the age.

### The river of fire and the river of life

Returning to Daniel's vision, a striking connection emerges when we juxtapose its image of a river of fire with an image from the final chapter of Revelation:

> Then the angel showed me *the river of the water of life, bright as crystal, flowing from the throne of God and of the Lamb* through the middle of the street of the city; also, on either side of the river, the tree of life with its twelve kinds of fruit, yielding its fruit each month. The leaves of the tree were for the healing of the nations. No longer will there be anything accursed, but the throne of God and of the Lamb will be in it, and his servants will worship him. They will see his face, and his name will be on their foreheads. And night will be no more. They will need no light of lamp or sun, for the Lord God will be their light, and they will reign forever and ever. (Revelation 22:1–5 ESV)

Both a river of fire *and* a river of water proceed from the throne of the Lamb.[7] In the divine presence model, these two "rivers" are identical; they are in fact one and the same reality, experienced very differently by those in communion with Christ (an experience of love, peace, rest, refreshment, and life) and those in disunion with him (an experience of wrath, judgment, restlessness, torment, and punishment). Once again, the symbolism of the passage—in this case, the juxtaposition of fire and water as both contrasting and complementary metaphors of the same reality—is not limited to Revelation, or even to other apocalyptic portions of Scripture. We've already noted the repeated claim that "God is a consuming fire" in both the Old and New Testaments,[8] and yet Jesus describes God's presence among humankind as "living water." He tells the Samaritan woman

---

6. In Orthodox theology, this is referred to as "Tabor light," because the transfiguration of Jesus is thought to have taken place on Mount Tabor.

7. The river of fire is often prominently featured in Orthodox icons of the final judgment. In some icons, both rivers are depicted as flowing from Jesus' throne. The river of fire always flows to Jesus' left; the river of life, if it's depicted in the icon, always flows to Jesus' right (see Matthew 25:31–33).

8. Deuteronomy 4:24; Hebrews 12:29.

at the well, "Indeed, the water I give them will become in them a spring of water welling up to eternal life" (John 4:7–14).[9] Elsewhere, Christ tells his followers that those who believe in him will have "rivers of living water" flowing out of them, and the gospel writer identifies this as a reference to the Spirit (John 7:37–39). Yet the very same Spirit is also depicted as a fire: in Matthew's Gospel, John the Baptist is quoted as saying,

> "I baptize you with water for repentance. But after me comes one who is more powerful than I, whose sandals I am not worthy to carry. *He will baptize you with the Holy Spirit and fire.* His winnowing fork is in his hand, and he will clear his threshing floor, gathering his wheat into the barn and *burning up the chaff with unquenchable fire.*" (Matthew 3:11–12)[10]

Interestingly, the context of these remarks suggests that they were not spoken only to John's disciples; the most immediate addressees seem to be "many of the Pharisees and Sadducees coming to where he was baptizing," whom he addresses as "You brood of vipers!" (Matthew 3:7). It is thus possible to interpret John the Baptist as teaching that *everyone* will be "baptized" by Christ (recall the apocalyptic imagery of the divine presence as a river, a lake, and a sea—symbols of immersion), but that for some it will be an experience of "burning up . . . with unquenchable fire," even as for others it will be an experience of "rivers of living water [flowing] from within them." Those who freely receive God's Spirit within themselves experience life through Him;[11] but for those who do not—those who commit "blasphemy against the Spirit"[12] by hardening their hearts, rejecting the truth about themselves that the Spirit reveals to them, calling it a lie, and refusing to repent even to the very end—they will experience the "baptism" into Christ's presence on the day of judgment as a tormenting fire.[13]

---

9. Compare Psalm 36:9. Note also, in light of this teaching, the poignant symbolism of an event recorded later in John's Gospel: "one of the soldiers pierced Jesus' side with a spear, bringing a sudden flow of blood *and water*" (John 19:34).

10. Again, compare Isaiah 33:10–11:

> "Now I will arise," says the LORD,
> "Now I will be exalted, now I will be lifted up.
> *You have conceived chaff, you will give birth to stubble;*
> *My breath* [lit. spirit] *will consume you like a fire.*" (NASB)

11. Compare Romans 8:11: "If the Spirit of him who raised Jesus from the dead dwells in you, he who raised Christ Jesus from the dead will also give life to your mortal bodies through his Spirit who dwells in you" (ESV).

12. Matthew 12:31–32.

13. In this light, note the references to the flood (a kind of "baptism") and the destruction of Sodom (a consuming fire) in the following passage, in which Jesus

The aforementioned passage from Revelation 22 brings together three of the most important images associated with the divine presence in Scripture: the face of Christ, the light of God, and the tree of life. The first two we've already discussed. The third image, the tree of life, is especially striking, because it ties together the vision of the eschaton with the opening chapters of Genesis. Once banished from the garden of Eden, lest they "take also from the tree of life and eat, and live forever" in their fallen state, redeemed humanity finally will "have the right to the tree of life" and will "take the free gift of the water of life."[14] The river of life and the tree of life are intertwined images of the presence of God ("On each side of the river stood the tree of life").[15] The tree is described as "bearing twelve crops of fruit, yielding its fruit every month," and "the leaves of the tree are for the healing of the nations" (Revelation 22:2). There's a striking similarity between this image and one of the self-descriptions of Jesus:

> "I am the bread of life. Your ancestors ate the manna in the wilderness, yet they died. But here is the bread that comes down from heaven, which anyone may eat and not die. I am the living bread that came down from heaven. Whoever eats this bread will live forever. *This bread is my flesh, which I will give for the life of the world.*" (John 6:48–51)

It seems, then, that the fruit of the tree of life is the same as "the bread of life," "the true bread from heaven," "the flesh of the Son of Man," which Christ describes to his disciples "the day the Son of Man is revealed":

> "For the Son of Man in his day will be like the lightning, which flashes and lights up the sky from one end to the other.... Just as it was in the days of Noah, so also will it be in the days of the Son of Man. People were eating, drinking, marrying and being given in marriage up to the day Noah entered the ark. Then the flood came and destroyed them all. It was the same in the days of Lot. People were eating and drinking, buying and selling, planting and building. But the day Lot left Sodom, fire and sulfur rained down from heaven and destroyed them all. *It will be just like this on the day the Son of Man is revealed.*" (Luke 17:24, 26–30)

14. Genesis 3:22; Revelation 22:14, 17. In the divine presence model, it's an act of *mercy* that God banishes Adam and Eve from His presence, for in their fallen state they experience the close dwelling with God that's constitutive of paradise to be instead an experience of judgment. Banishment from Eden is necessary to prevent this state from becoming permanent ("He must not be allowed to reach out his hand and take also from the tree of life and eat, and live forever"), which would be an experience of hell. By banishing them from His presence, God is instituting the conditions that are necessary for Adam and Eve's ultimate restoration.

15. Revelation 22:2. It's possible to interpret this image in Trinitarian terms: the river is an image of the Spirit (as we've discussed) and the tree is an image of the Son (to be discussed next).

offers to his disciples. ("Very truly I tell you, unless you eat the flesh of the Son of Man and drink his blood, you have no life in you" [John 6:53].) To be in communion with Christ is to receive into oneself not only his Spirit, but also his body and blood; thus Jesus goes on to tell his disciples,

> "Whoever eats my flesh and drinks my blood *remains in me, and I in them.* Just as the living Father sent me and I live because of the Father, so the one who feeds on me will live because of me. . . . [W]hoever feeds on this bread will live forever." (John 6:56–58)[16]

God's intention from the beginning is that humans partake of the fruit of the tree of life—that all "become partakers of the divine nature" (2 Peter 1:4 ESV)—but only at the appointed time, when a permanent state of union with Himself has been achieved. Jesus provides a way back to God, through his death on the cross, for those who "remain" in him. By receiving his Spirit into themselves and continually abiding in him, believers are sanctified, conformed to his image, and enabled finally to live in a state of perfect and holy communion with God and with other saints: an eternal communion of love.[17]

This is eternal life, in its simplest terms: to be in perfect communion with God, the Source of all life, and with those who are likewise united to Him. God is eternal (*aiónios* in New Testament Greek), and to be in communion with God is *aiónios* life, a participation in the life of the Trinity: "Now this is eternal life: that they know you, the only true God, and Jesus Christ, whom you have sent" (John 17:3). This is the end for which humans are created: a divine life, received by grace, through faith in the Son of God. The dawn of the new creation is the final abolishing of death in all of its facets; hence, "No longer will there be any curse" (Revelation 22:3a). The state of seeing God "face to face" is both humanity's original state and the state for which all are eventually destined (for better or worse): a state, like the garden of Eden, in which God dwells among us:

> Then I saw "a new heaven and a new earth," for the first heaven and the first earth had passed away. . . . And I heard a loud voice from the throne saying, "Look! God's dwelling place is now among the people, and he will dwell with them. They will be his

---

16. For helpful insight into the nature of the connection between union with God and participation in the Eucharist, see Stump, *Atonement*, chapter 9.

17. Consider in this light the closing line of Jesus' high priestly prayer: "I have given them the glory that you gave me, that they may be one as we are one—I in them and you in me—so that they may be brought to complete unity" (John 17:22–23a).

people, and God himself will be with them and be their God."
(Revelation 21:1–3)

The experience of God's dwelling among humankind is not an experience of *aiónios* life for all, however, as some will thwart God's desire and intention for them even to the end, refusing to be reconciled to Him. For such individuals, the experience of the new creation is akin to the experience of Adam and Eve in the wake of the fall: an experience of guilt and shame, of exposure and abasement, of realization and self-deception, of fear and dread. Hell is a separation not from God's presence but from communion with Him; it is an inability—made permanent through hardness of heart and persistence in sin—to experience God's love *as love*. For those who have set their wills against Truth, the very presence of God is an experience of judgment; for those who remain in their sins, the loving presence of Christ is experienced only as wrath. There is nothing arbitrary or artificial about the reward of heaven, nor the punishment of hell. Jesus is the light that shines in the darkness (John 1:5), but those in the "outer darkness" will not receive him, and so cannot understand him or perceive him as he is. They are unable to reflect his glory; they cannot participate in his nature, which is love (1 John 4:8). The experience of unrepentant sinners in the presence of a loving God is one of *aiónios* punishment, "eternal destruction that comes from the presence of the Lord and from the glory of his might."

# Recommended Further Reading

## Books

Copan, Paul, and Christopher M. Date, eds. *What Is Hell? A Multidisciplinary Dialogue.* Forthcoming from IVP Academic.

>*Opposing perspectives on hell from a variety of different disciplines. Contains an essay by the author that introduces the problem of hell and the divine presence model.*

Kalomiros, Alexander. *The River of Fire: A Reply to the Questions: Is God Really Good? Did God Create Hell?* Seattle: St. Nectarios Press, 1980.

>*A short work that helped to popularize the core idea of the divine presence model among English-speaking Orthodox Christians.*

Lewis, C. S. *The Great Divorce.* New York: HarperCollins, 2001.

>*A short work of fantasy that insightfully depicts the various forms that pride and self-deception can take, and the ways they can alienate a person from God and from other people. The closing paragraph is suggestive of the divine presence model.*

Manis, R. Zachary. *Sinners in the Presence of a Loving God: An Essay on the Problem of Hell.* Oxford: Oxford University Press, 2019.

>*An extensive, scholarly development and defense of the divine presence model.*

Talbott, Thomas. *The Inescapable Love of God*. 2nd ed. Eugene, OR: Cascade, 2014.

*A rigorous but accessible defense of universalism by a Christian philosopher.*

Walls, Jerry L. *Heaven, Hell, and Purgatory: Rethinking the Things That Matter Most*. Grand Rapids: Brazos, 2015.

*A rigorous but accessible defense of the choice model, as well as insightful discussions of heaven and purgatory, by a (Protestant) Christian philosopher.*

## Articles and Book Chapters

Adams, Marilyn McCord. "The Problem of Hell: A Problem of Evil for Christians." In *Reasoned Faith: Essays in Philosophical Theology in Honor of Norman Kretzmann*, edited by Eleonore Stump, 301–27. Ithaca, NY: Cornell University Press, 1993.

*A powerful argument for universalism by a Christian philosopher.*

Hart, Matthew J. "Calvinism and the Problem of Hell." In *Calvinism and the Problem of Evil*, edited by David E. Alexander and Daniel M. Johnson, 248–72. Eugene, OR: Pickwick, 2016.

*A Calvinist perspective on the problem of hell.*

Hick, John. "Soul-Making and Suffering." In *The Problem of Evil*, edited by Marilyn McCord Adams and Robert Merrihew Adams, 168–88. Oxford: Oxford University Press, 1990.

*An excerpt from Hick's influential book* Evil and the God of Love, *which presents the main ideas of the soul-making theodicy.*

Hopko, Thomas. "The Kingdom of Heaven." In *The Orthodox Faith: An Elementary Handbook on the Orthodox Church*, vol. 4, *Spirituality*, 189–99. New York: Department of Religious Education, the Orthodox Church in America, 1976.

*A concise presentation of the main ideas of the divine presence model by an influential Orthodox priest and theologian.*

Lewis, C. S. "Hell." In *The Problem of Pain*, 119–31. New York: HarperCollins, 2001.

*An accessible and influential discussion of the problem of hell whose proposed solution combines elements of the choice model and annihilationism.*

Louth, Andrew. "Eastern Orthodox Eschatology." In *The Oxford Handbook of Eschatology*, edited by Jerry L. Walls, 233–47. Oxford: Oxford University Press, 2008.

*Another helpful introduction to the divine presence model from an Orthodox perspective.*

Stump, Eleonore. "Dante's Hell, Aquinas's Moral Theory, and the Love of God." *Canadian Journal of Philosophy* 16 (1986) 181–98.

*An important argument by a Christian philosopher that a version of the choice model is developed in the writings of Dante and Aquinas.*

Swinburne, Richard. "A Theodicy of Heaven and Hell." In *The Existence and Nature of God*, edited by Alfred J. Freddoso, 37–54. Notre Dame, IN: University of Notre Dame Press, 1983.

*An insightful development of a natural consequence model of heaven and hell by a Christian philosopher.*

# Glossary of Terms

**agape**  A selfless and sacrificial kind of love that, according to the Bible, God has for us and commands us to have for one another.

**annihilationism**  The view that those consigned to hell are completely annihilated, either immediately or following a finite period of punishment.

**apocalypse**  The unveiling of the glorified Christ to all the world at the final judgment, the event that marks the definitive end of *divine hiddenness*.

**artificial consequence**  A consequence that follows an action not as a natural effect, but rather because of the intervening action of some other person or group. Receiving a ticket and being forced to pay a fine is an example of an artificial consequence of speeding. See also *natural consequence*.

**beatific vision**  A direct perception of God that includes an experience of God's infinite goodness and love and an experience of perfect *communion* with Him, an experience that results in the greatest possible happiness and joy.

**Calvinism**  A Christian theological system based on the ideas of the sixteenth-century theologian and reformer John Calvin. According to Calvinism, some people are finally lost, but God is in complete control of everything that happens in the world, including every individual's decision to either accept or reject God; hence it is God's will that some are finally lost.

**choice model** The view that damnation is not a state that God imposes on the damned against their wills, but rather a state that the damned freely choose for themselves. In consigning some to hell, God is merely respecting human free will, allowing people to experience the natural consequences of their own wicked choices. See also *natural consequence model of hell*.

**communion** Fellowship, union, or friendship based on *agape* love. According to Christian theology, the highest good of every human being, and the condition of true and permanent happiness, is a state of eternal communion with God and other people.

**conscious torment thesis** The claim that existence in hell involves intense suffering of some kind. An essential part of the view of hell known as *traditionalism*.

**consignment thesis** The claim that some people are (or will be) consigned to hell. An essential part of the view of hell known as *traditionalism*.

**culpability** Moral guilt or blameworthiness.

**defense** A strategy of defending a certain belief (for example, that some people will be consigned to hell) by demonstrating that it does not logically contradict other accepted beliefs (for example, that God is perfectly good and loving).

**divine hiddenness** The experience that God is neither easily nor fully perceived.

**divine presence model** The view that heaven and hell are the various ways that the righteous and the wicked will experience the presence of God after the final judgment.

**edification principle** The claim that anything that God reveals to be true is edifying (spiritually beneficial) to those who accept it.

**elect, the** Those who have been chosen by God for some special purpose or end. See *election*.

**election** God's selection of a person or group for some special purpose or end. On some theological systems, such as *Calvinism*, election is a matter of being chosen by God to receive salvation.

**experiential knowledge** The type of knowledge that is acquired by having a firsthand experience of something. See also *propositional knowledge*.

**freedom-communion principle** The claim that the human capacity for spiritual *communion* is directly proportional to the amount of moral freedom that humans possess. See also *freedom-harm principle*.

**freedom-harm principle** The claim that the extent of human moral freedom is directly proportional to the amount of harm that humans are capable of causing. See also *freedom-communion principle*.

**free-will theodicy** An explanation of God's reasons for allowing evil and suffering in the world that focuses on the conditions that are necessary for humans to possess genuine free will. An expanded version of the free-will theodicy, such as the *soul-making theodicy*, focuses on a specific good, such as moral and spiritual development, which is achievable only if humans possess free will.

**hardness of heart** A stubborn refusal to accept divine correction; an unwillingness to repent of wrongdoing or even to accept some unwelcome truth that God reveals. See also *self-deception*.

**human flourishing** The deepest and most permanent type of human happiness, which consists in the fulfillment of one's nature as a human being. Understood in Christian terms, human flourishing is a matter of being united to God and to other people in relationships of loving *communion*. This is so because human beings are made in the image of God, whose nature is love.

**intermediate state** The period between a person's death and resurrection. On the usual way of developing a *natural consequence model of hell*, an individual's moral and spiritual development continues into the intermediate state.

**judgment of transparency** The understanding of final judgment on the divine presence model, according to which being in the unmitigated presence of God, beginning with the revelation of Christ in glory at the end of the age, has the effect of finally and fully revealing the deepest moral and spiritual truth about everyone.

**justification** Being forgiven of one's sins and coming into a right relationship with God. A part of the process of salvation. See also *sanctification*.

**moral agent** A being who is capable of forming moral judgments, making morally significant choices, and performing morally significant actions—and who is rightly held accountable for these judgments, choices, and actions.

**natural consequence** A consequence that follows an action in virtue of the laws of nature. Losing control of one's car and wrecking it is an example of a natural consequence of speeding. See also *artificial consequence*.

**natural consequence model of hell** A view of hell in which damnation is the *natural consequence* of persistence in sin and rebellion against God, rather than an *artificial consequence* that God inflicts upon the damned. Both *the choice model* and *the divine presence model* are natural consequence models of hell.

**natural punishment** A punishment in which an authority figure (such as a parent) intentionally allows someone under their authority (such as a child) to experience the painful natural consequences of their own misbehavior, in order that a certain moral good might thereby be realized.

**new creation** The endless age that follows the return of Christ, the general resurrection, and the final judgment; an age in which everything in creation is restored to its original glory. Also known as "the new earth" or "the age to come."

**no escape thesis** The claim that once a person is consigned to hell, there is no possibility of escape; consignment to hell is a final, irreversible, and everlasting condition. An essential part of the view of hell known as *traditionalism*.

**omnibenevolent** Perfectly good. Omnibenevolence, or perfect goodness, is traditionally considered to be an attribute of God (that is, part of God's nature).

**omnipotent** All-powerful. Omnipotence, or maximal power, is traditionally considered to be an attribute of God.

**omnipresent** Everywhere present. Omnipresence, being present at every time and place in creation, is traditionally considered to be an attribute of God.

**omniscient** All-knowing. Omniscience, or complete knowledge, is traditionally considered to be an attribute of God.

**perfect being theology** The dominant way of understanding God's nature in the Christian tradition, according to which God is the greatest possible being. Each of God's attributes is some perfection (e.g., knowledge, power, goodness) in its maximal form (e.g., *omniscience, omnipotence, omnibenevolence*).

**personal identity** See *self-identity*.

**problem of divine hiddenness** The problem of explaining why a perfectly good and loving God remains hidden to many people, despite the suffering this experience causes to some and the barrier to belief in God—and thus the barrier to salvation—that it can pose.

**problem of evil** The problem of explaining why the world includes evil and suffering, given that it is created by an all-powerful, all-knowing, and perfectly good God. Atheists often allege that the existence of suffering is logically incompatible with the existence of God, and thereby proves that God does not exist.

**problem of hell** The problem of explaining why a perfectly good and loving God would consign anyone to hell.

**proportionality principle** The claim that a punishment is morally just and fitting only if it is proportionate to the severity of the wrongdoing that is being punished. Commonly considered to be a fundamental principle of justice.

**propositional knowledge** Knowledge of some truth—that is, knowing that something is the case. Everything that can be known *about* God falls into the category of propositional knowledge. See also *experiential knowledge*.

**providence** God's guidance (i) of the world and its unfolding history, (ii) of the church and its development, and (iii) of the lives of individual believers, especially in regard to making "all things to work together for good to those who love God."

**psychologically impossible** Something that a person simply could not bring themselves to do, because the action, though physically within their power to perform, conflicts so strongly with their character, personality, values, beliefs, or desires. What qualifies as psychologically impossible is different from one person to the next and can change over time for an individual.

**purgatory** An intermediate state between death and resurrection in which the moral and spiritual development of a person is brought to completion, making them finally and fully ready for heaven.

**reprobation** The Calvinist doctrine that God has chosen some people for eternal damnation from before the creation of the world, and that God brings this about by His own power, through a process of divine determination, in order to bring glory to Himself. See also *theological determinism*.

**retribution thesis** The view that consignment to hell is a punishment that God freely selects and imposes upon some people as a just recompense for the evil deeds they committed during their earthly lives. An essential part of the view of hell known as *traditionalism*.

**retributive justice** The view that justice is achieved through the retributive punishment of wrongdoers: that is, through the infliction of a proportionate loss, harm, or pain upon those who have unjustifiably caused others to suffer some loss, harm, or pain.

**revealed doctrine** Something revealed in the Bible to be true which could not be known on independent grounds such as reason or common experience.

**sanctification** The process of moral and spiritual development by which a person is completely freed from the bondage of sin and "conformed to the image" of Jesus Christ—that is, perfected in love—by a transforming work of the Holy Spirit. A part of the process of salvation. See also *justification*.

**self-deception** Actions by which one hides the truth from oneself: that is, causing oneself to consciously believe something that, at a deeper level, one knows to be false, because the truth conflicts with one's strong preferences or desires.

**self-identity** A person's unique identity as an individual. Also referred to as *personal identity*.

**soul-making** The process of moral and spiritual formation whereby a person's character and *self-identity* are formed.

**soul-making theodicy** An explanation of God's reasons for allowing evil and suffering in the world that focuses on the conditions that are necessary for *soul-making*.

**sovereignty** Absolute authority, traditionally considered to be an attribute of God (that is, part of God's nature). Sovereignty is sometimes mistakenly understood, especially by Calvinists, to mean "control"; according to this view, divine sovereignty entails that God determines everything that happens in the world. See also *theological determinism*.

**theist** Someone who believes in the existence of an all-powerful, all-knowing, and perfectly good God who is the Creator of everything that exists. The term "theism" is short for "monotheism": the view that there is only one God. Christianity, Judaism, and Islam are all versions of theism.

**theodicy** A plausible explanation of God's reasons for allowing evil and suffering in the world. A theodicy of hell is an explanation of this type which addresses, more narrowly, God's reasons for allowing the suffering of hell.

**theological determinism** The view that God determines every event that happens in the world. A key component of *Calvinism*.

**theosis** The process whereby those who are united to God in Christ become "partakers of the divine nature": that is, becoming more and more like Jesus in being wholly and perfectly loving, more and more filled with the Holy Spirit, increasingly participating in the life of the Trinity.

**thought experiment** A description of a possible scenario, whether real or imaginary, whose features highlight or help to clarify something of philosophical significance.

**traditionalism** The view that some people are consigned to hell for all eternity as a just punishment for the evil they committed in their earthly lives. On this view, hell involves intense suffering, and those consigned to hell have no chance or possibility of ever escaping.

**universalism** The view that everyone who is consigned to hell will eventually be saved. On this view, the purpose of hell is to reform sinners and reconcile them to God, and the mechanism of hell (whatever it might be) is always successful in achieving this end (though in some cases, it might take a very long time).

**vice** A character trait that disposes one to think, feel, and behave in ways that are contrary to human flourishing. In the Christian tradition, all of the vices are rooted in pride.

**virtue** A character trait that disposes one to think, feel, and behave in ways that promote human flourishing. In the Christian tradition, all of the virtues are rooted in love. Moreover, many if not all of the virtues can be construed either as specific forms of love or capacities that enable one to love well.

# Bibliography

Calvin, John. *Institutes of the Christian Religion*. Edited by John T. McNeill. Translated by Ford Lewis Battles. Philadelphia: Westminster, 1960.
*Catechism of the Catholic Church: Revised in Accordance with the Official Latin Text Promulgated by Pope John Paul II*. Vatican City: Libreria Editrice Vaticana, 1997.
Dostoevsky, Fyodor. *The Brothers Karamazov*. Translated by Constance Garnett. New York: Macmillan, 1922.
Evans, C. Stephen. *Kierkegaard on Faith and the Self: Collected Essays*. Waco, TX: Baylor University Press, 2006.
Fudge, Edward William. *The Fire That Consumes: A Biblical and Historical Study of the Doctrine of Final Punishment*. 3rd ed. Eugene, OR: Cascade, 2011.
Fudge, Edward William, and Robert A. Peterson. *Two Views of Hell: A Biblical and Theological Dialogue*. Downers Grove, IL: InterVarsity, 2000.
Hart, David Bentley. *That All Shall Be Saved: Heaven, Hell, and Universal Salvation*. New Haven: Yale University Press, 2019.
Hart, Matthew J. "Calvinism and the Problem of Hell." In *Calvinism and the Problem of Evil*, edited by David E. Alexander and Daniel M. Johnson, 248–72. Eugene, OR: Pickwick, 2016.
Hick, John. *Evil and the God of Love*. New York: Palgrave Macmillan, 2010.
———. "Soul-Making and Suffering." In *The Problem of Evil*, edited by Marilyn McCord Adams and Robert Merrihew Adams, 168–88. Oxford: Oxford University Press, 1990.
Hopko, Father Thomas. *The Orthodox Faith: An Elementary Handbook on the Orthodox Church*. Vol. 4, *Spirituality*. New York: Department of Religious Education, Orthodox Church in America, 1976.
Kierkegaard, Søren. *The Sickness unto Death: A Christian Psychological Exposition for Upbuilding and Awakening*. Edited and translated by Howard V. Hong and Edna H. Hong. Princeton, NJ: Princeton University Press, 1980.
Lewis, C. S. *The Great Divorce*. New York: Macmillan, 1963.
———. *Mere Christianity*. New York: Macmillan, 1977.
———. *Till We Have Faces: A Myth Retold*. Boston: Houghton Mifflin Harcourt, 2012.

Lossky, Vladimir. *The Mystical Theology of the Eastern Church*. Crestwood, NY: St. Vladimir's Seminary Press, 1997.

MacDonald, Gregory. *The Evangelical Universalist: The Biblical Hope that God's Love Will Save Us All*. 2nd ed. Eugene, OR: Cascade, 2012.

Manis, R. Zachary. *Sinners in the Presence of a Loving God: An Essay on the Problem of Hell*. Oxford: Oxford University Press, 2019.

Orwell, George. *1984*. Boston: Houghton Mifflin Harcourt, 1949.

Puhalo, Lazar. *On the Nature of Heaven and Hell according to the Holy Fathers*. Dewdbey, Canada: Synaxis, 1995.

Sproul, R. C. *Classic Teachings on the Nature of God*. Peabody, MA: Hendrickson, 2010.

Stump, Eleonore. *Atonement*. Oxford: Oxford University Press, 2018.

Talbott, Thomas. *The Inescapable Love of God*. 2nd ed. Eugene, OR: Cascade, 2014.

Teresa, Mother. *Mother Teresa: Come Be My Light; The Private Writings of the "Saint of Calcutta."* Edited by Brian Kolodiejchuk. New York: Doubleday, 2007.

van Inwagen, Peter. *The Problem of Evil: The Gifford Lectures Delivered in the University of St Andrews in 2003*. Oxford: Clarendon, 2006.

Walls, Jerry L. *Heaven, Hell, and Purgatory: Rethinking the Things That Matter Most*. Grand Rapids: Brazos, 2015.

———. *Purgatory: The Logic of Total Transformation*. Oxford: Oxford University Press, 2012.

Walls, Jerry L., and Joseph R. Dongell. *Why I Am Not a Calvinist*. Downers Grove, IL: InterVarsity, 2004.

# Subject Index

agape, 16, 19–20, 77–78, 97, 101, 110, 130n2, 209–10
annihilationism, 43–45, 54–56, 59–60, 206, 209
apocalypse, 71, 84, 89, 110, 137, 160, 178, 187, 191, 209
artificial consequence, *See* consequence, artificial

beatific vision, 71, 152–54, 177, 209

Calvinism, x, 16–19, 26, 31–43, 45, 131, 206, 209–10, 214–15, 217–18
*Catechism of the Catholic Church*, 59n7, 154n2, 177n21, 187n6, 217
Catholicism, ix, 25n2, 48, 56n3, 59n7, 97n4, 98n5, 154n2, 177n21, 187n6
choice model, 50–54, 59–60, 78–79, 95–96, 109, 113, 135–37, 180, 199n5, 206–7, 210, 212
Christ, *See* Jesus
coercion, problem of, 23–28, 38, 44–45, 47, 49, 51, 63, 78, 142–45
communion, 21, 40, 49–50, 59n7, 73, 90, 96–99, 101, 103, 110, 114, 124, 129–30, 138, 144, 146, 152, 161, 171–73, 175, 177, 200, 203–4, 209–11
consequence, artificial, 45–47, 50–51, 54, 67, 72, 75, 83n2, 97n4, 142–43, 145, 180, 204, 209, 212
consequence, natural, 46, 48–53, 67, 72, 76–79, 86, 91, 95–97, 103–14, 121, 128–30, 135, 148–50, 159, 176, 183, 207, 209–12

day of judgment, *See* judgment, final
defense, 62, 112n6, 210
destruction, 32, 44, 115, 155, 158, 178–80, 192, 199n5, 201n13, 204
determinism, theological, x, 17, 26, 42, 45, 214–15
disclosure, divine, 141–47, 152–55, 158–63, 167–71, 185–88, 191–93, 196–200
divine hiddenness, *See* hiddenness, divine

Eastern Orthodoxy, *See* Orthodoxy
eschatology, 70, 207
edification principle, xi, 23–24, 26, 63, 68, 210
election, 17n3, 18n4, 19, 32–33, 39–41, 210

# SUBJECT INDEX

eternal punishment, *See* punishment
evil, 4–6, 8–9, 23, 49, 62, 74f7, 76–78, 86n11, 95–96, 98–110, 117–18, 127–29, 138, 140, 146, 151, 155, 161–62, 168–69, 176, 178, 182f1, 184–85, 192f17, 192f18, 206, 211, 213–15, 217–18
evil, moral, 9, 23, 76–77, 86n11, 98–102, 105–6, 129, 162, 176, 178, 184
evil, natural, 102
evil, problem of, 4–5, 8, 62, 95–96, 98, 102–3, 138, 146, 151, 155f4, 161–62, 206, 211, 213, 215, 217–18

face of God, 69–71, 87, 147, 168–70, 174–80, 187, 197, 199–200, 202–3
final judgment, *See* judgment, final
fire, 6, 52, 55n1, 69–70, 85, 86n12, 87, 88n17, 167, 176–78, 186, 191, 193–202, 205, 217
flourishing, human, 49–50, 96, 100n7, 211, 216
freedom-communion principle, 101, 129, 211
freedom-harm principle, 100, 129, 211
free will, 6, 17, 25–28, 32, 44, 46–47, 50–52, 59n7, 63, 67, 72–75, 79, 95, 98–102, 104, 108n3, 109–10, 113–15, 118–19, 121, 123–28, 131, 135, 142–46, 148, 157–59, 161, 171, 180, 190, 201, 210–11, 214

Hades, 89n17, 136–37, 198
hardness of heart, 49, 82, 104, 110, 116–17, 171–76, 178, 180, 183–84, 187–88, 204, 211
hiddenness, divine, 71, 83, 88, 95, 135, 137–63, 170, 209–10, 213
human flourishing, *See* flourishing, human

impossibility, logical, 26, 73–74, 104, 124, 146n3, 148, 153, 162
impossibility, psychological, 27–28, 49, 106–12, 126, 213

intermediate state, 98n5, 108–9, 112n6, 211, 214

Jesus, 11n1, 11n2, 16n1, 19, 22, 37, 39n2, 47, 51–52, 69–71, 72n5, 73, 75, 77, 80, 83–86, 88–91, 97–98, 108n4, 109–11, 112n6, 116n3, 119, 122n6, 125, 130n2, 136n3, 137, 142, 152–55, 157n8, 158, 160, 162, 169, 172–75, 177–78, 180–93, 197–204, 209, 211–12, 214–15
judgment, final, 47, 52–53, 67–74, 83–85, 98n5, 109, 111, 112n6, 137, 160, 175–76, 178, 185–88, 190, 192n17, 192n18, 193, 198n3, 199, 200n7, 201, 209–12
judgment of transparency, 81, 83–86, 181–93, 199, 211
justice, problem of, 8–16, 22–23, 28, 44–45, 47, 50, 78–79, 114,
justice, retributive, 5–6, 8–9, 13, 15–16, 32, 34–37, 41, 43, 45–48, 50, 54, 57–59, 67, 72, 75–78, 143, 160, 162, 214
justification, doctrine of, 83n2, 97, 211, 214

love, problem of, 15–23, 28, 44–45, 50, 78–79

momentum, spiritual, 104–7, 126–28, 135

natural consequence, *See* consequence, natural
natural punishment, *See* punishment
new creation, 72–73, 75, 85, 88–91, 112n6, 161–63, 174, 203–4, 212

omnipresence, 87–88, 135–37, 212
Orthodoxy, ix–x, 68–70, 98f5, 154n2

parousia, 71, 178
perfect being theology, 18–19, 34, 62, 75, 213
personal identity, *See* self-identity
proportionality principle, 9, 13, 45, 213

# SUBJECT INDEX

Protestantism, ix–x, 25n2, 56, 97n4, 98n5, 154n2, 206
providence, 56–58, 131, 213
psychological impossibility, *See* impossibility, psychological
punishment, 5–6, 8–9, 11–13, 15–16, 19–23, 25, 32, 35, 39n2, 41, 43–54, 55n1, 57, 59n9, 67, 68n2, 72, 75–78, 83n2, 97n4, 138, 142–44, 145n2, 177–80, 190–93, 199n5, 200, 204, 209, 212–15, 217
purgatory, 48, 98n5, 109n4, 193, 206, 214, 218

Reformed epistemology, 147–50, 157, 159
repentance, 18, 26–27, 48, 73–74, 76, 81, 85, 104, 107–12, 121–23, 126, 128, 153, 171, 173, 175, 181–82, 184, 188, 201
reprobation, 33–35, 39–41, 214
retribution, *See* justice, retributive
retributive justice, *See* justice, retributive

sanctification, 97, 98f5, 105, 111, 112n6, 126, 153–54, 158–60, 173, 193, 211, 214
self-deception, 12, 82, 85–86, 95, 104, 110, 114–25, 128, 135, 139n5, 150, 156–57, 159, 162, 171, 183–84, 187, 188n9, 204–5, 211, 214
self-identity, 107, 125–28, 158, 213, 214

Shekinah, 87
Sheol, 136–37
soul-making, 95–109, 112n6, 113, 124–29, 135, 142–44, 146, 148, 153, 158–60, 206, 211, 214–15, 217
sovereignty, 16–17, 31–37, 42–43, 54, 67, 215
spiritual momentum, *See* momentum, spiritual
suffering, 3–6, 9, 15, 17, 20–21, 23, 28n4, 32–33, 44–45, 50–51, 56–62, 67, 68n3, 69–72, 75–80, 85, 91, 95–96, 98, 100–102, 104, 108n4, 109–11, 112n6, 121, 137n3, 138, 146, 151, 153–54, 160–63, 168, 178–80, 182n1, 187, 199n5, 200–01, 206, 210–11, 213, 215, 217

theodicy, 62–63, 95–104, 109, 112n6, 113, 124, 126–27, 129, 135, 146, 206–7, 211, 215
theological determinism, *See* determinism, theological
theosis, x, 89f18, 154, 173–75, 215
torment, *See* suffering
traditionalism, 5–28, 44–47, 50, 54, 55n2, 59–60, 135–37, 142–43, 145n2, 180, 210, 212, 214–15

universalism, 48, 54–56, 59–60, 103, 112–31, 206, 215

# Author Index

Barth, Karl, 17n3
Basil, Saint, 86n12

Calvin, John, 40–41, 209, 217

Dostoevsky, Fyodor, 117n4, 217

Evans, C. Stephen, 156n7, 217

Fudge, Edward William, 55n1, 68n2, 217

Hart, David Bentley, 55n1, 217
Hart, Matthew J., 33n3, 206, 217
Hick, John, 96n1, 103n1, 206, 217
Hopko, Thomas, 69, 80, 177, 206, 217

Isaac, Saint, 68

Kierkegaard, Søren, 84, 156n7, 217

Lewis, C. S., x, 50, 52, 68, 85n8, 119n5, 154n1, 205–6, 217

Lossky, Vladimir, 68n3, 218
Luther, Martin, 68

MacDonald, Gregory, *See* Parry, Robin
Manis, R. Zachary, 4n2, 33n4, 167n1, 170n3, 205, 218

Orwell, George, 26n3, 218

Parry, Robin, 55n1, 218

Sproul, R. C., 17n3, 218
Stump, Eleonore, 203n16, 206–7, 218

Talbott, Thomas, 55n1, 113n1, 179n25, 206, 218
Teresa, Mother, 150, 157n8, 218

van Inwagen, Peter, 155n4, 218

Walls, Jerry, 40n3, 98n5, 109n4, 206–7, 218

www.ingramcontent.com/pod-product-compliance
Lightning Source LLC
Chambersburg PA
CBHW031811220426
43662CB00007B/599